Cambridge Lower Secondary

Computing

9

Ben Barnes
Margaret Debbadi
Pam Jones
Tristan Kirkpatrick

SERIES EDITOR:
Lorne Pearcey

HODDER EDUCATION
AN HACHETTE UK COMPANY

Endorsement indicates that a resource has passed Cambridge International's rigorous quality-assurance process and is suitable to support the delivery of a Cambridge International curriculum framework. However, endorsed resources are not the only suitable materials available to support teaching and learning, and are not essential to be used to achieve the qualification. Resource lists found on the Cambridge International website will include this resource and other endorsed resources.

Any example answers to questions taken from past question papers, practice questions, accompanying marks and mark schemes included in this resource have been written by the authors and are for guidance only. They do not replicate examination papers. In examinations the way marks are awarded may be different. Any references to assessment and/or assessment preparation are the publisher's interpretation of the curriculum framework requirements. Examiners will not use endorsed resources as a source of material for any assessment set by Cambridge International.

While the publishers have made every attempt to ensure that advice on the qualification and its assessment is accurate, the official curriculum framework, specimen assessment materials and any associated assessment guidance materials produced by the awarding body are the only authoritative source of information and should always be referred to for definitive guidance. Cambridge International recommends that teachers consider using a range of teaching and learning resources based on their own professional judgement of their students' needs.

Cambridge International has not paid for the production of this resource, nor does Cambridge International receive any royalties from its sale. For more information about the endorsement process, please visit www.cambridgeinternational.org/endorsed-resources

Cambridge International copyright material in this publication is reproduced under licence and remains the intellectual property of Cambridge Assessment International Education.

Third-party websites and resources referred to in this publication have not been endorsed by Cambridge Assessment International Education.

Hachette UK's policy is to use papers that are natural, renewable and recyclable products and made from wood grown in well-managed forests and other controlled sources. The logging and manufacturing processes are expected to conform to the environmental regulations of the country of origin.

Orders: please contact Hachette UK Distribution, Hely Hutchinson Centre, Milton Road, Didcot, Oxfordshire, OX11 7HH. Telephone: +44 (0)1235 827827. Email education@hachette.co.uk Lines are open from 9 a.m. to 5 p.m., Monday to Friday. You can also order through our website: www.hoddereducation.com

ISBN: 978 1 3983 6982 5

© Margaret Debbadi and Pam Jones 2023

First published in 2023 by
Hodder Education,
An Hachette UK Company
Carmelite House
50 Victoria Embankment
London EC4Y 0DZ

www.hoddereducation.com

Impression number   10 9 8 7 6 5 4 3

Year   2027 2026 2025 2024 2023

All rights reserved. Apart from any use permitted under UK copyright law, no part of this publication may be reproduced or transmitted in any form or by any means, electronic or mechanical, including photocopying and recording, or held within any information storage and retrieval system, without permission in writing from the publisher or under licence from the Copyright Licensing Agency Limited. Further details of such licences (for reprographic reproduction) may be obtained from the Copyright Licensing Agency Limited, www.cla.co.uk

Cover photo © ZinetroN - stock.adobe.com

Illustrations by Aptara, Inc.

Typeset in India by Aptara, Inc.

Produced by DZS Grafik, Printed in Slovenia

A catalogue record for this title is available from the British Library.

Contents

	Introduction	4
9.1	Presenting choices: Combining constructs	8
9.2	Design your own network: Shape and size	55
9.3	Coding and testing: Game development for the micro:bit	88
9.4	Drilling down: How the processor handles instructions	129
9.5	Big Data modelling and analysis: Databases and spreadsheets	160
9.6	An array of skills	198
	Glossary	236
	Index	242

Introduction

About this book

Computer science is the study of computers, computing hardware and software, computer networks and the design of computer programs. It also includes the study of the way humans interact with computers and computing technology.

Computer science is linked to all areas of the world you live in today. It helps you to make positive changes to the world you live in, and provides important tools and applications to help you solve a wide range of problems. Computer science is continually evolving to provide new and valuable ways of improving your life and your interactions with the world around you.

This Student's Book will help you to understand some of the key areas of computer science, such as:
- network design
- algorithms and **sub-routines**
- **machine learning** and **Industry 4.0**
- **one-dimensional arrays** and **string manipulation**
- databases, spreadsheets and **Big Data**
- software **prototype** development.

This book also supports the learning objectives within the five strands of the Cambridge Lower Secondary Computing framework:

- **Computational thinking** is built into the tasks in this book. It looks at how computing can be used to explore and analyse data collected from the world around you. It is also about the development of skills to support problem-solving, for example how to describe a problem, and the data needed to solve that problem, in a way that a computer can understand.
- **Programming** explores the steps involved in designing and creating a computer program that can be used to carry out a particular task. In this book, you will study text-based programming languages such as Python and explore how to program a physical computing device to solve a problem.
- **Managing data** looks at how computers and computer programs can be used to store, organise and manage different **types of data**. It also explores how that data can be used to support problem-solving. In this book, you will learn how to use, edit and create databases and spreadsheets to help with managing different types of data.
- **Networks and digital communication** focuses on the methods used to transfer digital data between different computing devices and on how these devices are used to support communication. In this book, you will explore how different computing devices can be linked together to support data transfer and find out about the methods used to ensure that data is transferred securely and accurately.
- **Computer systems** is about how computer hardware devices and computer programs work together to support users in solving problems. It involves considering how the hardware and software and the data input is processed, stored and then output, to help a user solve a problem. In this book, you will explore the network and communications devices used to transmit data and information around a computer, and around the world, in the process of solving a problem.

KEYWORDS

sub-routine: standalone section of code that can be called from the main program
machine learning: ability of a computer system to learn over time
Industry 4.0: refers to how industry is combining electronics with new technologies, e.g. machine learning, artificial intelligence, robotics and green energy
one-dimensional array: series of items grouped together under one identifier
string manipulation: process of changing the format of a variable/string to allow it to be analysed

Big Data: datasets that are too large or complex for traditional data-processing applications, e.g. databases or spreadsheets, to process
prototype: initial product created for testing and reviewing, before a final product is released
data type: classification applied to a data item specifying which type of data that item represents, e.g. in a spreadsheet some of the data types available include currency, text and number

This Student's Book has six units:

9.1 Presenting choices: Combining constructs develops knowledge and skills using Python to understand how to use a count-controlled loop and an array. You will plan an algorithm and program with Python to act as a chatbot and ask a sequence of questions to help a student make a decision on which options or areas of study to focus on.

9.2 Design your own network: Shape and size investigates how networks can be structured in a variety of environments, providing scope to scale. It also covers ways in which networks can be protected through design: how error-checking can work to improve transmission, how machine learning is continuously improving the efficiency of utilities software and how networks can be kept secure.

9.3 Coding and testing: Game development for the micro:bit develops your knowledge and skills with the BBC micro:bit and MicroPython using count-controlled iteration and arrays. You will create a MicroPython program to utilise the micro:bit as an element of a 'What am I?' game, developing your knowledge of using physical devices as part of game development.

9.4 Drilling down: How the processor handles instructions looks at the steps a processor carries out during the execution of a computer program. You will learn about the fetch–decode–execute cycle and how program instructions are stored in lists that are run one at a time. You will also learn why a range of language translators are needed to ensure that the processor can understand and carry out program instructions users write. You will explore logic circuits and learn about the benefits of machine learning and computerisation in a range of industry and manufacturing areas.

9.5 Big Data modelling and analysis: Databases and spreadsheets explores the concept and applications of 'Big Data'. You will develop your data-modelling skills to create relational databases of real-life models. You will learn how to use functions such as MAX, MIN, COUNT and IF in spreadsheet models. You will investigate how to manipulate relational-database models and spreadsheet models using complex queries and formulae, respectively.

9.6 An array of skills focuses on iterative development and developing a program over time to meet a set of requirements. You will make use of all three programming constructs (sequence, selection and iteration) and use arrays in the development of your program. You will develop a game to improve knowledge of times tables and systematically debug and test the solution using trace tables.

How to use this book

In each unit, you will learn new skills by completing a series of tasks.

These features appear in each unit:

Get started!

This box introduces the unit and gives you some questions to discuss in pairs or small groups.

Learning outcomes

This box lists the learning outcomes that you will achieve in the unit.

Warm up

This box provides a task to do in pairs or small groups to get the learning started.

SCENARIO

This box contains a scenario that puts the tasks in the unit into a real-world context.

DID YOU KNOW?
This box provides an interesting or important fact about the task or section.

Do you remember?

This box lists the skills you should already be able to do before starting the unit.

Learn

This box introduces new concepts and skills.

Practise
This box contains tasks to apply and practise the new skills and knowledge from the 'Learn' box.

Go further
This box contains tasks to enhance and develop the skills you have previously learned in the unit.

Challenge yourself
This box provides challenging tasks with additional instructions to support new skills.

Final project
This box contains a final project that encompasses all the skills you have developed over the unit, in the context of the Scenario. The tasks in this box can be used to support teacher assessment of the learning objectives from the 'Learning outcomes' box.

Evaluation
This box provides guidance on how to evaluate and, if necessary, test the Final project tasks.

What can you do?
This box provides a summary of the skills you have learned in the unit and can be used to support self/peer assessment of the learning objectives.

Computational thinking
Most computational thinking skills are embedded into the Practise tasks. However, where you see this box, an individual computational thinking skill is highlighted for your attention.

KEYWORDS
Important words are shown in **emboldened orange font** and are defined in this box. They also appear in the Glossary at the back of the book.

These speech bubbles provide hints and tips as you complete the tasks.

Student resource files, used in some of the 'Practise' boxes, are available at www.hoddereducation.com/cambridgeextras

Unit 9.1 Presenting choices: Combining constructs

Get started!

Have you ever wondered how a computer program can help you to make a decision? How does a sequence of questions help you work out what to do?

Questioning allows you to ask specific questions and gain insight through the answers. If structured correctly, these questions can help you to find a solution to a problem or make a decision.

Try this game in pairs: One student should think of an object and the other student must ask up to 20 questions to try to guess what the object is. The questions can have a response of only 'Yes' or 'No'.

Discuss with your partner:
- How did the questions help to narrow down what the object was?
- What questions did you start with and why?
- Did you plan the questions you would ask before you started?
- What would you do differently if you were to do this activity again?

Questioning is an effective tool and, when used correctly, can help you find out about something or help to narrow down a selection.

In this unit, you will develop a Python program to act as a **chatbot**. A chatbot is a program that asks the user a series of questions, stores the answers and then uses the information to help the user to make a decision.

KEYWORD

chatbot: software application that uses text to ask questions to help a user

DID YOU KNOW?

A chatbot is a software application that carries out an online conversation with a human user and, through questioning, helps to identify a suitable solution to a problem.

You may have interacted with a chatbot on a website that enables you to have a conversation without human involvement. For example, if you do not want to wait on a phone for someone to answer a query about a product, a chatbot allows you to type in specific questions and guides you to a solution.

A chatbot is also used by the music application Spotify to allow users to search for, listen to and share music.

Unit 9.1 Presenting choices: Combining constructs

Learning outcomes

In this unit, you will learn to:
- follow, understand, edit and correct algorithms that are presented as pseudocode
- follow flowchart or pseudocode algorithms that use loops
- create algorithms using flowcharts and pseudocode
- use and explain iteration statements with count-controlled loops in either pseudocode or flowcharts
- predict the outcome of algorithms that use iteration
- compare and contrast two algorithms for the same solution and decide which is better suited to a task
- create an algorithm as a flowchart or pseudocode using more than one of these constructs: sequence, selection and count-controlled iteration
- identify and explain the purpose of a one-dimensional array
- identify and describe data types in Python programs, including integer, real, character, string and Boolean
- develop a Python program with count-controlled loops
- access data from an array using Python
- develop Python programs using string manipulation, including length, uppercase and lowercase
- use iterative development on Python prototypes to create solutions to problems
- develop and apply test plans that include normal, extreme and invalid data
- identify test data that covers normal, extreme and invalid data
- identify and describe a range of errors, including syntax, logic and runtime errors
- use a trace table to debug errors in a Python program.

Warm up

You make decisions every day, such as what clothes to wear, what to have for breakfast, what to take to school, and many more. Some decisions can be difficult to make and you may need to answer some questions to help you to choose. For example, the flowchart on the next page could help you to decide what to have for breakfast.

Each question helps to narrow down your options. The questions lead on from one another in a sequence, and every question has a 'Yes' or 'No' path to follow. These paths lead either to another question or to the final output – the decision.

In pairs, create a **flowchart** to help you to make a decision, such as choosing a topping for a pizza.

KEYWORD

flowchart: visual representation of an algorithm

CAMBRIDGE LOWER SECONDARY COMPUTING 9

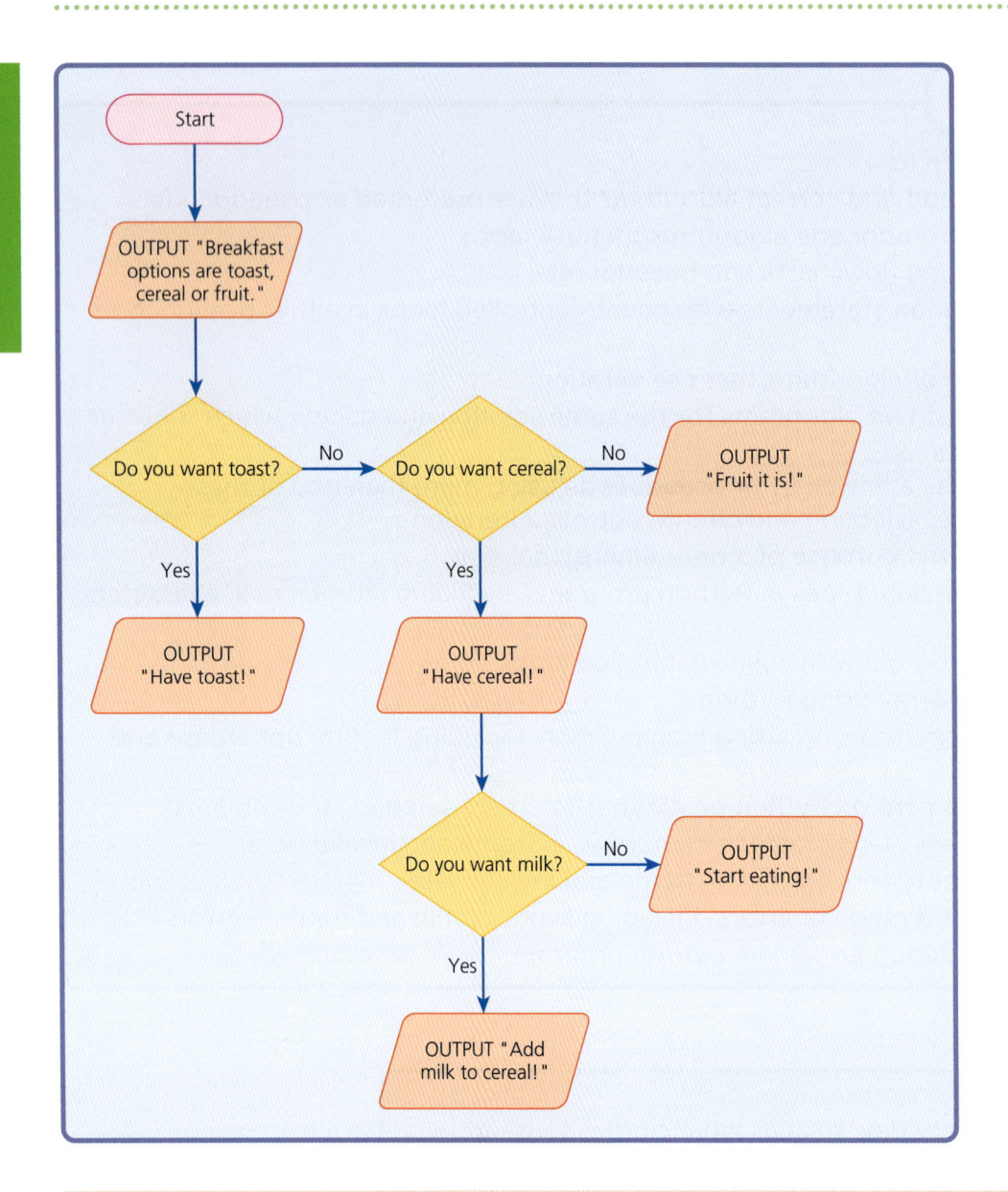

```
Start
  │
  ▼
OUTPUT "Breakfast options are toast, cereal or fruit."
  │
  ▼
Do you want toast? ──No──▶ Do you want cereal? ──No──▶ OUTPUT "Fruit it is!"
  │                          │
  Yes                        Yes
  │                          │
  ▼                          ▼
OUTPUT "Have toast!"      OUTPUT "Have cereal!"
                             │
                             ▼
                          Do you want milk? ──No──▶ OUTPUT "Start eating!"
                             │
                             Yes
                             │
                             ▼
                          OUTPUT "Add milk to cereal!"
```

SCENARIO

You use technology in a wide range of ways, and when you need help it is not always possible to speak to a person. A chatbot allows a company to support their customers to find a solution to their problem through questioning.

Your school has asked you to create a chatbot program to interact with students during the selection of options or subject areas to continue to study. The chatbot will ask the user a series of questions, store their answers and use this to help make a final decision. The solution will:

- be presented as pseudocode to show the algorithm for your chatbot program
- use variables and/or an array to store the answers to the questions asked of the user
- use a count-controlled loop
- follow an iterative process to design, develop, test and review to create a final prototype.

Unit 9.1 Presenting choices: Combining constructs

> **Do you remember?**
>
> Before starting this unit, you should be able to:
> ✔ develop a Python program using an iterative process
> ✔ follow and understand an algorithm presented as pseudocode
> ✔ explain and use the rules AND, OR and NOT to create logic within an algorithm
> ✔ follow flowcharts and pseudocode algorithms that use conditional statements
> ✔ predict the outcome of algorithms that use pseudocode
> ✔ create a Python program that uses conditional statements
> ✔ create a program in Python that uses a range of different data types
> ✔ develop a Python program that uses rules involving AND, OR and NOT
> ✔ decompose a problem into smaller sub-problems to make it easier to solve
> ✔ identify and describe the data types in a Python program
> ✔ develop and apply a test plan to ensure a Python program or algorithm works correctly.

In this unit, you will use the Python programming language.

Python's Integrated Development and Learning Environment (IDLE) provides features for creating, editing and running programs. Before using Python, you will need to install IDLE on your own personal device:

1 Go to **www.python.org/downloads**
2 Select `Download Python`.
3 Once downloaded, double-click on the file to open it and then choose `Install Now`.
4 Once IDLE has installed, it should appear in your Start Menu.

Chatbots

> **Learn**

Chatbots have become increasingly useful to growing businesses as they strive to meet customer demands. Instead of a customer sitting in a queue to speak to someone about the questions they have, they can use a chatbot to answer their questions and receive possible solutions. This is a developing technology that has limitations, so if the chatbot is unable to help it will direct the customer to speak to a person. In this way, chatbots filter the calls that need to be answered by a person by offering quick answers to the problems they can solve.

For example, an IT helpline may be able to support a selection of customers by asking some key questions about the issues they have and using this to offer possible ways for the customers to solve the problem themselves.

There are two main types of chatbot:
- Rule-based chatbots
- Chatbots with artificial intelligence.

Rule-based chatbots have predefined questions built in, so they are structured and less conversational. The questions do not **evolve** with the user's answers and are limited to the set questions that have been programmed to be asked. Examples include IT first-line support to gain an understanding of a system error or a health chatbot asking questions to determine the level of a health issue or how to advise on the next steps.

Chatbots with **artificial intelligence** (AI) offer intelligent conversations as the AI learns from your selections and answers to guide the next question or offer advice. It is called **machine learning** when a device learns over time. This type of chatbot is a developing technology, but more of the basics of AI are being integrated into chatbots where they learn from the user's choices, for example song selections or programme selections guide suggestions for future choices.

Practise

1. Discuss with your partner the difference between a rule-based chatbot and an artificial-intelligence chatbot.
2. Chatbots are integrated into websites to help the customer. In pairs, investigate how chatbots are used in retail and support, and consider the following questions.
   a. What is the chatbot's main function?
   b. Who is the chatbot for (what type of user, for example, a teenager)?
   c. How does it use questions to offer a solution?
   d. What is good about this type of chatbot?
3. Discuss as a class the range of chatbots you have found and any similarities or differences between them.

KEYWORDS

rule-based chatbot: chatbot with a set of questions built in that it asks and the user answers

evolving: changing and improving

artificial intelligence: ability of a computer system to learn and develop its own programming from the experiences it encounters

machine learning: ability of a computer system to learn over time

Data types and collecting variable data

Learn

You have previously used different **data types**, such as string and integer, when developing **programs**. Remember: you need to consider the data type of any variable when planning an **algorithm**.

The data types are:
- **string**: a series of characters surrounded by quotation marks
- **character**: a single letter, digit or symbol
- **integer**: a whole number
- **real**: also known as a **float**; this is a decimal number
- Boolean – True or False.

KEYWORDS

data type: classification applied to a data item specifying which type of data that item represents, e.g. in a spreadsheet some of the data types available include currency, text and number

program: instructions that tell a computer system how to complete a task

Unit 9.1 Presenting choices: Combining constructs

A string is a series of characters, and the characters are placed inside quotation marks, for example: `"string"`. Some programming languages, such as Java, include a character data type that is used to store a single letter, digit or symbol. However, Python does not use this data type. Here is an example showing a character data type being set up in the C programming language: `char variableName = 'A'`. The content of the variable is a single character defined by the code `char`, and the content following the `=` is the single letter `A`.

If you want to use a number in an equation or comparison, you must set it as either an integer or a real data type. The integer data type stores whole numbers, and the real data type stores numbers that contain decimal places, for example 15.75. You should also be familiar with the Boolean data type that stores either True or False; for example, `if age > 20:` would generate a True or False outcome.

It is important to set the data type when creating a variable. The following program should store two numbers the user enters, add them together and display the total.

```
num1 = input("Enter a number: ")
num2 = input("Enter a number: ")
total = num1 + num2
print(total)
```

However, when this program is run and the user enters 5 and 3, the output is shown as 53.

```
Enter a number: 5
Enter a number: 3
53
```

Python assumes that an input is a string unless it is told otherwise. Therefore, in this program it has linked the numbers together to form a longer string, rather than adding them. This is called **concatenation**. To add the values together, the computer needs to be told to store each input as an integer. Remember: this is done by adding `int` to the input statement. When you convert the value from one data type to another, it is called **casting** because you **cast** it.

```
num1 = int(input("Enter a number: "))
num2 = int(input("Enter a number: "))
total = num1 + num2
print(total)
```

Now when the program is run it gives the result expected:

```
Enter a number: 5
Enter a number: 3
8
```

> **KEYWORDS**
>
> **algorithm:** step-by-step instructions to solve a particular problem
>
> **string:** sequence of characters that can be text, numbers or symbols; quotation marks around the characters define it as a string
>
> **character:** single letter, digit or symbol
>
> **integer:** whole number
>
> **real:** also known as a *float*; a decimal number
>
> **float:** decimal number
>
> **concatenation:** joining two strings together
>
> **cast:** change the data type of a variable

Consider a chatbot that is going to ask you how many hours you have free, what your favourite activity is and how long the activity will take, and then output as a sentence how much time you will have left when you have completed the activity. A table can be created to plan the variables required and their data types. Here is an example.

Variable name	Data type
hours	Integer
activity	String
activityTime	Real
timeLeft	Real

These values can be used to plan the algorithm as **pseudocode**:

```
START
hours = INPUT "How many hours do you have free?"
activity = INPUT "What is your favourite activity?"
activityTime = INPUT "How long will the activity take?"
timeLeft = hours - activityTime
OUTPUT "When you have completed" ,activity, "you will have" ,timeLeft, "hours left"
STOP
```

The data type is not shown in the pseudocode, so having a table with the variable names and data types planned out clearly can help the programmer when they are creating the code.

You have already used `int` to set the data type to an integer in Python. To set the data type as a real number, you use `float` instead of `int`. In the program below, you can see that the variable 'hours' has been set as an integer and the variable 'activityTime' has been set as a float (real). The variable 'activity' does not have a data type set as it will be stored as a string by default.

Remember: the name of a variable is important to ensure that it tells you what it is storing. There are two main **naming conventions**:
camelCase: all lowercase; from the second word, the first letter is capitalised
snake_case: all lowercase; spaces are replaced with an underscore (_)

```
hours = int(input("How many hours do you have free? "))
activity = input("What is your favourite activity? ")
activityTime = float(input("How long will the activity take? "))

timeLeft = hours - activityTime
print("When you have completed",activity,"you will have",timeLeft,"hours left")
```

Notice that the output uses both text and the contents of variables. The text is encased in quotation marks and a comma is placed between this and the name of the variable to be used. A comma is added whenever the output changes between text and a variable.

> **KEYWORDS**
>
> **pseudocode:** textual representation of an algorithm
> **naming convention:** the way a variable or array is named in programming
> **camelCase:** all lowercase, and from the second word the first letter is capitalised
> **snake_case:** all lowercase, and spaces are replaced with underscores (_)

Unit 9.1 Presenting choices: Combining constructs

Practise

1. Discuss with your partner what this flowchart algorithm will do.
2. Copy the table below and add the variables and data types that will be required when creating the program.

Variable name	Data type

3. Create the pseudocode to match the flowchart algorithm.
4. Write the program code for the algorithm in Python and save it as **activityChatbotV1.py**.
5. Test, using a **test plan**, that your program works as expected.
6. Discuss with your partner how planning the variables and data types can help when creating the program code.
7. Discuss with your partner the different data types, with examples, and identify which data type is not used in Python.

> **KEYWORD**
>
> **test plan:** document that details the tests to be carried out when a program is complete and whether or not they are successful

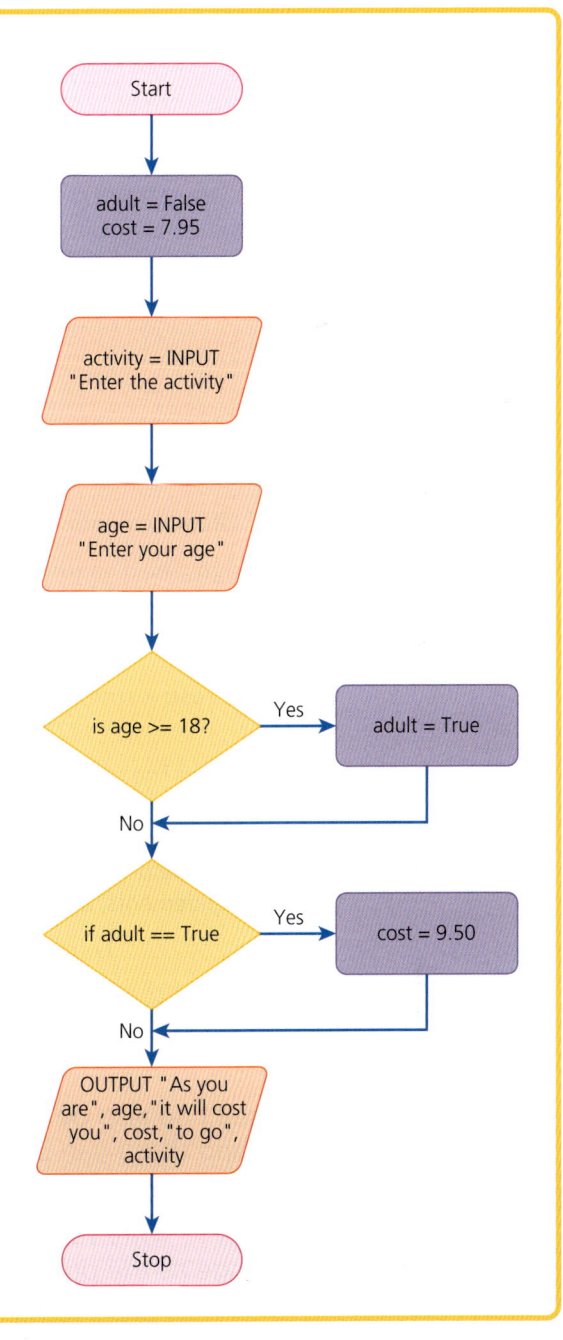

Flowchart:

- Start
- adult = False; cost = 7.95
- activity = INPUT "Enter the activity"
- age = INPUT "Enter your age"
- is age >= 18? — Yes → adult = True
- No ↓
- if adult == True — Yes → cost = 9.50
- No ↓
- OUTPUT "As you are", age, "it will cost you", cost, "to go", activity
- Stop

Developing in iterations

Learn

You have seen that a program is developed from an algorithm to program code. The initial idea for the program can **evolve** throughout this process. When the programmer receives the initial **requirements**, they have a starting vision. This vision, through development into a **prototype**, may change or be adjusted. That is where the programmer needs to work iteratively to take in any adjustments and apply them to the development. **Iterative** means 'to repeat', and the development steps are repeated until the prototype is ready to be released.

A project can follow this iterative process.

Requirements: What does the finished product need to do?

Design: The algorithm is developed using flowcharts or pseudocode; a **trace table** is used to help check the algorithm.

Develop: The program code is written.

Test: A structured test plan is used to check the program's functionality.

Review: The test plan outcomes are looked at and anything that is not working as expected is fixed; any potential improvements that are identified are added to the requirements for the next iteration; there is a general review of whether the final program meets the initial requirements, or whether another development cycle is needed.

Launch: The final program is released.

The program code itself can also be developed iteratively. The code can be broken down into smaller sections, and these can be developed, tested and reviewed before the next section of code is added.

As a programmer starts to write the code, developments can be considered. The initial idea may grow or change as the program develops, and a new development iteration may be required.

To develop the opening of a chatbot program for selecting the type of support a user requires, you would start with the pseudocode.

Unit 9.1 Presenting choices: Combining constructs

Step 1: Investigate the pseudocode

The pseudocode shows the algorithm for a program to select from a range of options, and the user's answer is used to give a response.

```
START
OUTPUT "Welcome to this support chatbot"
OUTPUT "Please select from one of the following options"
OUTPUT "1 for products"
OUTPUT "2 for store locations"
OUTPUT "3 for special offers"
selection = INPUT

IF selection == 1 THEN
    OUTPUT "Welcome to store products"
ELSEIF selection == 2 THEN
    OUTPUT "The store locations are UK and USA"
ELSE
    OUTPUT "Welcome to the special offers"
ENDIF
STOP
```

Step 2: Identify the variable and data type required in the program

Variable name	Data type
Selection	Integer

Step 3: Use the pseudocode to write the Python program

```python
print("Welcome to this support chatbot")
print("Please select from one of the following options")
print("1 for products")
print("2 for store locations")
print("3 for special offers")
selection = int(input())

if selection == 1:
    print("Welcome to store products")
elif selection == 2:
    print("The store locations are UK and USA")
else:
    print("Welcome to the special offers")
```

Step 4: Identify areas for improvement

When this program is run, the text is output and the cursor stays on the next line waiting for the user to input their selection. It would help the user to have a prompt, for example, stating the possible inputs: **1, 2 or 3**.

```python
print("Welcome to this support chatbot")
print("Please select from one of the following options")
print("1 for products")
print("2 for store locations")
print("3 for special offers")
selection = int(input("1, 2 or 3: "))

if selection == 1:
    print("Welcome to store products")
elif selection == 2:
    print("The store locations are UK and USA")
else:
    print("Welcome to the special offers")
```

The program is developed iteratively through testing and reviewing.

KEYWORDS

evolving: changing and improving

user requirements: tasks a user expects of an application

prototype: initial product created for testing and reviewing, before a final product is released

iterate/iterative/iteration: repeat/repeated/repetition

trace table: technique for predicting step by step what will happen as each line of an algorithm or program is run, and to identify errors

---

Practise

1. A pizza shop wants to develop a chatbot to allow customers to select their pizza. Customers may choose between chicken and sweetcorn, spicy lamb, and margherita.
   a. Discuss with your partner how you can use iterative development to create a prototype chatbot for the pizza shop.
   b. Make a list of the requirements for the finished chatbot.
   c. Plan the algorithm for the chatbot using pseudocode.
2. a. Use your pseudocode algorithm to write the program code for the chatbot and save it as **pizzaChatbotV1.py**.
   b. Test your code to make sure that it works as you expect.
   c. Review your chatbot prototype to make sure that it meets your list of requirements.
3. a. The pizza shop have decided that they would also like to offer a veggie pizza. Develop your program code to include this option and save it as **pizzaChatbotV2.py**.
   b. Review your chatbot protype to make sure it meets this new requirement.

Code tracers

Learn

When developing a solution from algorithm to program, it is important to test both the algorithm and the program code. When testing the finished program, it can be easier to see errors when you use a structured test plan to document the output based on a range of inputs.

An algorithm is the plan for a program that needs to be created and can be developed visually using a **flowchart** or textually as **pseudocode**. The algorithm needs to be checked and tested before it is handed over to the programmer to develop the program code.

A **variable** is a temporary storage location in memory whose contents can be called and edited at any time in the program. The contents of each variable can be mapped out in a trace table to show where they change as a program runs. A **trace table** is a structured approach like a test plan that can be used to look at the algorithm, or program code, and follow the variables and conditions.

Look at the structure of a trace table.

Line	Variable	Condition	Output

- **Line:** The line in the pseudocode algorithm or the step in the flowchart.
- **Variable:** You can put the name of the variable in the heading and make a note of the value of the variable in the column each time it changes.
- **Condition:** The conditional statement that completes a check to see whether the variable meets the set **criteria**; the output will be either True or False.
- **Output:** Where the program outputs the value stored in a variable.

Follow these steps to test this pseudocode using a trace table.

```
1    START
2    number = 5
3    IF number < 10 THEN
4        OUTPUT number + 5
5    ELSE
6        OUTPUT number - 5
7    ENDIF
8    STOP
```

Step 1: You can see that there is one variable in this pseudocode example: 'number'. This can be added to the second column in the trace table, under the heading 'Variable'.

There is also a condition being tested ('Is the number less than 10?'). This can be added to the third column in the trace table, under the heading 'Condition'.

CAMBRIDGE LOWER SECONDARY COMPUTING 9

Line	Variable	Condition	Output
	number	number < 10	

> Remember that a conditional statement such as `number < 10` is generating a Boolean output, as the outcome can be only True or False.

Step 2: Look at the first line of the pseudocode. This just defines the 'START' and is not added to the trace table.

Line 2: Here, the value 5 is set against the variable 'number'. This is added to the first row of the table. The line number is added to column 1 and the value stored in the variable is added to column 2.

Line	Variable	Condition	Output
	number	number < 10	
2	5		

Step 3: Line 3 has the condition `IF number < 10 THEN`. The value that is stored in the variable 'number' at this time is 5, and this is less than 10, so the output is True. This is added to the next row of the table.

Line	Variable	Condition	Output
	number	number < 10	
2	5		
3		True	

Step 4: Line 4 has an output. It will output the value that is stored in the variable 'number' plus 5. This is added to the next row of the trace table.

Line	Variable	Condition	Output
	number	number < 10	
2	5		
3		True	
4			10

Steps 5–6: Lines 5 and 6 would not be used in this instance as they would run only if the condition on line 3 was False. This is not added to the trace table.

Steps 7–8: Lines 7 and 8 do not use the variable as they define the end of the **selection** section and the end of the algorithm, so they are not added to the trace table.

Unit 9.1 Presenting choices: Combining constructs

The trace table is complete, and the algorithm has been tested. You can see the flow of the variable 'number' and how it is used throughout the program when it is run.

The lines are easily seen in pseudocode. Now look at an example with a flowchart. In the previous example, the value stored in the variable 'number' was an **integer** (a whole number). In this next example, the value stored is a **string** (a series of characters).

Step 1: Create the table with the headings for the variables, condition and output.

Line	Variable	Variable	Condition	Output
	password	userInput	password == userInput	

Step 2: Look at instruction 1, which would be line 1 of the code. This is the 'start' shape on the flowchart and is not added to the trace table.

Line 2: The variable 'password' is created and the string 'enter123' is assigned to it.

Line	Variable	Variable	Condition	Output
	password	userInput	password == userInput	
2	enter123			

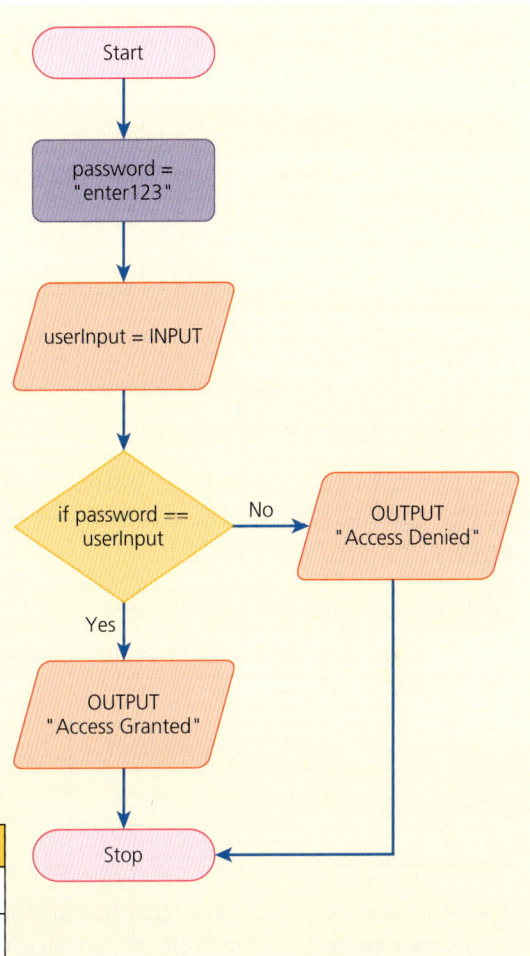

Step 3: Line 3: The user enters their password, and the string they input is stored in the variable 'userInput'. For this test, the user is inputting the string 'enter123'.

Line	Variable	Variable	Condition	Output
	password	userInput	password == userInput	
2	enter123			
3		enter123		

Step 4: Line 4: The condition is `if password == userInput`. This is checking whether the string stored in the 'password' variable matches the string stored in the 'userInput' variable. This will generate a Boolean outcome of True or False. The two variables do match so the outcome is True. This is added to the next line of the **truth table**.

Line	Variable	Variable	Condition	Output
	password	userInput	password == userInput	
2	enter123			
3		enter123		
4			True	

Step 5: Line 5: As the outcome to the condition is True, the output is 'Access Granted', and this is added to the next line of the truth table.

Line	Variable	Variable	Condition	Output
	password	userInput	password == userInput	
2	enter123			
3		enter123		
4			True	
5				Access Granted

The trace table is complete.

A trace table can also be created to check what will happen if the user enters a different string for their input; for example, the trace table below shows the output if the user enters the string 'enter321'.

Line	Variable	Variable	Condition	Output
	password	userInput	password == userInput	
2	enter123			
3		enter321		
4			False	
5				Access Denied

Trace tables are a useful tool for anyone planning a program. They help the programmer to carry out a **dry-run** test on an algorithm, to check the values of variables through a run of a program, and to find and fix any errors.

> **KEYWORDS**
> **flowchart:** visual representation of an algorithm
> **pseudocode:** textual representation of an algorithm
> **variable:** named memory location that can store a value
> **trace table:** technique for predicting step by step what will happen as each line of an algorithm or program is run, and to identify errors
> **criteria:** set of rules that must be met
> **selection:** choice to be added to a program using `if… elif… else` and the next instruction executed in the program is decided by the outcome of a condition
> **integer:** whole number
> **string:** sequence of characters that can be text, numbers or symbols; quotation marks around the characters define it as a string
> **truth table:** breakdown of a logic circuit, listing all possible operations the logic circuit can carry out
> **dry run:** process of working through an algorithm manually to trace the values of variables

Unit 9.1 Presenting choices: Combining constructs

Practise

You have seen that a trace table can be used to trace the flow of a variable through an algorithm displayed as pseudocode or as a flowchart. A trace table can also be used with a Python prototype program to find and fix errors.

1. Open the file **FoodSelectionChatbot.py** provided by your teacher. The program is a prototype for a chatbot to help you to select a food to eat. Using the file:
   a. Copy and complete the trace table below when the input is 1.
   b. Complete the trace table when the input is 2.
   c. Complete the trace table when the input is 3.
   d. Complete the trace table when the input is 4.

Line	Variable	Condition	Condition	Condition	Condition	Output
	food	food == 1	food == 2	food == 3	else	

2. Discuss with your partner the error that the trace table has helped to identify.
3. Edit the Python program to correct the error, and save it as **FoodSelectionChatbotV2.py**.
4. Repeat the trace table to check that the program now works correctly.
5. Annotate your trace table to identify where the integer and Boolean data types are used.
6. Discuss with your partner how you can use trace tables as you use iterative development to create your software prototype.

Error processing

Learn

In the previous section, you learned about trace tables and how they can be used to check algorithms and Python program prototypes. This is a useful process to follow to identify errors and fix them.

The main focus of iterative development is to produce a fully working prototype and then a finished solution that is free from error. If a chatbot is released that has not been thoroughly tested, it may not work properly and this would mean that it is not able to ask

CAMBRIDGE LOWER SECONDARY COMPUTING 9

the necessary questions to help the user to find a solution. As a program is developed, a series of processes are followed to find and fix errors, for example, using trace tables.

Errors that are introduced at the design stage can filter through to the development stage if they are not identified early on. This could result in the product needing to be redeveloped, which could be very costly and would take extra time. Therefore, it is important to find and fix any errors as early as possible in the process.

Errors can be categorised in three ways:
- **Logic errors**: The program will run but does not output what is expected; an example of a logic error is the inclusion of an incorrect conditional operator.
- **Syntax errors**: Errors in the program code that stop the program from running; an example of a syntax error is where the code has been typed incorrectly, for instance, missing brackets, colons or indentation or incorrect spelling, to name a few.
- **Runtime errors**: Errors that occur while the program is running as the instructions cannot be completed; an example of a runtime error is where the variable name has not been added correctly in one aspect of the program – it would not generate an error until it is used.

Testing an algorithm before it is developed into the program code can help to find and fix any errors early on.

In the previous section, you looked at trace tables. Trace tables can also be used to find any logic errors in an algorithm. A logic error does not stop the program from running, but the program doesn't do what you expect it to.

One area that can cause a logic error is the use of **conditional operators** in **conditional statements**.

Here's a reminder of the conditional operators.

Conditional operator	Description
==	equal to
!=	not equal to
>	greater than
>=	greater than or equal to
<	less than
<=	less than or equal to

KEYWORDS

logic error: error that allows a program to run but not output what is expected

syntax error: error in program code that stops the program from running

runtime error: error that occurs while a program is running; the instructions cannot be completed

conditional operator: symbol, e.g. >, < and =, used to carry out comparisons between two values

conditional statement: completes a check to see whether set criteria is either True or False

If these operators are used incorrectly, the outcome of comparisons could be wrong, and this would result in the wrong output from the program. For example, if a chatbot asks for a value to be added, then the correct value needs to be detected in the comparison `if food == 1`.

24

Unit 9.1 Presenting choices: Combining constructs

Look at the example below of an algorithm (presented as pseudocode) and a trace table to find and fix the logic error. The pseudocode has been developed as a plan for a chatbot program to allow a student to enter their score and output the level they are working at, along with a message of encouragement.

```
1  START
2  OUTPUT "Student score chatbot"
3  score = INPUT "Enter your recent score."
4  IF score > 90 THEN
5    OUTPUT "You are working at a Distinction level."
6    OUTPUT "Keep the focus on new subject areas."
7  ELSEIF score >= 51 AND <= 89 THEN
8    OUTPUT "You are working at a Merit level."
9    OUTPUT "You are doing well. Focus on revision techniques."
10 ELSEIF score >= 20 AND <= 50 THEN
11   OUTPUT "You are working at a Pass level."
12   OUTPUT "Some extra sessions may help improve your understanding."
13 ELSE
14   OUTPUT "You have not passed this assessment."
15   OUTPUT "Some one-to-one time would help with looking at content."
16 ENDIF
17 STOP
```

In the same way as you would test program code with a test plan and a range of data inputs, you need to use a range of inputs to test the algorithm. Each input will require a new trace table.

Test 1: Trace table for input of score 10

Line	Variable	Condition	Condition	Condition	Condition	Output
	Score	score > 90	score >= 51 and <= 89	score >= 20 and <= 50	else	
3	10					
4		False				
7			False			
10				False		
13					True	
14						You have not passed this assessment.
15						Some one-to-one time would help with looking at content.

25

The trace table shows that when a score of 10 is entered, the conditions on lines 4, 7 and 10 are all False. The program moves to the `else` section and generates an output of 'You have not passed this assessment.' and 'Some one-to-one time would help with looking at content.' The trace table shows that the algorithm works correctly for this value.

Test 2: Trace table for input of score 20

Line	Variable	Condition	Condition	Condition	Condition	Output
	score	score > 90	score >= 51 and <= 89	score >= 20 and <= 50	else	
3	20					
4		False				
7			False			
10				True		
11						You are working at a Pass level.
12						Some extra sessions may help improve your understanding.

The trace table shows that when a score of 20 is entered, the conditions on lines 4 and 7 are both False. The condition on line 10 is True and generates an output of 'You are working at a Pass level.' and 'Some extra sessions may help improve your understanding.' The trace table shows that the algorithm also works correctly for this value.

Test 3: Trace table for input of score 89

Line	Variable	Condition	Condition	Condition	Condition	Output
	score	score > 90	score >= 51 and <= 89	score >= 20 and <= 50	else	
3	89					
4		False				
7			True			
8						You are working at a Merit level.
9						You are doing well. Focus on revision techniques.

The trace table shows that when a score of 89 is entered, the condition on line 4 is False. The condition on line 7 is True and generates an output of 'You are working at a Merit level.' and 'You are doing well. Focus on revision techniques.' The trace table shows that the algorithm also works correctly for this value.

Unit 9.1 Presenting choices: Combining constructs

Test 4: Trace table for input of score 90

Line	Variable	Condition	Condition	Condition	Condition	Output
	score	score > 90	score >= 51 and <= 89	score >= 20 and <= 50	else	
3	90					
4		False				
7			False			
10				False		
13					True	
14						You have not passed this assessment.
15						Some one-to-one time would help with looking at content.

When a score of 90 is input, the expected output would be for the student to receive the level of Distinction. However, from tracking the variable in the trace table, you can see that the condition is not producing the correct outcome. This is a logic error. The conditional operator has been set as greater than (>) when it should be set as greater than or equal to (>=).

```
 1 START
 2 OUTPUT "Student score chatbot"
 3 score = INPUT "Enter your recent score."
 4 IF score >= 90 THEN
 5   OUTPUT "You are working at a Distinction level."
 6   OUTPUT "Keep the focus on new subject areas."
 7 ELSEIF score >= 51 AND <= 89 THEN
 8   OUTPUT "You are working at a Merit level."
 9   OUTPUT "You are doing well. Focus on revision techniques."
10 ELSEIF score >= 20 AND <= 50 THEN
11   OUTPUT "You are working at a Pass level."
12   OUTPUT "Some extra sessions may help improve your understanding."
13 ELSE
14   OUTPUT "You have not passed this assessment."
15   OUTPUT "Some one-to-one time would help with looking at content."
16 ENDIF
17 STOP
```

If this error had not be found at this stage, the wrong operator would have been used in the program code and the error would not have been spotted until much further through the process. If you are using conditions that involve comparisons, it is important to test the algorithm using a wide range of data inputs. In this example, some specific numbers were used in the dry-run testing, but it would be better to test each value that is used in a conditional statement and a selection of other values in between.

> **Practise**
>
> 1 Open the file **StudentScoreChatbot.py** provided by your teacher.
>   a Run the program to find the syntax error.
>   b Correct the program and save it as **StudentScoreChatbotV2.py**.
> 2 Create trace tables for the following inputs:
>   a 95   b 15   c 25   d 80
> 3 a Annotate the trace table to identify where the logic error is.
>   b Correct the program and save it as **StudentScoreChatbotV3.py**.
> 4 a Discuss with your partner how trace tables helped to identify the logic compared with how you identified the syntax error.
>   b Evaluate how effective a trace table can be to identify errors and help development.

Iteration introduction

> **Learn**
>
> So far, you have created Python programs using two programming constructs: **sequence** and **selection**.
>
> Another programming construct is **iteration**. You have seen that iteration in program development is about repeating a series of steps to develop the program continuously until the final solution is reached. In programming, *iteration* is a set of instructions that are repeated, and it is also referred to as a *loop*.
>
> Remember: *sequence* is the order in which the program code needs to be to work correctly; *selection* allows a choice to be added to the program using `if… elif… else` so that the next instruction **executed** in the program is decided by the outcome of a condition.
>
> A **count-controlled loop** is where a series of program instructions is repeated a set number of times. This type of loop is also called a **for loop**.
>
> Here's an example of a for loop:
>
> ```python
> for i in range(5):
>     print ("Loop", i)
> ```

The structure of a for loop is important:
- `for` tells the computer that it will be running a for loop.
- `i` is a variable that is used to count how many times the code in the loop has been repeated; it starts at 0 and increases by 1 each time the loop has finished running – the variable 'i' is often used as it is short for 'iteration', but you can use any variable name of your choice here.
- `in` is used to separate the variable from the number of times the loop will run.
- `range(5)` defines the number of times the loop will run.
- `:` is used to signal the beginning of the code that will be repeated.

All the lines of code that need to be repeated when the loop runs are indented underneath, in the same way that code is indented after `if`, `elif` and `else`.
- `print("This is loop," i)` outputs the text 'This is loop' followed by the value stored in the variable 'i' to show the iteration that the program is on.

Program output

When the program above is run, the output displayed would be:

```
Loop 0
Loop 1
Loop 2
Loop 3
Loop 4
```

The **loop variable** always starts at 0 and the loop is executed until the value of the loop variable is the same as the number in the brackets after `range()`. In the example above, to output the number 5 the range would need to be increased to 6.

A chatbot may need to ask the same set of questions more than once. You can use a for loop to set the number of times a question is asked and test the input using selection. It is important that the conditional statements are indented inside the for loop.

In the pseudocode below, the program outputting the iteration number is developed to check the value stored in the variable 'i'. If the value of i is greater than 3, then the output is 'This is loop', the value of i and 'Iterations complete'. If the value of i is 0, 1, 2 or 3, then the output is 'This is loop' and the value of i. In pseudocode, the actual values of the count variable are stated.

```
START
FOR i = 0 TO 4
    IF i > 3 THEN
        OUTPUT "This is loop",i,"Iterations complete"
    ELSE
        OUTPUT "This is loop",i
    ENDIF
ENDFOR
STOP
```

It is important that the selection statements are indented inside the for loop. The output if the conditional statement is True or False is indented under the `IF` and `ELSE` sections.

This pseudocode can be developed into a Python program, ensuring that the same indentation is used.

```python
for i in range (5):
    if i > 3:
        print("This is loop",i,"Iterations complete")
    else:
        print("This is loop",i)
```

> **KEYWORDS**
>
> **sequence:** order that program code needs to be in to work correctly
>
> **selection:** choice to be added to a program using `if… elif… else` and the next instruction executed in the program is decided by the outcome of a condition
>
> **execute:** carry out the instructions described in a computer program
>
> **iterate/iterative/iteration:** repeat/repeated/repetition
>
> **count-controlled loop:** set of instructions repeated a set number of times
>
> **for loop:** the Python or MicroPython loop for a count-controlled loop
>
> **loop variable:** variable that counts the number of times code has been repeated in a count-controlled loop

Practise

Open your file **FoodSelectionChatbotV2.py** from the earlier section 'Code tracers'.

1. Discuss with your partner how a count-controlled loop could be added to allow the question and selection program code to be run twice.
2. Edit the program code to include a for loop. Save your new program development as **FoodSelectionChatbotV3.py**.

Iteration in algorithms

Learn

Using a loop can avoid the need to rewrite lines of program code multiple times. Look at the two flowcharts below. Compare them to identify their similarities and contrast them to identify the differences between them.

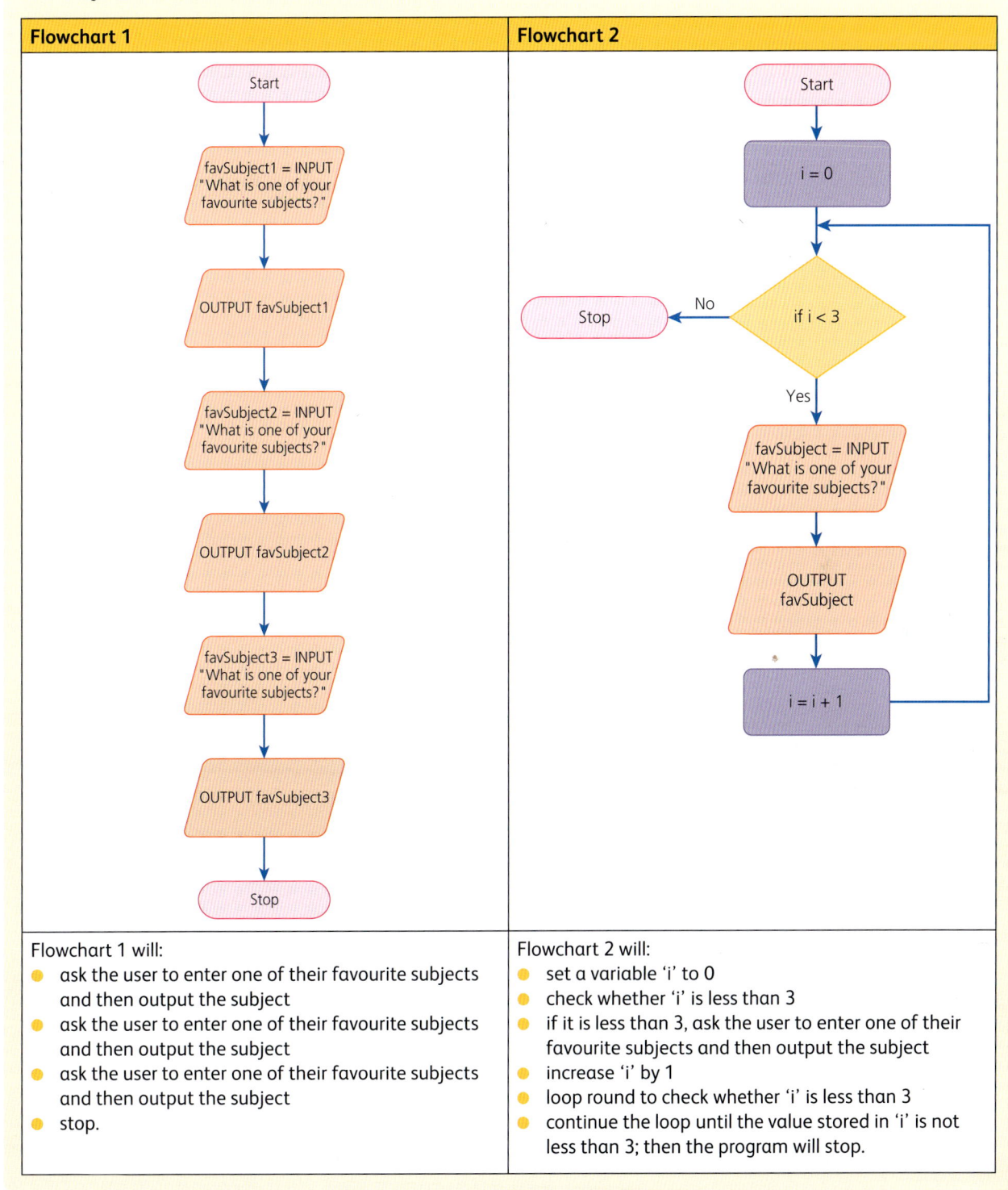

Flowchart 1	Flowchart 2
Start → favSubject1 = INPUT "What is one of your favourite subjects?" → OUTPUT favSubject1 → favSubject2 = INPUT "What is one of your favourite subjects?" → OUTPUT favSubject2 → favSubject3 = INPUT "What is one of your favourite subjects?" → OUTPUT favSubject3 → Stop	Start → i = 0 → if i < 3 (No → Stop; Yes → favSubject = INPUT "What is one of your favourite subjects?" → OUTPUT favSubject → i = i + 1 → loop back to if i < 3)
Flowchart 1 will: • ask the user to enter one of their favourite subjects and then output the subject • ask the user to enter one of their favourite subjects and then output the subject • ask the user to enter one of their favourite subjects and then output the subject • stop.	Flowchart 2 will: • set a variable 'i' to 0 • check whether 'i' is less than 3 • if it is less than 3, ask the user to enter one of their favourite subjects and then output the subject • increase 'i' by 1 • loop round to check whether 'i' is less than 3 • continue the loop until the value stored in 'i' is not less than 3; then the program will stop.

CAMBRIDGE LOWER SECONDARY COMPUTING 9

Both flowcharts have asked the user to enter their favourite subject and output what it is three times. However, the use of a loop in flowchart 2 makes the algorithm more **efficient**. The efficiency of a program is measured by how long it takes to run. Usually, if the code can be written in fewer lines, it is more efficient.

You can use the flowchart to create pseudocode to represent the same algorithm.

Flowchart 1

Each shape of the flowchart is represented on a single line in pseudocode. Remember to capitalise the words INPUT and OUTPUT and define the START and STOP.

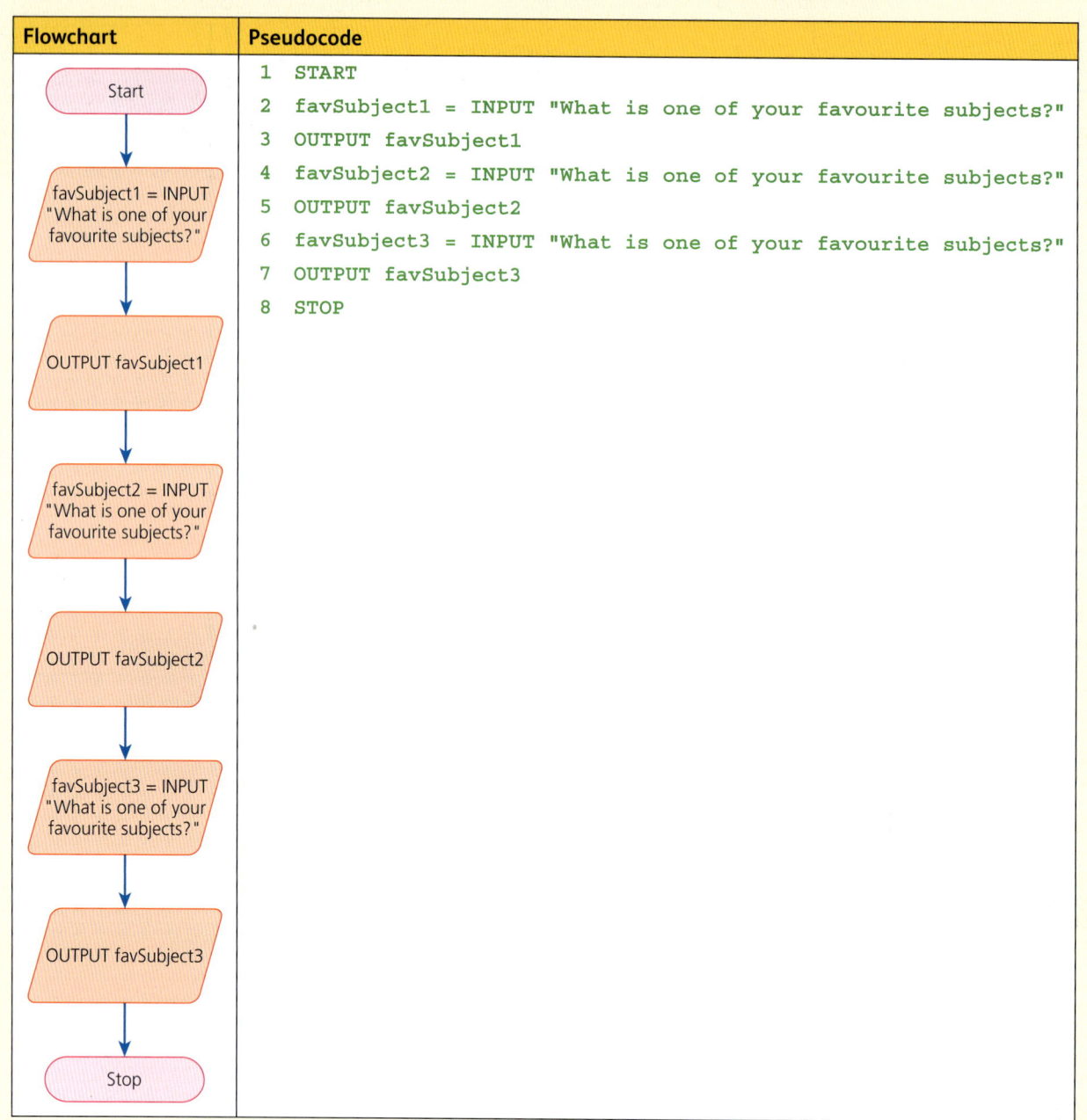

Flowchart	Pseudocode
Start → favSubject1 = INPUT "What is one of your favourite subjects?" → OUTPUT favSubject1 → favSubject2 = INPUT "What is one of your favourite subjects?" → OUTPUT favSubject2 → favSubject3 = INPUT "What is one of your favourite subjects?" → OUTPUT favSubject3 → Stop	1 START 2 favSubject1 = INPUT "What is one of your favourite subjects?" 3 OUTPUT favSubject1 4 favSubject2 = INPUT "What is one of your favourite subjects?" 5 OUTPUT favSubject2 6 favSubject3 = INPUT "What is one of your favourite subjects?" 7 OUTPUT favSubject3 8 STOP

32

Unit 9.1 Presenting choices: Combining constructs

Flowchart 2

The for loop in pseudocode is defined using the starting value of the variable 'i' and the value that it needs to count to. The end of the for loop is shown using **ENDFOR**.

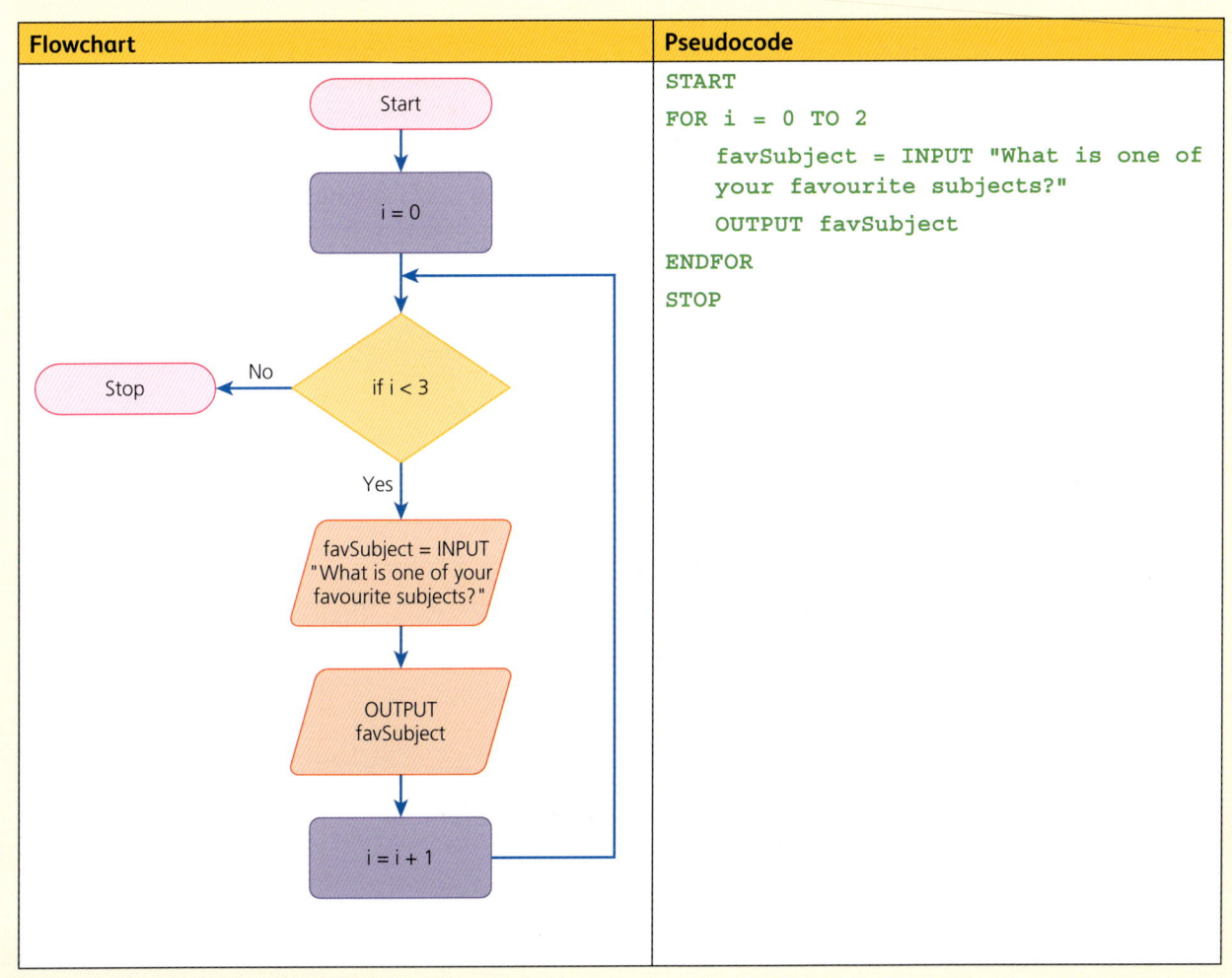

Flowchart	Pseudocode
| (Flowchart showing: Start → i = 0 → if i < 3 (No → Stop; Yes → favSubject = INPUT "What is one of your favourite subjects?" → OUTPUT favSubject → i = i + 1 → loops back to if i < 3)) | ```
START
FOR i = 0 TO 2
    favSubject = INPUT "What is one of
    your favourite subjects?"
    OUTPUT favSubject
ENDFOR
STOP
``` |

The use of a loop can make the flowchart seem more complicated. However, the use of a loop means that less code is going to be needed and makes the algorithm easier to follow.

You can take the pseudocode and use this to create the program in Python.

Pseudocode	Python code
`FOR i = 0 TO 2`	`for i in range(3):`
`favSubject = INPUT "What is one of your favourite subjects?"`	`favSubject = input("What is one of your favourite subjects? ")`
`OUTPUT favSubject`	`print("One of your favourite subjects is",favSubject)`

The program code is written using three lines of code. If you wrote this without using a for loop, it would require six lines of code. You can see this in the comparison below. The program with the count-controlled loop (for loop) is more efficient.

33
```

| Program **with** a for loop | ```
for i in range(3):
    favSubject = input("What is one of your favourite subjects? ")
    print("One of your favourite subjects is",favSubject)
``` |
| Program **without** a for loop | ```
favSubject1 = input("What is one of your favourite subjects? ")
print("One of your favourite subjects is",favSubject1)
favSubject2 = input("What is one of your favourite subjects? ")
print("One of your favourite subjects is",favSubject2)
favSubject3 = input("What is one of your favourite subjects? ")
print("One of your favourite subjects is",favSubject3)
``` |

> **KEYWORD**
>
> **efficient:** the efficiency of a program can be measured by how quickly it runs

Practise

Pseudocode 1	Pseudocode 2
1 START 2 import time library 3 4 countdown = 3 5 OUTPUT countdown 6 countdown = countdown - 1 7 wait 1 second 8 OUTPUT countdown 9 countdown = countdown - 1 10 wait 1 second 11 OUTPUT countdown 12 wait 1 second 13 OUTPUT "Let's start" 14 STOP	1 START 2 import time library 3 4 countdown = 4 5 FOR i = 0 to 2 6 OUTPUT countdown - 1 7 wait 1 second 8 ENDFOR 9 OUTPUT "Let's start" 10 STOP

1 Follow the pseudocode above and predict with your partner what each program is designed to do.
2 Discuss how a countdown could be used at the start of a chatbot.
3 Compare and contrast the two algorithms with your partner. Copy and complete the table below to identify the similarities and differences between the two algorithms.

Similarities	Differences

Unit 9.1 Presenting choices: Combining constructs

4. Decide which algorithm on the previous page is more efficient and explain why.
5. For pseudocode 2, using the count-controlled loop, complete the following variable and data type table.

Variable	Data type

6. Use pseudocode 2 to create the Python program using a count-controlled loop. Save the file as **CountdownChatbotStart.py**.
7. Complete the trace table using the Python program.

Line	Variable	Variable	Output
	i	countdown	

8. Discuss with your partner how a count-controlled loop could be used to create a loading-style beginning to a program or a countdown to the start of a chatbot.

Iterations and arrays

Learn

In the previous program you looked at, a for loop was used to output the same question three times, which reduced the amount of code needed. However, the program doesn't store all three answers in separate variables. Instead, each input from the user overwrites the content of the variable 'favSubject'. This is fine if the user needs just to see the output to their question, but what if you want to store and use the answers again?

A solution to this is to use an **array**. An array is a data structure that can store more than one item of data under a single identifier. In most programming languages, an array holds just one type of data, such as strings. However, Python uses **lists** that can include items of any data type.

A Python list is defined in a similar way to a variable. You give the list a name followed by an equals sign (=), and then square brackets ([ ]) are used to show the start and end of the **data items**.

Look at this shopping-list array with three items: bread, milk and apples.

```
shoppingList = ["bread", "milk", "apples"]
```

Each item has quotation marks around it as they are all strings. This is the same as you would use on an individual string being stored in a variable. The items in the list are separated by commas.

Once you have created a list, there are various ways in which you can manipulate the contents. The `append()` method is used to add an item to the end of a list. A full stop and `append()` are added to the list name, and the item to be added is put inside the brackets. In the example below, `append()` is used to add grapes to the list.

```
shoppingList = ["bread", "milk", "apples"]

shoppingList.append("grapes")
print(shoppingList)
```

When the program is run, the `print` command outputs the contents of the list on one line, including the square brackets and quotation marks.

```
['bread', 'milk', 'apples', 'grapes']
```

To improve the presentation of the output, you can use a for loop to display each item of the list on a separate line. This will also remove the square brackets, commas and quotation marks.

Instead of using 'i' as the variable, you can use a more specific variable name. The example below uses 'item', as each item in the shopping list will be printed.

```
shoppingList = ["bread", "milk", "apples"]

shoppingList.append("grapes")

for item in shoppingList:
    print(item)
```

The output is now in a vertical list with just the items showing.

```
bread
milk
apples
grapes
```

The `len()` function can be used to find out how many items are in a list. In the program below, the value is stored in a variable called 'num'.

```
num = len(shoppingList)
```

It can be used in an output to say how many values are in the list.

```
print("There are",num,"items in the list.")
```

```
There are 4 items in the list.
```

Unit 9.1 Presenting choices: Combining constructs

Look again at the chatbot program from the previous section that asks the user three times what their favourite subject is and stores their answers. An empty list called 'favSubjects' can be set up at the start of the program:

```
favSubjects = [ ]
```

A for loop can be set up to run three times:

```
for i in range(3):
```

> Remember: A count-controlled loop is set to run the indented code a set number of times. In Python, this is a *for loop*.

On each iteration, the program needs to ask the user what one of their favourite subjects is and then add their answer to the list. This can be done in a single line of code, indented below the code to run the loop:

```
for i in range(3):
    favSubjects.append(input("What is your favourite subject at school? "))
```

A second for loop can be used to print out the subjects:

```
for subject in favSubjects:
    print(subject)
```

The program now makes use of an array and two for loops to get the inputs from the user, store them and then output them.

KEYWORDS

array: data structure in a program that can store more than one item of data of the same data type under a single identifier; data items can be changed

list: data structure that stores multiple items of data in a single variable; the values can be changed

data item: piece of information that represents part of the data that makes up a person, place or thing, e.g. some of the data items that represent a person are their first name and second name

---

Practise

A chatbot has been created to use an array to store a range of colours that a user enters.

```
START
ARRAY rainbow = [red, orange]

FOR i = 0 TO 4
        Add INPUT to ARRAY "Add a colour"
ENDFOR
```

37

```
OUTPUT "_ _ _ _ _ _ _ _ _ _ _ _ _ _ _ _ _ _ _ _ _ _ _ _"
OUTPUT "Your rainbow colours are:"

FOR each colour in ARRAY rainbow:
    OUTPUT colour
ENDFOR

STOP
```

1 Look at the pseudocode and discuss these questions with your partner.
   a What is the content of the array at the start of the program?
   b How many times will the user be asked to enter a colour?
   c What will the output be at the end of the program?
   d What is the purpose of the dashed line?
   e What will be the content of the array at the end of the program when you add the colours: yellow, green, blue, indigo and violet?
2 Predict the expected output at the end of the program.
3 Use the pseudocode to create the Python program code for the chatbot, and save it as **rainbowColoursChatbotV1.py**.
4 Discuss with your partner whether your output prediction was correct.
5 Discuss with your partner the purpose of the array in this program and how the program accesses the data stored in the array.

Developing the chatbot further

Learn

You have used all the key programming concepts across this and previous stages: sequence, selection and iteration.

Chatbot programs need to use selection to allow the user's answer to determine the next step in the program. For example, the user could be asked questions about the sort of activity they prefer to do, and the chatbot could suggest a new activity for them to try.

Look at this example, which shows how a chatbot would use questioning to narrow down the possible options and aid the decision-making process.

Program development iteration 1

First, the algorithm is planned using either a flowchart or pseudocode. The algorithm uses sequence, selection and iteration.

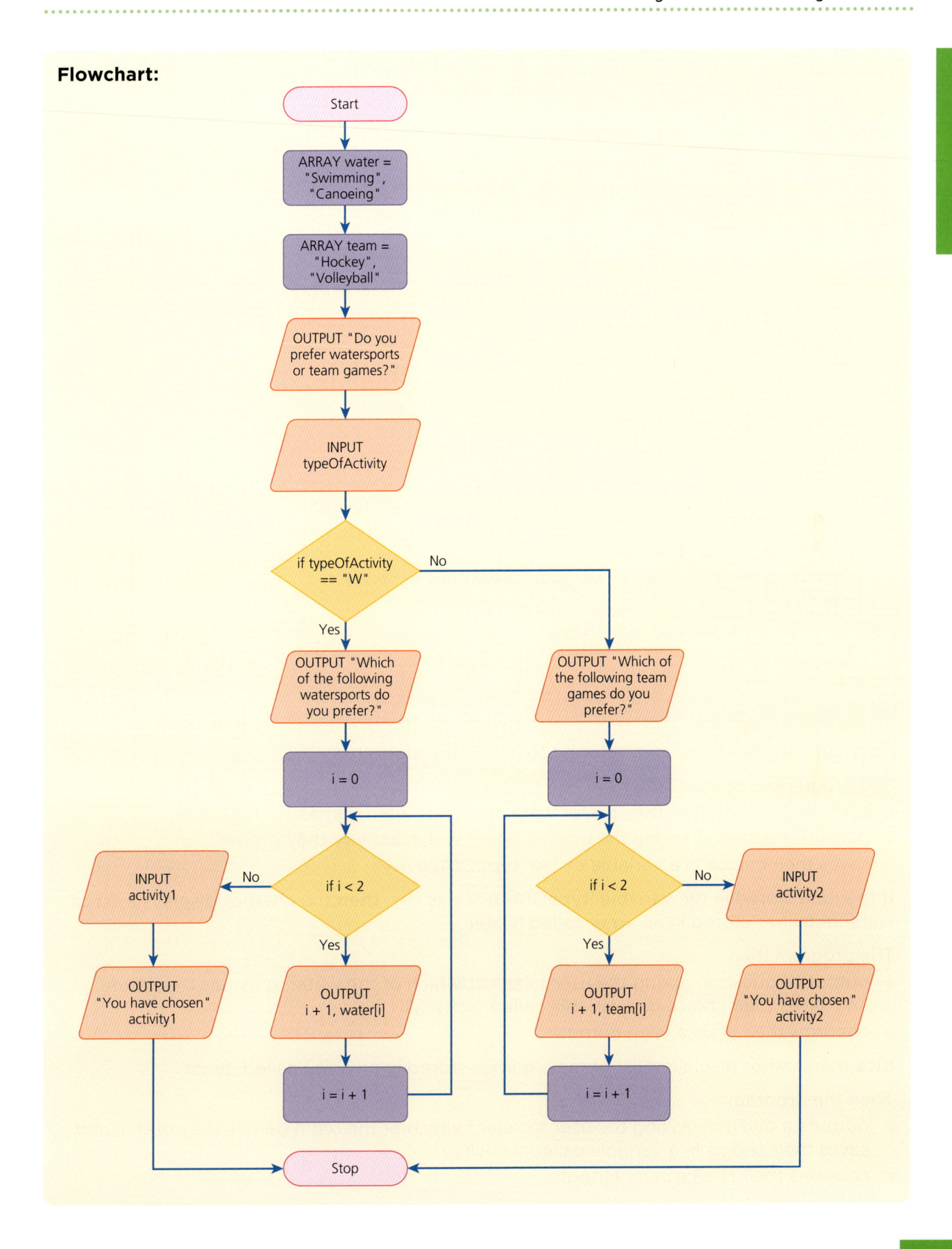

Flowchart:

```
Start
  ↓
ARRAY water = "Swimming", "Canoeing"
  ↓
ARRAY team = "Hockey", "Volleyball"
  ↓
OUTPUT "Do you prefer watersports or team games?"
  ↓
INPUT typeOfActivity
  ↓
if typeOfActivity == "W"
  ├── Yes ──→ OUTPUT "Which of the following watersports do you prefer?"
  │              ↓
  │            i = 0
  │              ↓
  │            if i < 2
  │              ├── Yes ──→ OUTPUT i + 1, water[i]
  │              │              ↓
  │              │            i = i + 1 ──┐ (loop back to if i < 2)
  │              │
  │              └── No ───→ INPUT activity1
  │                             ↓
  │                           OUTPUT "You have chosen" activity1
  │                             ↓
  │                           Stop
  │
  └── No ───→ OUTPUT "Which of the following team games do you prefer?"
                 ↓
               i = 0
                 ↓
               if i < 2
                 ├── Yes ──→ OUTPUT i + 1, team[i]
                 │              ↓
                 │            i = i + 1 ──┐ (loop back to if i < 2)
                 │
                 └── No ───→ INPUT activity2
                                ↓
                              OUTPUT "You have chosen" activity2
                                ↓
                              Stop
```

Pseudocode:

```
START
ARRAY water = [Swimming, Canoeing]
ARRAY team = [Hockey, Volleyball]
OUTPUT "Do you prefer watersports or team games?"
INPUT typeOfActivity

IF typeOfActivity == "W" THEN
    OUTPUT "Which of the following watersports do you prefer?"
    FOR i = 0 to 1
        OUTPUT i + 1, water[i]
    OUTPUT "Enter the number of your preferred activity."
    INPUT activity1
    OUTPUT "You have chosen" activity1

ELSE
    OUTPUT "Which of the following team games do you prefer?"
    FOR i = 0 to 1
        OUTPUT i + 1, team[i]
    OUTPUT "Enter the number of your preferred activity."
    INPUT activity2
OUTPUT "You have chosen" activity2

ENDIF
STOP
```

Next, the program code is developed to match the algorithm.

The program:
- asks the user whether they prefer watersports or team games
- outputs a question asking the user to select which activity they prefer
- saves their choice in a variable called 'typeOfActivity'.

If the item stored in the variable 'typeOfActivity' is `"W"`, **then** the chatbot displays a list of water activities stored in an array called 'water'.

The program then:
- outputs a question asking the user to select which of the water activities they prefer, and saves their choice in a variable called 'activity1'
- confirms their choice in an output.

Else the chatbot displays a list of team games stored in an array called 'team'.

Then the program:
- outputs a question asking the user to select which of the team games they prefer, and saves their choice in a variable called 'activity2'
- confirms their choice in an output.

Unit 9.1 Presenting choices: Combining constructs

The program code matches the algorithm using variables, selection and iteration in a Python program.

```python
water = ["Swimming","Canoeing"]
team = ["Hockey","Volleyball"]

print("Do you prefer watersports or team games?")
typeOfActivity = input("Enter W or T: ")

if typeOfActivity == "W":
    print("Which of the following watersports do you prefer?")
    for i in range(2):
        print(i+1,water[i])
    activity1 = int(input("Enter the number of your preferred activity: "))
    print("You have chosen",water[activity1-1])

elif typeOfActivity == "T":
    print("Which of the following team games do you prefer?")
    for i in range(2):
        print(i+1,team[i])
    activity1 = int(input("Enter the number of your preferred activity: "))
    print("You have chosen",team[activity1-1])
```

If the program is developed to ask the user to choose between three types of activity, then an additional comparison will be needed. This will mean adding `elif` to the algorithm and program.

Program development iteration 2

A new iteration of the algorithm is planned to refine the chatbot further by using the value stored in 'activity1' or 'activity2' to suggest an alternative activity that the user might like to try.

Flowchart

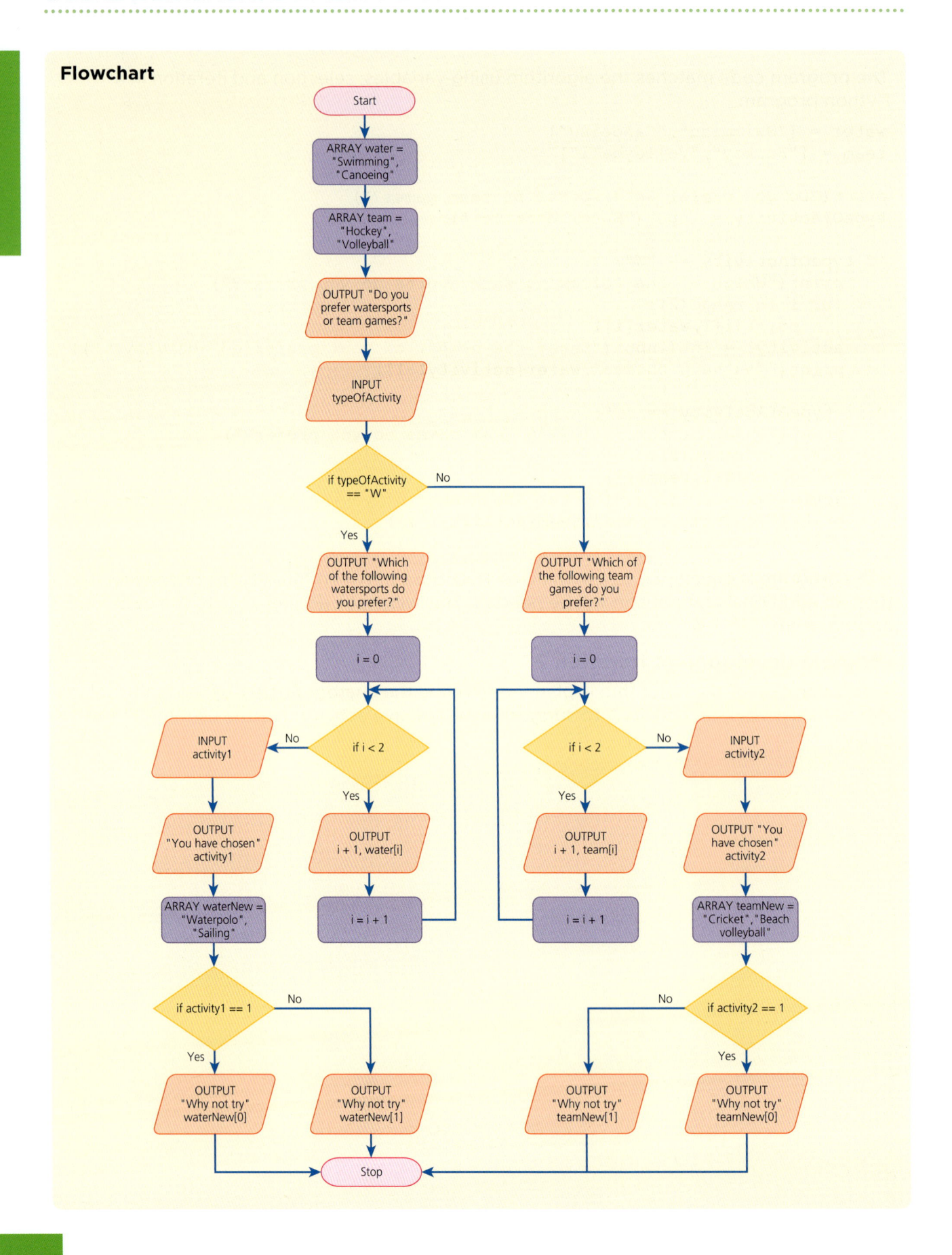

```
Start
  ↓
ARRAY water = "Swimming", "Canoeing"
  ↓
ARRAY team = "Hockey", "Volleyball"
  ↓
OUTPUT "Do you prefer watersports or team games?"
  ↓
INPUT typeOfActivity
  ↓
if typeOfActivity == "W"
  ├── Yes ──→ OUTPUT "Which of the following watersports do you prefer?"
  │              ↓
  │            i = 0
  │              ↓
  │            if i < 2
  │              ├── Yes ──→ OUTPUT i + 1, water[i]
  │              │              ↓
  │              │            i = i + 1 ──┐ (loops back to if i < 2)
  │              │
  │              └── No ──→ INPUT activity1
  │                           ↓
  │                         OUTPUT "You have chosen" activity1
  │                           ↓
  │                         ARRAY waterNew = "Waterpolo", "Sailing"
  │                           ↓
  │                         if activity1 == 1
  │                           ├── Yes ──→ OUTPUT "Why not try" waterNew[0]
  │                           └── No  ──→ OUTPUT "Why not try" waterNew[1]
  │
  └── No ──→ OUTPUT "Which of the following team games do you prefer?"
                ↓
              i = 0
                ↓
              if i < 2
                ├── Yes ──→ OUTPUT i + 1, team[i]
                │              ↓
                │            i = i + 1 ──┐ (loops back to if i < 2)
                │
                └── No ──→ INPUT activity2
                             ↓
                           OUTPUT "You have chosen" activity2
                             ↓
                           ARRAY teamNew = "Cricket", "Beach volleyball"
                             ↓
                           if activity2 == 1
                             ├── Yes ──→ OUTPUT "Why not try" teamNew[0]
                             └── No  ──→ OUTPUT "Why not try" teamNew[1]
                                           ↓
                                         Stop
```

Unit 9.1 Presenting choices: Combining constructs

Pseudocode

```
START
ARRAY water = [Swimming, Canoeing]
ARRAY team = [Hockey, Volleyball]
ARRAY waterNew = [Water polo, Sailing]
ARRAY teamNew = [Cricket, Beach volleyball]
OUTPUT "Do you prefer watersports or team games?"
INPUT typeOfActivity

IF typeOfActivity == "W" THEN
   OUTPUT "Which of the following watersports do you prefer?"
   FOR i = 0 to 1
      OUTPUT i + 1, water[i]
   OUTPUT "Enter the number of your preferred activity."
   INPUT activity1
   OUTPUT "You have chosen" activity1
   IF activity1 == 1 THEN
      OUTPUT "Why not try" waterNew[0]
   ELSE
   OUTPUT "Why not try" waterNew[1]
    END IF

ELSE
   OUTPUT "Which of the following team games do you prefer?"
   FOR i = 0 to 1
      OUTPUT i + 1, team[i]
   OUTPUT "Enter the number of your preferred activity."
   INPUT activity2
   OUTPUT "You have chosen" activity2
   IF activity2 == 2 THEN
      OUTPUT "Why not try" teamNew[0]
   ELSE
   OUTPUT "Why not try" teamNew[1]
    END IF

END IF
STOP
```

Then the program code is developed to match the algorithm.

The program uses the value of the variable 'activity1' or 'activity2' to output the name of the activity that the user might like to try.

The program code has now been developed to use the answer from one question to decide which question to ask next, and then uses the answer from the second question to

43

advise the user which activity they might like to try. The program uses several variables, conditional statements and count-controlled loops to allow different pathways through the chatbot program. Note that the extra arrays have been set up at the start of the program so that they can be accessed easily at any point when the program is run.

```python
water = ["Swimming","Canoeing"]
waterNew = ["Water Polo","Sailing"]
team = ["Hockey","Volleyball"]
teamNew = ["Cricket","Beach Volleyball"]

print("Do you prefer watersports or team games?")
typeOfActivity = input("Enter W or T: ")

if typeOfActivity == "W":
    print("Which of the following watersports do you prefer?")
    for i in range(2):
        print(i+1,water[i])
    activity1 = int(input("Enter the number of your preferred activity: "))
    print("You have chosen",water[activity1-1])
    if activity1 == 1:
        print("Why not try",waterNew[0])
    else:
        print("Why not try",waterNew[1])

elif typeOfActivity == "T":
    print("Which of the following team games do you prefer?")
    for i in range(2):
        print(i+1,team[i])
    activity1 = int(input("Enter the number of your preferred activity: "))
    print("You have chosen",team[activity1-1])
    if activity1 == 1:
        print("Why not try",teamNew[0])
    else:
        print("Why not try",teamNew[1])
```

This program has now gone through two development iterations.

Practise

As a chatbot program is developed, the different concepts are integrated. For example, if you need a conditional statement to check what the user enters, then you need to use selection. If you want to run program code for a set number of times, then you need to use a count-controlled loop.

1 Discuss with your partner how this program could be developed to include additional activities for the user to choose between.

2 Plan a new iteration of the chatbot algorithm that asks the user to choose from three different watersports or team games and gives a suggestion for a new activity to try for each activity chosen. Do this as pseudocode.

Unit 9.1 Presenting choices: Combining constructs

> 3 Compare and contrast your pseudocode development with your partner. Test each other's algorithm using a trace table, fixing any errors that you identify.
> 4 Open **ActivitiesChatbot.py** provided by your teacher. Develop the program code in Python to create a software prototype to match your pseudocode, and save it as **ActivitiesChatbotV2.py**.
> 5 Discuss with your partner:
>   a how using a selection allows you to have different pathways through your program
>   b the purpose of the **one-dimensional arrays** in this chatbot program.

> **KEYWORD**
>
> **one-dimensional array:** series of items grouped together under one identifier

Testing times

Learn

As you already know, it is particularly important to test the programs that you write to make sure that they run and that they produce the correct outputs. This is an important process in developing a new prototype.

To recap, there are different types of errors that can be found when creating programs:
- Syntax
- Logic
- Runtime.

If a program contains a **syntax error**, it will not run. A syntax error occurs where the programmer has written the code incorrectly. Possible syntax errors include a missing bracket, a missing colon or missing indentation.

The program below is a chatbot to guide a user on what to do at the weekend. It contains a syntax error on line 3 as the colon (:) is missing from the end of the line.

```
1  activities = []
2
3  for i in range(3)
4      activities.append(input("Enter a possible activity: "))
5
6  print(activities)
7  decision = input("Which do you prefer? ")
8
9  for item in activities:
10     if item == decision:
11         print("At the weekend you should do", item)
12     else:
13         print("That is not a possible activity.")
```

45

The error is detected as soon as the program is run, and an error message is produced. Different **integrated development environments (IDEs)** present the error message in different ways. For example, in IDLE the place where the program has failed is highlighted and a pop-up suggests what the problem may be:

```
1 activities = []
2
3 for i in range(3)
```

expected ':'

OK

In a different IDE, the following error message is produced:

```
File "<ipython-input-1-f40285fcd492>", line 3
    for i in range(3)
                     ^
SyntaxError: invalid syntax
```

Both error messages give a hint to the location and an indication of what type of error has been encountered.

As you saw with trace tables, a **logic error** is linked to the **conditional operator** that is used. The program will run but the output will not be as expected if the wrong operator has been used.

A **runtime error** occurs during the running of a program when Python cannot execute an instruction. For example, look at this program code for the chatbot program to select a possible activity for the weekend.

Program code	``` 1 activities = [] 2 3 for i in range(3): 4 activities.append(input("Enter a possible activity: ")) 5 6 print(activities) 7 decision = input("Which do you prefer? ") 8 9 for item in activity: 10 if item == decision: 11 print("At the weekend you should do", item) 12 else: 13 print("That is not a possible activity.") ```
When executed	``` Enter a possible activity: swimming Enter a possible activity: running Enter a possible activity: walking ['swimming', 'running', 'walking'] Which do you prefer? walking Traceback (most recent call last): File "/Users/Lorne/Documents/testingTimes.py", line 9, in <module> for item in activity: NameError: name 'activity' is not defined. Did you mean: 'activities'? ```

Unit 9.1 Presenting choices: Combining constructs

The first part of the program runs correctly, but the program encounters a problem at line 9. The program output stops and a **traceback message** is displayed that helps to identify where the error occurred. Here, 'activity' has been used in the for loop instead of 'activities' for the name of the array.

Finding and fixing errors is an important part of a programmer's role, as all aspects of a program need to work correctly.

When you test a program, you should use a range of test data to check that the program runs as expected. However, a programmer cannot test every possible input a user might add to a program, so they must decide carefully which data to use when they create their test plan.

Look at a chatbot program that asks the user to guess a number between 1 and 10.

```
number = 6
print("I have chosen a number between 1 and 10")
guess = int(input("What do you think it is? "))
if guess == number:
    print("You guessed correctly!")
elif guess > 0 and guess < 10:
    print("Not correct")
else:
    print("Not a valid guess")
```

There are three possible types of test data that should be used in a test plan for this program.

- **Normal data**: A sensible input that the program should accept: any number between 1 and 10.
- **Extreme data**: Still an acceptable input but at the ends of the possible input range: using 1 or 10 as the input.
- **Invalid data**: An input that should not be accepted: using a value outside the acceptable range, such as 20.

These values can be added to a test plan and then used to test the program. This test plan has been completed for the program above using a range of test data:

Test	Test data	Expected outcome	Pass/fail
Normal	5	Not correct	Pass
Normal	6	You guessed correctly!	Pass
Extreme	1	Not correct	Pass
Extreme	10	Not a valid guess	Fail
Invalid	20	Not a valid guess	Pass

CAMBRIDGE LOWER SECONDARY COMPUTING 9

The test plan has shown that the program ran all the way from start to finish. This shows that there are no syntax errors or runtime errors. However, one of the tests did fail. The extreme test data used the input 10, which should produce the output 'Not correct', but instead the output was 'Not a valid guess'. This shows that a logic error has been found.

> Checking the conditional operator used in the `elif` conditional statement shows that it has been set as less than 10 (< 10). To include 10, the conditional operator needs to be amended to be less than or equal to 10 (<= 10). Once this has been changed, the programmer should test the program again to ensure that it now works correctly.

KEYWORDS

syntax error: error in program code that stops the program from running

integrated development environment (IDE): software that includes all the tools needed to develop a program in a particular language

logic error: error that allows a program to run but not output what is expected

conditional operator: symbol, e.g. >, < and =, used to carry out comparisons between two values

runtime error: error that occurs while a program is running; the instructions cannot be completed

traceback message: displayed when a runtime error is encountered to help identify where the error occurred and what went wrong

normal test data: data of the correct type that should be accepted by a program

extreme test data: acceptable input but at the ends of the possible input range

invalid test data: data that should be rejected by a program

Practise

1. Open the file **TestProgram.py** provided by your teacher.
   a. Discuss with your partner what normal, extreme and invalid data you would use to test this program.
   b. Create a test plan that uses normal, extreme and invalid test data.
   c. Complete the test plan.
   d. Identify and fix the syntax, runtime and logic errors in the code.
   e. Save the corrected file as **TestProgramV2.py**.
   f. Test the program again to make sure that it works correctly.
2. Discuss with your partner the benefits of using normal, extreme and/or invalid test data for a program's development.
3. Discuss with your partner the different types of program errors and how a programmer can find each one.
4. Evaluate in pairs the importance of using a range of test data as a process in program development.

Unit 9.1 Presenting choices: Combining constructs

Go further

When a user inputs into a program an answer to a question, the answer is either stored in a variable or added to an array. The input is stored exactly as the user types it. A user may input their answer using uppercase or lowercase or a mix of both.

If you are using a conditional statement to compare two variables, the way the user enters their answer may affect the outcome.

In the chatbot program below, the user is asked to enter a possible activity for the weekend.

```
activity = input("Enter a possible activity: ")

if activity == "swimming":
    print("A great choice")
else:
    print("Nice idea, but have you thought about trying swimming?")
```

The conditional statement is looking for 'swimming' as the input. If swimming was added using uppercase letters or with an uppercase letter at the start, then the program would not recognise it as a True outcome as the string would not be an exact match.

As the input is being stored as a string data type, **string manipulation** can be used to adjust aspects of the stored string. For, example, no matter how the user enters their answer, the whole input can be converted to lowercase letters by adding `.lower()` to the end of the input. This is useful in a chatbot program where you need to test the input using selection or need all items in an array to have the same format.

```
activity = input("Enter a possible activity: ").lower()
```

Likewise, the input can be converted to uppercase letters by adding `.upper()` to the end of the input.

```
activity = input("Enter a possible activity: ").upper()
```

It is also possible to convert the first letter of a string to uppercase and the rest of the string to lowercase by adding `.capitalize()` to the end of the input.

```
activity = input("Enter a possible activity: ").capitalize()
```

String-manipulation code can also be used to output the length of the string, for example, the length of the word being stored in a variable.

```
activity = "swimming"
print(len(activity))
```

Or it can be used to find out the length of the array, that is, the number of items being stored in the array.

```
activity = ["swimming", "running", "walking"]
print(len(activity))
```

In pseudocode, this would be written by defining the way the input should be entered.

```
START
activity = INPUT lowercase "Enter a possible activity."

IF activity == "swimming" THEN
      OUTPUT "A great choice!"
ELSE
      OUTPUT "Nice idea, but have you thought about trying swimming?"
ENDIF
STOP
```

1 Look at the pseudocode you used in the 'Iterations and arrays' section.

```
START
ARRAY rainbow = [red, orange]

FOR i = 0 TO 4
      Add INPUT to ARRAY "Add a colour"
ENDFOR

OUTPUT " _ _ _ _ _ _ _ _ _ _ _ _ _ _ _ _ _ _ _ _ _ "
OUTPUT "Your rainbow colours are:"

FOR each colour in ARRAY rainbow:
      OUTPUT colour
ENDFOR
STOP
```

> Remember that this program has an array to store the input from the user. The user is asked to enter five colours, as the for loop iterates five times over the input question.

2 Open your file **rainbowColoursChatbotV1.py** from the 'Iterations and arrays' section. Discuss with your partner how you think a user would enter their answers when this program is run.

3 Open the file **RainbowColoursChatbot.docx** provided by your teacher. Annotate the pseudocode to show where you could use string manipulation to alter the user's input. Add to the algorithm so that it tells the user how many items are in the array after each new item has been added.

4 Develop your program file so that it matches your new iteration of the pseudocode algorithm and save it as **rainbowColoursChatbotV2.py**.

5 Discuss with your partner how you would test the program and identify test data that would be suitable.

6 Create a test plan with normal, extreme and invalid data and use this to test your rainbow colours chatbot program.

KEYWORD

string manipulation: process of changing the format of a variable/string to allow it to be analysed

Unit 9.1 Presenting choices: Combining constructs

Challenge yourself

You can now add items to an array and use a **for loop** to access the items. You can have more than one array in a program and the items can be used multiple times in different ways. For example, a chatbot may ask you to enter items of clothing you are looking for and then your favourite colours. This could be used to show you clothes items in the colours you entered.

Previously, you have used an array in a chatbot program to store three favourite subjects. In this next iteration of the chatbot, the program is going to ask for the name and favourite subject of three friends. The chatbot will then output the individual answers.

The pseudocode for the algorithm shows that:
- two empty arrays are set up at the start of the program
- the user is asked three times to enter a friend's name and their favourite subject
- each name is stored in the array 'names'
- each subject is stored in another array 'favSubjects'
- there is an output acting as a separation using dashed lines and a title stating that the details will follow
- the relevant items from both arrays are located and output in the same sentence.

```
START
ARRAY names = [ ]
ARRAY favSubjects = [ ]

FOR i = 0 to 2
    Add INPUT to ARRAY names "Enter your friend's name"
    Add INPUT to ARRAY favSubjects "Enter their favourite subject"
ENDFOR

OUTPUT "_ _ _ _ _ _ _ _ _ _ _ _ _ _ _ _ _ _ _"
OUTPUT "Your friend's details are:"
OUTPUT "_ _ _ _ _ _ _ _ _ _ _ _ _ _ _ _ _ _ _"

FOR each item in ARRAY names and ARRAY favSubjects
    OUTPUT name "likes" subject
ENDFOR
STOP
```

To create the final count-controlled loop that looks at both arrays, you need to use a new function: `zip()`.

The loop needs to look at each item in each array. Two variables can be set at the start of the for loop to store the item in the list being looked at: **for name, subject in**. It is important that the two variables (shown in green here) are separated by a comma.

The two array names are placed inside the brackets of the `zip()` function, again separated by a comma. Remember to add the colon at the end of the line to tell the program that the for loop has been set up: **for name, subject in** `zip(names, favSubjects):`

The output is placed in a print function. The variables defined at the start of the for loop, to store the items from the arrays, are used in the output.

```
for name,subject in zip(names,favSubjects):
    print(name,"likes",subject)
```

1 Write a program in Python to match the pseudocode algorithm shown above.
2 Choose suitable test data and develop a test plan to check that your program works correctly.
3 Save the file as **challengeYourself.py**.
4 Discuss with your partner the types of test data used in your test plan.

Final project

The skills you have learned in this unit are all about using iterative development to produce solutions to problems. You have learned how to trace the variables through a program using a trace table and how a count-controlled loop and an array can develop your Python programming further.

Look back to the start of this unit to remind yourself of the Scenario.

You are going to create a program to help students during the selection of options or subject areas to continue to study. The chatbot will ask the user a series of questions, store their answers and use this to help them to make a final decision.

- The solution will be presented as pseudocode to show the algorithm for your chatbot program.
- Use variables and/or an array to store the answers to questions asked of the user.
- Use a count-controlled loop.
- Follow an iterative process to design, develop, test and review towards a final prototype.

Part 1: Planning

1 Plan and list the questions that your chatbot will need to ask. Think about how you might help someone to choose between three different subjects.
2 List the variables and data types that are going to be used in your program.
3 Identify suitable names for one or more arrays to be used in your program. Add these to your list.

Part 2: Develop the algorithm

1 Plan the algorithm using pseudocode.
2 Annotate your pseudocode to show how your program will use an array and a count-controlled loop.
3 Annotate your pseudocode to describe the data types that are being used and which are not being used and why.
4 Add a caption to your pseudocode to explain how you will use string manipulation to adjust a user's input.

Part 3: Test the algorithm

1 Create a trace table and use this to check the contents of variables,

Unit 9.1 Presenting choices: Combining constructs

arrays and the outcome of conditional statements in a **dry run** of the pseudocode.
2. Identify suitable test data, including normal, extreme and invalid inputs, and create a test plan to be used on your program once it has been written.
3. If necessary, correct any logic errors identified by the dry run of your program and work through the trace table again. Ensure that you save any developments as a new iteration of the pseudocode.

Part 4: Development
1. When you are sure that the pseudocode algorithm is complete and correct, start the development of your Python code.
2. Continuously test, debug and improve your program code.
3. Create a trace table and use this to check the contents of variables, arrays and the outcome of conditional statements as the program is run.
4. Use your test plan to test the program using normal, extreme and invalid data.
5. Using both the trace table and test plan, identify any logic, syntax or runtime errors.
6. Save each development as a new iteration of the program.

Part 5: Evaluation of the prototype
Once you have created, tested and reviewed your prototype program solution, **evaluate** the impact of the different parts of the process that you have followed to create your final version of the program. Create a short report that explains:
1. the iterative process you used to develop your final program code
2. how you used trace tables
3. how you used test plans with normal, extreme and invalid data
4. the difference between a logic error, a runtime error and a syntax error and how you have tested for these throughout the program development.

Evaluation

1. Swap programs with your partner and test their program. Comment on the following:
   a. Does it cover all the requirements?
   b. Is the solution easy to use?
   c. Do the inputs work as expected?
   d. Are the questions suitable for the Scenario at the start of the unit?
   e. Are the variables clear to understand?
   f. What extra features have they added, such as arrays/string manipulation, and what impact do they have on the final program?
2. Open your program and look at the code. Reflect on what you could improve in your own program following feedback from your partner.
3. Based on the evaluations, make a list of recommendations to improve your final program.

KEYWORDS

dry run: process of working through an algorithm manually to trace the values of variables

evaluation: checking the suitability of a solution to a problem

53

What can you do?

Read and review what you can do.
- ✔ I can follow, understand, edit and correct algorithms that are presented as pseudocode.
- ✔ I can follow flowchart or pseudocode algorithms that use loops.
- ✔ I can create algorithms using flowcharts and pseudocode.
- ✔ I can use and explain iteration statements with count-controlled loops in either pseudocode or flowcharts.
- ✔ I can predict the outcome of algorithms that use iteration.
- ✔ I can compare and contrast two algorithms for the same solution and decide which is best suited to the task.
- ✔ I can create an algorithm as a flowchart or pseudocode using more than one construct: sequence, selection and count-controlled iteration.
- ✔ I can identify and explain the purpose of a one-dimensional array.
- ✔ I can identify and describe data types in Python programs, including integer, real, character, string and Boolean.
- ✔ I can develop a Python program with count-controlled loops.
- ✔ I can access data from an array using Python.
- ✔ I can develop Python programs using string manipulation, including length, uppercase and lowercase.
- ✔ I can use iterative development on Python prototypes to create solutions to problems.
- ✔ I can develop and apply test plans that include normal, extreme and invalid data.
- ✔ I can identify test data that covers normal, extreme and invalid data.
- ✔ I can identify and describe a range of errors, including syntax, logic and runtime errors.
- ✔ I can use a trace table to debug errors in a Python program.

Unit 9.2 Design your own network: Shape and size

Get started!

Have you ever wondered how computer **networks**, both big and small, are designed, or what the boxes full of wires and other devices that are found in classrooms, offices and homes across the world actually do? Who decided where to position them and why did they set up the network in the way that they did? How do we make sure that **data** transmitted across networks is secure?

Discuss the following with your partner:
- How are devices connected to networks?
- When a device is connected to a network, what type of address is assigned to it?
- Are there ways of knowing whether data has been transmitted accurately?

In this unit, you will develop your understanding of the ways in which networks can be designed and expanded. You will look at how the design of a network can affect the way in which devices work on the network. You will investigate how devices communicate and how **data packets** are transmitted. Importantly, you will learn how networks can be built **sustainably**, so they can be expanded and developed to ensure that they are always **fit for purpose**.

KEYWORDS

network: collection of computing devices connected to each other, either by wires or wirelessly

data: raw facts and figures

data packet: small unit of data that is packaged to be sent across a network

sustainably: when a network is built in a way that it is easy to maintain in the future

fit for purpose: something that is well designed for its purpose

Learning outcomes

In this unit, you will learn to:
- explain how different network topologies (bus, ring and star) transfer information between devices
- explain the role of protocols in data transmission
- explain what scalability factors are and how scalability can affect a network
- explain why scalability should be considered when designing networks and how networks can be designed to scale up
- explain what a parity bit is and its role in error detection
- perform parity bit and parity block calculations and identify errors in data transmission
- explain the choices that must be made when securing information on a network, including cost, accessibility and the relative security requirements of different datasets.

CAMBRIDGE LOWER SECONDARY COMPUTING 9

Warm up

Connecting devices to a network brings a whole range of possibilities to their use. Some devices simply wouldn't work as intended without an active network connection, such as an internet-connected smart lightbulb or the online services of a games console.

Discuss the following with your partner:
- What devices do you use that connect to a network?
- Does the device require an **active internet connection** to work?
- If the device has an internet connection, does it require a **high-bandwidth** connection?
- What would happen if the internet connection disconnected due to **interference**?

KEYWORDS

active internet connection: where a device has a working connection to the internet

high bandwidth: connection that can send and receive a large amount of data per second

interference: when electronic signals disrupt data transmissions

network topology: diagram that shows how devices in a network are connected to one another, and shows the network hardware

SCENARIO

A local youth-recreation centre has opened, with the aim of providing a facility for young people who wish to game, interact and hang out in a safe, monitored and flexible online environment. The centre has asked the IT department in your school for advice on networking and security. They also need advice about the hardware they will need to ensure that members can be connected in a network. The group hopes that students can link up using any electronic device they have access to, for example mobile phones, tablets, gaming consoles, PCs or even smart watches!

The network should be able to support a large number of members in the youth centre, with users connecting from a range of devices.

Your challenge is to learn all about **network topologies** (network layouts), technologies and the software required to support network communications, before you can advise them on their hardware needs for the network.

56

Unit 9.2 Design your own network: Shape and size

> **DID YOU KNOW?**
> The first network to connect different kinds of computers together was switched on in October 1969. It was named ARPAnet. The system was invented to connect large companies, universities and governments together so that they could share information via devices such as teletype machines.

> **Do you remember?**
>
> Before starting this unit, you should be able to:
> ✔ decide what type of network should be used in different scenarios
> ✔ understand the difference between copper and fibre cables
> ✔ explain whether wired or wireless networks should be used in certain scenarios
> ✔ understand the security features that different types of networks can have
> ✔ describe how an echo check can check for data accuracy in transmission
> ✔ understand how firewalls, antivirus and anti-spyware can provide protection to a network
> ✔ explain the purpose of operating systems
> ✔ understand what is meant by ASCII.

Building blocks of networking

Learn

People, companies, schools and governments rely on network connectivity to be dependable and fast. The type of network that is designed by network engineers is crucial to the network running reliably and speedily. Here's a recap of the different types of network.

PANs

Personal Area Networks are a type of network where devices communicate over a small area, usually no further than 10 metres or so. This type of network is often used for devices that the user wears, such as headphones or a smart watch.

CAMBRIDGE LOWER SECONDARY COMPUTING 9

LANs

Local Area Networks are a type of network where devices communicate over a small geographical area. You could think of this as a single building or a school site, for example. Devices within this network range are able to access services offered by the **server** on the same network, which is ideal for sharing files, printing or sharing a single internet connection. In your school network, it is likely that you can access a students' drive, or similar, where teachers can place files for you to use.

WANs

Wide Area Networks are a type of network where devices communicate over larger geographical areas. An example of this would be a company with a few offices at opposite sides of town, or even offices in different countries. These networks usually connect together via the internet, as it would be physically impossible to lay dedicated cables between the office buildings.

WANs rely on external networking equipment, usually provided via the **Internet Service Provider's (ISP's)** cabling, to create a 'virtual' link between the LANs of each office.

> Remember that there are also WPAN, WLAN and WWAN, which are the same as PAN, LAN and WAN but the devices connect wirelessly!

KEYWORDS

Personal Area Network (PAN): type of network where devices communicate over a small area of no more than 10 metres, usually connecting devices a person wears to a smartphone or computer

Local Area Network (LAN): type of network where devices communicate over a small geographical area, e.g. a single building

server: usually a powerful computer that offers a range of services to a network, e.g.
file storage, user management, printer sharing, email access or web servers

Wide Area Network (WAN): type of network where devices communicate over a large geographical area, such as across a city or country

Internet Service Provider (ISP): company that provides users access to the internet, and is often responsible for the network equipment that connects LANs to WANs

Network architecture

Network engineers are specialists in building networks so that they are fast, dependable and safe to use. It is likely that any business, school or government has used a network engineer to help them to create their network, so that the users can use it without having problems.

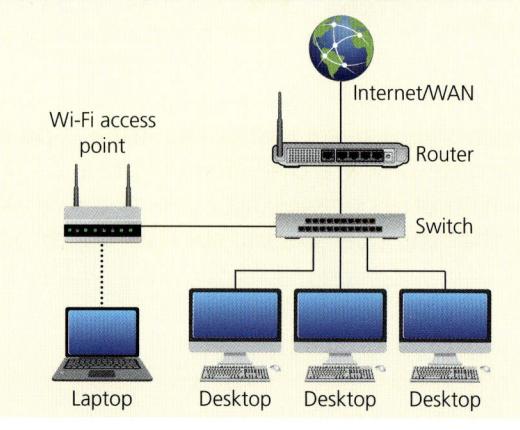

58

Unit 9.2 Design your own network: Shape and size

Network topologies show how a network is arranged and how the devices connect to each other. Some network topology diagrams can be extremely detailed, to show every aspect of a network, including **hardware**, devices and connection methods.

The example on the previous page shows a simple network topology diagram connecting three desktop computers and one laptop to a network. All the devices are connected to a switch, which forms a LAN. The **router** then joins the LAN to a WAN (the internet).

Imagine you were asked to create a network topology diagram for your school that contains every device and piece of network hardware. It is likely that it would be an exceptionally large document!

Network hardware

When network engineers are designing a network topology, they need to decide what network hardware to use to ensure that the network will be fast, dependable and secure.

> **KEYWORDS**
>
> **network topology:** diagram that shows how devices in a network are connected to one another, and shows the network hardware
>
> **hardware:** physical parts of a computer that you *can* touch and see, e.g. the processor, storage devices, input devices, output devices
>
> **router:** hardware device that connects networks together
>
> **network switch:** switch that connects devices together to form a wired network
>
> **network interface card (NIC):** every device that connects to a network includes a NIC, which has a pre-programmed MAC address so that it can be identified on the network
>
> **MAC address:** number programmed into a network interface card that identifies each device on a network
>
> **wireless access point:** allows devices to connect to a network using Wi-Fi

The common hardware components of a network are listed in the table below. You will recognise some of the device names from the basic topology diagram above.

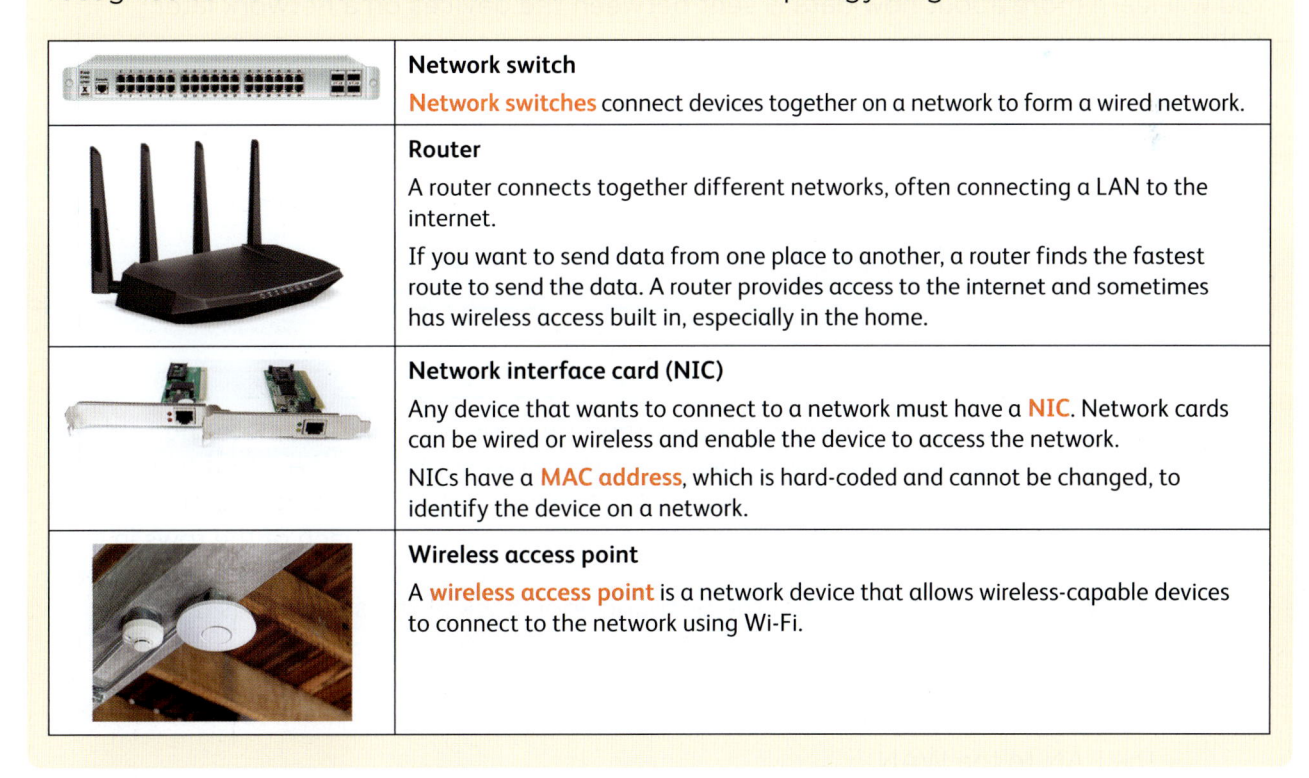

	Network switch **Network switches** connect devices together on a network to form a wired network.
	Router A router connects together different networks, often connecting a LAN to the internet. If you want to send data from one place to another, a router finds the fastest route to send the data. A router provides access to the internet and sometimes has wireless access built in, especially in the home.
	Network interface card (NIC) Any device that wants to connect to a network must have a **NIC**. Network cards can be wired or wireless and enable the device to access the network. NICs have a **MAC address**, which is hard-coded and cannot be changed, to identify the device on a network.
	Wireless access point A **wireless access point** is a network device that allows wireless-capable devices to connect to the network using Wi-Fi.

59

CAMBRIDGE LOWER SECONDARY COMPUTING 9

	Ethernet cabling These are cables that are designed to work with ethernet ports on a NIC to connect devices to a network. They are dependable for high-speed connections, with a maximum bandwidth of 10 Gbps (gigabits per second). The longer the cable, the worse the performance.
	Servers Servers are computers on a network that offer a service to other devices. Here are some common servers found on networks. **File servers**: These offer devices on a network a place to store and access files. On large networks, files are not usually stored on the device that the user is using, but on the file server. This can be especially useful in a business where a number of people need to access the same files, or where people may need to access their files from any computer on the network. **Print servers**: These enable devices on a network to share printers. In a large office it would not be feasible for every device to have its own printer. A print server manages which devices can print to each printer so that users can share them. **Mail servers**: These store email messages and allow users to log in to send and receive messages. **Web servers**: These provide internet-accessible files and transmit files to users over the world wide web.
	Firewall Most networks, especially business networks, use a hardware **firewall**. This examines the incoming and outgoing **network traffic** to check for security risks and block any suspicious activity.

You will learn more about how data is sent between the devices on a network later in this unit.

> **KEYWORDS**
>
> **file server:** server that stores users' files and enables them to be shared on a network
>
> **firewall:** restricts the network traffic entering and exiting a network, to ensure that it is safe
>
> **network traffic:** amount of data travelling through a network, split into small parts for transmission

Practise

1. Open the file **Network hardware.docx** provided by your teacher. Complete the table without using this book, where possible. Provide a brief summary of each of the network devices. Copy and paste images from the internet of the devices you find.
2. a Open the file **Network uses.docx** provided by your teacher. For each of the rows in the table, explain how the youth centre in the Scenario could use the device in their network. If you need to remind yourself of the Scenario, look back at the start of this unit.
   b Complete the diagram to show the following connections:
      i   the router to a port on the network switch
      ii   each of the laptops to the network switch to form a LAN
      iii the LAN to the WAN.

60

Unit 9.2 Design your own network: Shape and size

Topologies and architecture

Learn

You are probably used to using networks at home and at school. This gives you an excellent oversight of a small LAN (home) compared with a larger LAN (school). Both of these networks will probably link to the internet (a WAN), and **routers** are used to join your home or school network to the internet.

As you explored in the previous section, **network topology** is how the hardware devices are arranged and connected in a network. There are some well-known topologies that have been tried and tested over time. Each of these topologies has advantages and disadvantages.

Bus topology

In a **bus topology**, all the devices (servers, computers, printers) are joined to one cable (the bus). There is a **terminator** at each end of the cable to absorb the signals and stop them from being reflected back down the bus.

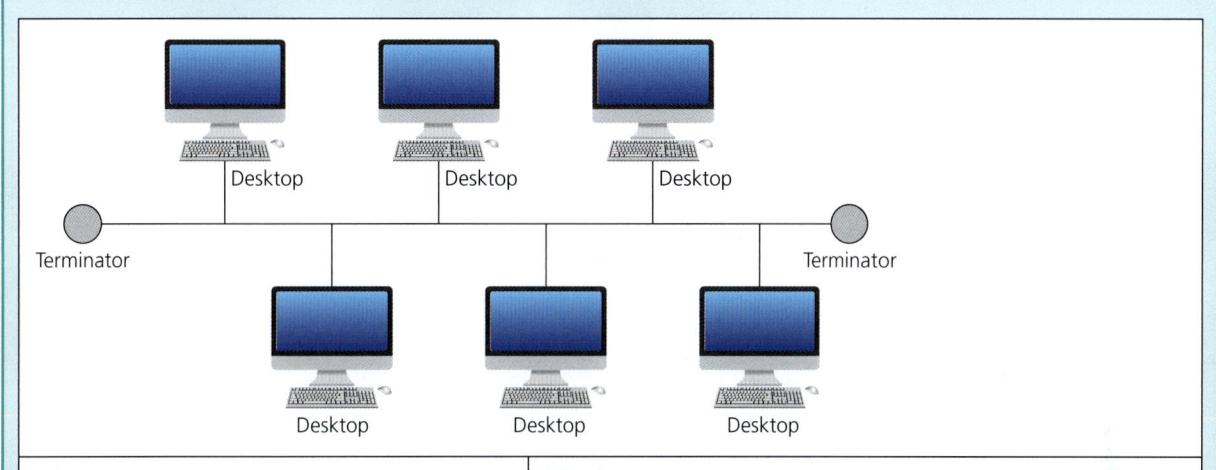

Advantages
- Bus networks are easy to install.
- They are cheap as they don't need a lot of cable.

Disadvantages
- If the main cable fails or is damaged, the whole network will stop working.
- As the network gets larger, it is more likely that data will **collide** and be corrupted as it is sent between devices. This reduces the performance of the network.
- All devices on the network are visible to each other, which could pose a security risk.

KEYWORDS

router: hardware device that connects networks together

network topology: diagram that shows how devices in a network are connected to one another, and shows the network hardware

bus topology: network in which all devices are connected together via a main cable running down the centre of the network

terminator: ending to a network cable that absorbs the signal to stop it bouncing back

colliding: when data 'bumps into' other data, which often causes errors or lost data

61

Ring topology

In a **ring topology**, each device is connected to two other devices, forming a ring for the data to travel around. The data travels in one direction and is passed through each device until it reaches its destination.

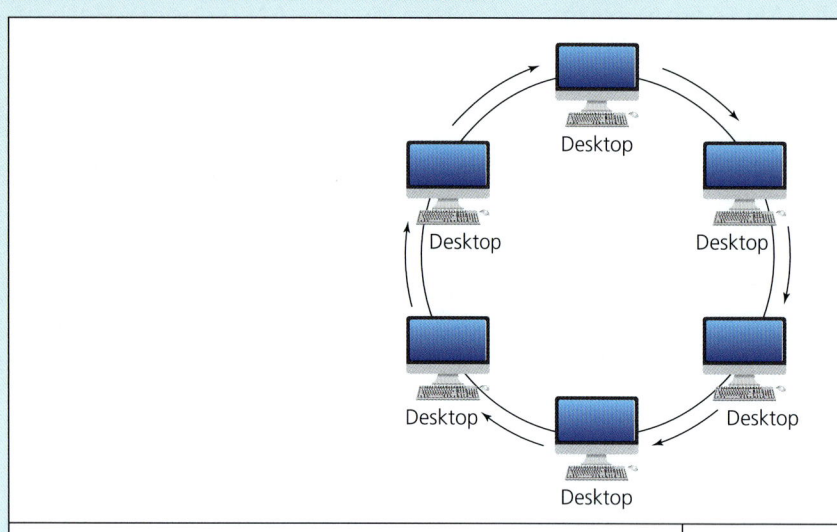

Advantages
- Data travelling on a ring network flows only one way, which means that data does not collide.
- Data can be transferred quite quickly, even if there are a large number of devices connected.

Disadvantages
- If the main cable of the ring network is broken, it will stop the entire network working for all devices connected to it.

Star topology

In a **star topology**, every device on the network has its own connection to a switch. The main switch sends data packets to the destination device only.

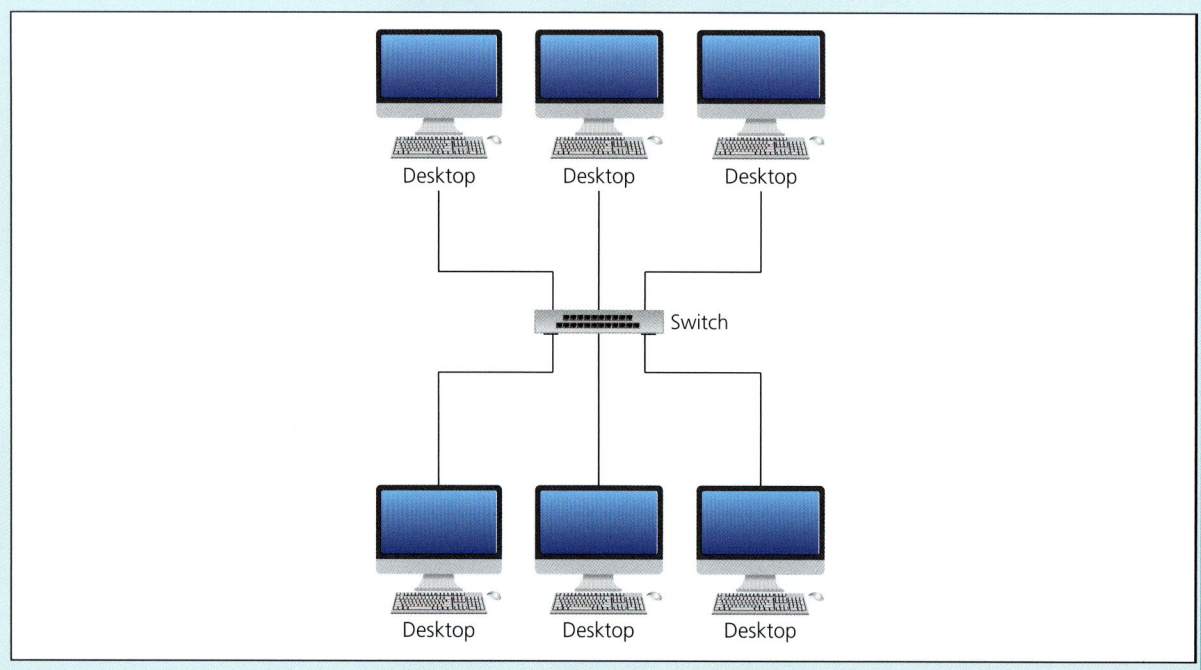

Unit 9.2 Design your own network: Shape and size

Advantages	Disadvantages
● Each device is connected separately. ● It is very dependable as the rest of the network will continue to work if a cable or device fails. ● Network performance is good as the switch directs data to the correct destination. ● It is easy to add new devices to the network, as they can be attached directly to the switch.	● If the main switch fails, then none of the devices can communicate. ● It can be expensive to install as more ethernet cabling is needed.

In modern networks, star topologies are usually used, as data collisions do not occur when a switch is performing its task of directing packets of data to the correct device only.

When designing networks, it is important to consider what will be the best topology to use before you start to create the network topology diagram.

Practise

1. Look around your classroom. Write a list of all the devices in the room, along with other devices that are used in your school network. Your teacher will help to identify these. Include how many there are of each device, for example 25 PCs, 5 tablets and 15 smartphones.

2. Create a network topology diagram for your school. Include:
   a. a basic icon and label for each of the devices
   b. any WAPs and switches
   c. lines to show how the devices are connected to a WAP or switch, labelled to show whether the device is connected by a wire (W) or wirelessly (WL).

   The WAP and/or switch may be visible to you in your classroom or might be in another room nearby.

3. Assume that your school has a router, connecting your LAN to the internet, and a firewall hardware device to improve its security.
   a. Add a firewall above the switch, and connect the devices together.
   b. Add a router above the firewall, and connect the devices together.
   c. Add a WAN/the internet above the router.
   d. Connect the LAN and WAN together.

4. In groups, discuss the type of network that has been designed.
   a. Is it a star, ring or bus network? Why has that type of network been used?
   b. What would be the disadvantages of using a ring network to redesign your school network?

KEYWORDS

ring topology: network in which all devices are connected together to form a ring

star topology: network in which each device is connected separately to a central switch

It's all in the protocol

Learn

Imagine if computer manufacturers created devices that could communicate only with other devices made by the same manufacturer. Smartphones wouldn't be able to join cellular networks unless the mast was made by that manufacturer. PCs wouldn't be able to communicate with each other unless the same company made them. Network switches would communicate only with devices that were made by the same company as the switch manufacturer.

Thankfully, this is where **protocols** step in to save the day! Protocols are an agreed set of rules for communicating over a network. The protocols used in modern technology allow all kinds of devices to communicate with each other, regardless of who manufactured them.

There are two main protocols that you need to know about, both of which have clear rules for how computers should communicate over a network.

TCP/IP Protocol

Transmission Control Protocol/Internet Protocol (TCP/IP) is a collection of rules that govern how computers can communicate with each other over a network.

When sending data from one device to another on a network, TCP/IP is the protocol used to break the data into **packets**, address the data, transmit the data, route the data and receive any data from other devices.

The Transmission Control Protocol (TCP) is responsible for breaking the data into smaller sections called *packets*. Imagine that you wanted to send an image file from one computer to another. TCP would send part of the image data in each data packet.

Each packet has extremely strict rules about how it should look. Along with the image data, the TCP protocol adds information to each packet, including how many packets there are in total and the number of each packet.

Think of a packet as being like a letter, which needs to include the address of where the packet is being sent. The Internet Protocol (IP) adds the **IP address** of the sender and the receiver to the packet. The example below shows a single packet that is ready to be sent over a network.

> **KEYWORDS**
>
> **protocol:** agreed set of rules that computers follow to communicate with each other over a network
>
> **Transmission Control Protocol/Internet Protocol (TCP/IP):** protocol for transferring data between devices
>
> **data packet:** small unit of data that is packaged to be sent across a network
>
> **IP address:** unique number assigned to a computer on a network

Unit 9.2 Design your own network: Shape and size

Sender IP address 83.23.55.31	Receiver IP address 54.211.90.1	Packet number 5/340
Data 01100110110110111101101011001101101101111011010110011011011011110110101100110110110111101101011001101101101111011010110011011011011110110101100110110110111101101011001101101101111011010110011011011011			

Sender IP address: The packet needs to include this so that devices on the network know where to forward the packet to.

Receiver IP address: This needs to be included in case of a 'dropped packet', which means a packet that did not reach its destination. If this is the case, then the receiver can request that the packet is sent again.

Packet number: This is included so that the receiving device can re-assemble the packets in the correct order. It also helps the receiving device to understand if there are any packets missing.

Packet switching

When data is transmitted across a network, it is split up into small packets. For example, if somebody wanted to transmit a video file across a network, the file would be split as follows:

Full video file				
Video file packet 1	Video file packet 2	Video file packet 3	Video file packet 4	Video file packet 5

In reality, packets are so small that a video file would likely be split into thousands of packets.

Packets contain the data that is being sent, and the sender IP address and receiver IP address, so that the data can be directed to the correct destination.

Video packet 1	
Sender IP address	88.34.23.3
Receiver IP address	212.51.22.2
Packet number	5/340
Data	01000010101111011010100010111101011010...

When the packets are assembled, they are sent across the network. Packets can be sent across the network using different routes, often travelling through many different devices before they reach their destination.

The receiving computer will put the packets in order to check that they have all been received. If there have been any 'dropped packets', the receiver will re-request that packet and it will be transmitted across the network again.

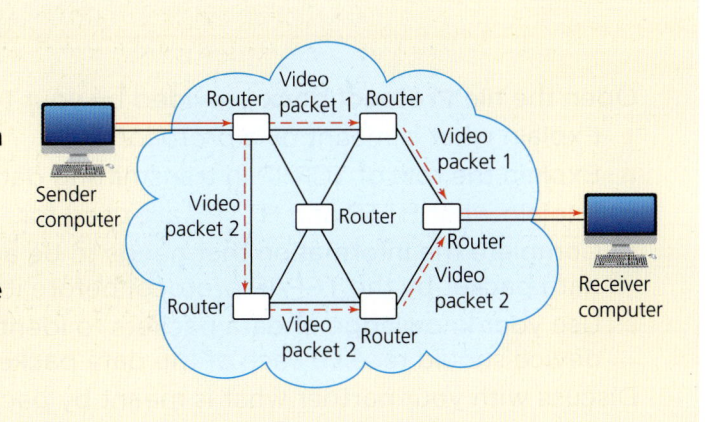

65

CAMBRIDGE LOWER SECONDARY COMPUTING 9

HTTP and HTTPS

Hypertext Transfer Protocol (HTTP) and **Hypertext Transfer Protocol Secure (HTTPS)** are protocols that exist to allow web browsers to fetch documents from web servers. Documents could include web pages, text, images or videos. HTTPS is encrypted, which can prevent unauthorised access if data is intercepted.

Each time a user on a web browser tries to view a document on the world wide web, the device sends a request to the web server for the information. Here is an example of a request that is sent when the browser tries to visit **www.google.com**:

```
Request headers
:authority: www.google.com
:method: GET
:path: /
:scheme: https
accept: text/html
accept-encoding: gzip, deflate, br
accept-language: en-US,en;q=0.9
upgrade-insecure-requests: 1
user-agent: Mozilla/5.0
```

KEYWORDS

Hypertext Transfer Protocol (HTTP): set of rules for communicating with web servers

Hypertext Transfer Protocol Secure (HTTPS): set of rules for communicating with web servers, with added encryption to improve security

domain name: part of a URL that specifies the location on the internet, e.g. **google.com**

You will notice that the request includes the **domain name**, but also includes some additional information, such as the type of document it is requesting (in this case, html, which is a webpage document). It also shows what type of web browser the user is using (Mozilla).

DID YOU KNOW?

The packet-switching concept was invented in the early 1960s by Paul Baran (left, receiving a National Medal of Technology and Innovation in 2008 from US president George W. Bush). The concept was designed to send and receive data successfully even if devices on the network failed, by redirecting the packets in a different direction from their destination.

Practise

1. Open the file **Protocol.docx** provided by your teacher.
   a. Explain what is meant by a *protocol*.
   b. Explain the role of TCP/IP in transmitting data.
   c. Explain what HTTP and HTTPS are used for.
   d. Complete the information that needs to be added to the data packet by the TCP/IP protocol before it can be sent.
   e. Use your knowledge of data packets to identify which device should receive each of the data packets shown.
2. Discuss with your partner what is meant by *packet switching*.

Unit 9.2 Design your own network: Shape and size

Scalable considerations

Learn

Imagine you are a network engineer and have spent a lot of time building the perfect, fast, reliable and safe network. Everything is running smoothly until your boss asks you to add another 100 devices to the network! Is it possible to add devices to a network without changing other aspects of the network? It's a good question and will need some investigation.

Network **scalability** means how well a network can cope if it suddenly needs to move a lot more data between more devices. If your school opened a new building full of classrooms, but didn't upgrade their network hardware, having lots more users on the same connection would slow down the speed. It could also make the network less secure. Think about the impact there would be if your school allowed all students to connect their smartphones to the Wi-Fi. It is important that scalability is considered when a network is being planned and built.

To assess the scalability of a network accurately, you need to consider the following.

Security

If the network becomes unstable due to a rapid increase in the number of devices connected and the amount of data being transmitted, it could cause network hardware to not operate properly. For example, if the network were unstable and caused the firewall to disconnect from the network, the network could be open to the threat of a **cyber-attack**.

It could be an excellent idea to use multiple **firewalls**. For example, in a school it might be useful to have a firewall for staff offices and a separate firewall for student computer rooms. This way, there is a more limited amount of data flowing through a single firewall at any time.

Storage solutions

What effect would adding lots more devices have on storing files on the network? If there is a **file server**, would this need to be expanded, so that the impact of having more users is avoided.

To improve scalability of storage, it would be important to add either more storage capability to the current file server or another file server into the network.

Accessibility of data

If the network is not scalable, then adding more devices that are transmitting a lot of data around the network could have an impact on the speed of data transmission, as the bandwidth has to be shared between all the devices. This could also make the network unstable, causing devices to become disconnected from the network. This may mean

KEYWORDS

scalability: capacity to make something larger, e.g. a network enlarged with more devices

cyber-attack: attempt to gain unauthorised access to a network, to damage or destroy a computer system

firewall: restricts the network traffic entering and exiting a network, to ensure that it is safe

file server: server that stores users' files and enables them to be shared on a network

that essential files cannot be accessed at crucial times. Imagine, for example, if this happened in a hospital just before a patient's operation.

It is important to make sure that the network hardware is not overloaded. This might mean adding more network switches, or more wireless access points for Wi-Fi devices, so that particular devices are not overused.

> Network **administrators** are often faced with the dilemma of whether to expand the network horizontally (adding new devices to the network to increase the scalability) or upgrading the devices they currently have to improve the capacity of the network.

Innovation in networking

Cloud computing makes use of servers on the internet to provide services to store, manage or process data. Lots of companies worldwide now use cloud servers, rather than having their own servers on their premises. Lots of smartphone users, for example, use cloud photo storage, rather than having to increase the storage available on their device.

Because of the challenges of scalability in networking, new solutions are constantly being developed. Lots of the most innovative solutions take advantage of cloud computing or use devices outside the network to do some of the work. For example, if your school were to open a new building, by using a file server on the internet there would be no reason to upgrade the file server that is in school. The school would simply pay for an online service to store staff and student files. Examples of **online storage services** include Microsoft OneDrive, Google Drive and Dropbox.

Network system software

Network operating systems (NOS) play an important role in keeping a network running quickly, reliably and safely. Network operating systems work in the same way as a normal **operating system**, but they are designed to be installed on servers. Often, the NOS manages the users on the network, maintains the network connections, manages file server features and provides **utilities software** for keeping the network running well.

> An operating system is a piece of **software** that manages the hardware (**device drivers**) and software on a computer system. Commonly used operating systems are Microsoft Windows, macOS, iOS, Linux and Android.

Unit 9.2 Design your own network: Shape and size

Network operating systems also manage resources such as the router, switches and firewalls.

A common task that the operating system carries out on a network file server is disc **defragmentation**. This organises files on a **hard disc drive**, which can improve the speed at which files can be accessed on the file server.

User management is essential on a well-maintained network. Network administrators can control which files, printers, software and other network facilities different types of user can access. The image on the previous page shows that network administrators have a number of tools at their disposal to keep the network running well, including file management. For example, it would not be a good idea to give students access to the confidential staff folders.

Network utilities software

Utilities software on an NOS works in a similar way to utilities software on a personal device. Networks still need to have **virus scanning**, **backup** and **encryption** software installed. Instead of performing this on individual devices, network utilities allow the network administrator to run scans, checks and tools on all of the devices on the network at the same time. They even allow network administrators to schedule the tasks to run at specific times of the day. For example, in a school it would be useful for these to run at 5 a.m., before staff and students have arrived.

> Encryption software on a network can be extremely important, especially if the network holds personal information about people. Encryption software can also be used if people connect to the network **remotely**, to make sure that the data cannot be intercepted.

KEYWORDS

administrator: account with top-level access, with the ability to change settings or add and remove users from a network

cloud computing: using servers on the internet for services

online storage services: using file storage servers on the internet to store files

network operating system (NOS): computer operating system that supports networks, often including additional administrator software and monitoring tools

operating system: software that manages all the computer hardware and software; it also acts as an interface between computer hardware components and the user, and provides a platform where applications can run

utilities software: software that helps maintain the smooth functioning of a digital device by helping the operating system manage tasks and resources

software: a program or a set of instructions that tell a computer what to do to complete a task; aspects of a device you *cannot* touch

device driver: software program that operates a hardware device connected to a computer

defragmentation: reorganising files stored on a hard drive to ensure that all parts of the same file are located one after the other on the drive

hard disc drive: removable disc in computers for storing large amounts of data, typically measured in gigabytes or terabytes

user management: adding or removing users to control access to a network

virus scanning: checking files on a computer system for malicious content

backup: copying files to another location in case the original is lost or damaged

encryption: converting information into a scrambled form, so that it cannot be understood if it is intercepted

remotely: connecting to a network from another location via an internet connection

CAMBRIDGE LOWER SECONDARY COMPUTING 9

Practise

1. Open the file **Scalability.docx** provided by your teacher. Read the scenario.

   > Ravi is the network administrator for a new company, which has an office. The company has started selling lots more of their products due to an increase in demand. They have taken on twelve new employees and need to open another office in the same building, containing twelve desktop computers.

   a. Add to the existing network topology diagram of Office 1 to show Ravi how he could scale up the network.

   b. Add a comment to the diagram to state the tasks that a network operating system could carry out on the network.

   c. Add a paragraph below the diagram to explain what utilities software could be used to keep the network secure or running more smoothly.

2. Ravi has been asked to remove four computers from Office 1, as they are no longer needed. Using **Scalability.docx**, make changes to the network topology diagram of Office 1 to accommodate the new request.

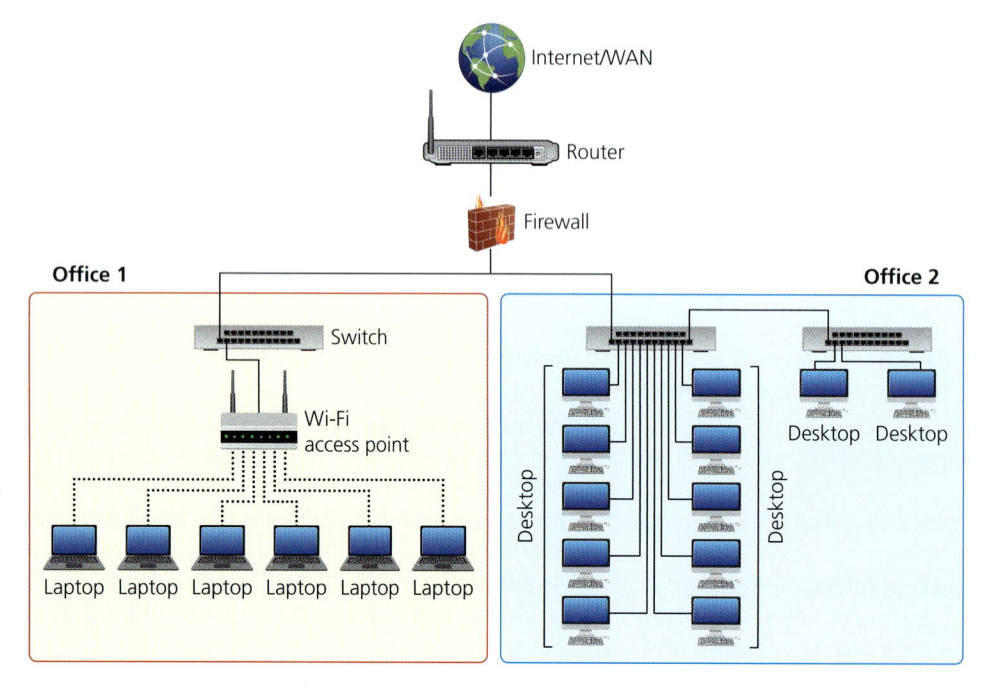

3. Ravi has designed the network topology, but a year later the network isn't running reliably. He investigates the issues and finds that the firewalls he is using are no longer powerful enough to run a network of this size. Ravi has also noticed that his users are running out of file storage space, so they are not able to save files on the network. In the office, he has noticed that the Wi-Fi speeds are very slow, due to the number of devices trying to access the network.

   Explain how Ravi can improve the network, based on the following factors. Write a paragraph under each heading.
   - Security
   - Storage
   - Accessibility

Unit 9.2 Design your own network: Shape and size

Checking for errors

Learn

With millions of **packets** of data transmitted over networks every second, it is to be expected that some will not reach their destination in one piece. Networks handle so much data that how devices deal with the errors becomes especially important to the reliability of a network.

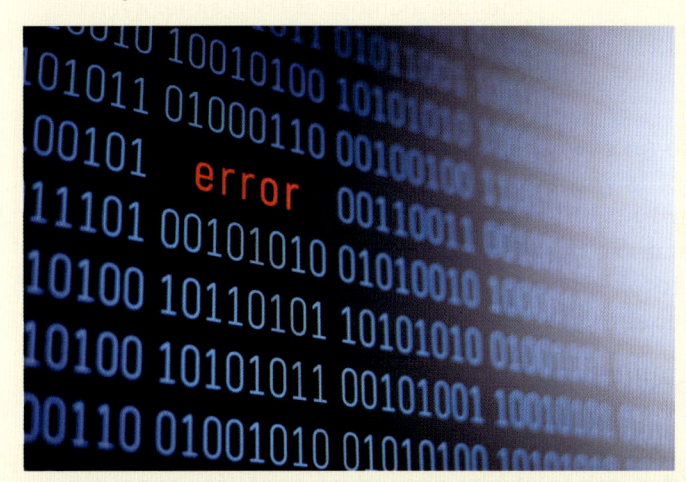

> **KEYWORDS**
> **data packet:** small unit of data that is packaged to be sent across a network
> **bit:** short for 'binary digit': 0 or 1
> **binary data:** data that is represented as a 1 or a 0
> **hacker:** somebody who tries to gain unauthorised access to a computer system or network

Electrical spikes or power surges
A power surge is a short burst of significantly more voltage coming through the electrical wire to an electrical device. Power surges can cause binary **bits** to flip between 0 and 1, causing an error in data transmission. They are usually caused by faulty wiring or lightning strikes.

> Remember: the only data that computers understand are 0s or 1s. If one of these bits is 'flipped' then this can cause errors.

Interference
Interference occurs when a number of electrical devices are being used in a small area. The electrical and radio waves can disrupt each other's signals. This can cause errors in **binary data**, or causes devices to disconnect from the network.

Security breaches
Security breaches can be caused by malware or by **hackers**. For example, if a firewall hardware device were hacked, its rules could be changed to allow any data into the network, which could result in the system being overloaded and could cause errors in the binary data being transmitted.

Hardware failure
If a network switch were to fail, this could cause errors in data transmission, with packets no longer routed to the correct places.

Parity-checking

How can we check that data is received accurately by another device? **Parity-checking**! Parity checks are used to make sure that data has been sent and received correctly. Devices transmitting data between each other agree to use either an **odd or even** protocol for parity-checking.

> **KEYWORDS**
>
> **parity-checking:** type of error check that ensures data has been transmitted correctly
>
> **byte:** eight bits of data, e.g. 01010011
>
> **parity bit:** bit added to a byte to make the total number of 1 bits either even or odd

If devices have agreed that they will use an **even** number of bits, then any data received should have an **even** number of 1s within it, so a **byte** would have two 1s, four 1s, six 1s or eight 1s in total. The **parity bit** is set to either 1 or 0 to ensure that the total number of 1s is even. For example, if the first 7 bits are 1001100, then the parity bit would be set to 1 to make four 1s in total; if the first 7 bits are 1001000, then the parity bit would be set to 0 as there is already an even number of 1s in this byte.

If any bytes are received that have an **odd** number of 1s, then this data has an error and would need to be sent again.

Where devices have agreed that an **odd** number of bits should be sent (for example one 1, three 1s, five 1s or seven 1s), if there are an **even** number of 1s, then the data contains an error and would need to be sent again.

Example 1

Computer 1 and Computer 2 have agreed to use an **even** checking system.

Computer 1 sends the byte:

| 0 | 1 | 0 | 1 | 0 | 1 | 0 | 1 |

Computer 2 receives the byte:

| 0 | 1 | 0 | 1 | 0 | 1 | 0 | 1 |

The byte received by Computer 2 has four 1s, which is an even number. There is no error.

Computer 2 receives the byte:

| 1 | 1 | 1 | 1 | 1 | 1 | 0 | 1 |

There has been an electrical surge and the byte received by Computer 2 has seven 1s, which is an odd number. There is an error.

Unit 9.2 Design your own network: Shape and size

> **Example 2**
> A mobile phone and a tablet device have agreed to use an **odd** checking system.
>
> The tablet device receives the byte:
>
> | 0 | 1 | 1 | 1 | 0 | 1 | 0 | 1 |
> |---|---|---|---|---|---|---|---|
>
> The byte received by Computer 2 has five 1s, which is an odd number.
> There is no error.

Parity checks give computers a way to check for errors. They can detect errors quickly and require little computing power. However, this check does not identify which bit is incorrect, if an error is detected, so the data has to be re-sent.

Practise

1. Answer the following questions in pairs.
   a. What is a parity bit?
   b. How can a parity bit help in error detection?
2. Look at each example below. Say whether an error would be detected and explain the reason for each answer.
   a. A smart watch and a mobile phone have agreed to use an **even** parity-checking system. The mobile phone receives the following byte:

0	1	1	1	1	1	0	1

   b. A PC and a server have agreed to use an **odd** parity-checking system. The server receives the following byte:

0	1	0	0	0	1	0	0

   c. A tablet and a PC have agreed to use an **odd** parity-checking system. The PC receives the following byte:

0	0	0	0	0	0	0	0

Keeping it all secure

Learn

In companies, schools or governments, the data contained in packets that speed around networks can be extremely valuable to the organisation that owns them. Often, the organisations rely on the data they have about their customers, students or products to be able to continue successfully. Some of the data is personal data, which means that companies have a legal responsibility to look after it carefully.

A **dataset** is a collection of data that is stored in a **table**, or multiple tables. An example of a simple dataset is shown below, and includes how much money an employee is paid per year, along with their personal details.

Full Name	Address	Country	Pay per year
Luis Garcia	PO Box 325, 2864 Enim St	Spain	$57,711.00
Athena Levy	Ap #426-1625 Erat. Rd	United Kingdom	$41,751.00
Dominic Compton	9665 Vitae Road	Canada	$35,326.00
Lenore Berg	PO Box 288, 4870 Natoque Ave	India	$65,103.00
Neve Hart	565-7129 Lectus Street	Austria	$59,849.00
Vera Townsend	271-2412 Et St	France	$51,792.00
Ju Yang	657-1640 Felis. Ave	China	$14,589.00
Aamandu Abebe	Ap #414-3963 Arcu. Rd	South Africa	$16,563.00
Porter Dickson	Ap #886-4114 Sed Ave	United States	$30,379.00
Nelle Sosa	Ap #537-5164 Pede Street	United States	$17,371.00

KEYWORDS

dataset: collection of related information that a computer can manipulate

table: set of facts or figures that are set out in a column and row structure

It is crucial that this information is kept safely and cannot be accessed by anyone who is not authorised to do so, as people could be identified from the information, and the information is private. Other examples of private information include:
- medical records
- school records
- police records
- customers' information kept by businesses
- bank details.

For example, would you be happy for your school records to be made publicly available for other people to see? What effect could this have on your opportunities in the future?

Network managers need to make sure that the datasets on their networks are kept safe, which is a challenging task when there are lots of threats to data.

Here are some ways in which organisations can keep datasets safe on networks.

Firewalls

Most networks, especially business networks, use a firewall. This is a special type of network hardware (or software) that examines the incoming and outgoing network traffic to check for security risks and blocks any suspicious activity.

Firewalls can protect datasets by blocking access to the data from outside the network, or from specific parts of the network.

User access controls

User access controls enable network managers to allow some users access to the datasets, but not others. This could be useful in a school, for example, by allowing teachers to view the datasets about student progress and parental contact details. It would not be a good idea to allow students access to this information, in case it was misused.

Often, some accounts will be grouped as **administrator** accounts, which is the type of account the network manager would have. In a school, it is likely that there would also be 'staff' and 'student' account groups, that could access different parts of the network.

Password policies

To prevent unauthorised access to a network, it is important that network managers create strong password policies for their users. This helps to make sure that users create stronger passwords.

Here are some of the rules that may be included in the policy.
- Passwords must
  - contain letters, numbers and symbols
  - be longer than ten **characters**
  - not contain the user's name
  - not contain a date.
- Users must change their passwords regularly.

Using long and unpredictable passwords helps to keep datasets secure, as it would take much longer for **hackers** to gain access using a **brute-force attack**.

Biometric security and two-factor authentication

Other methods that network managers could use to keep the network safe are **biometric security** and **two-factor authentication**.

> **KEYWORDS**
>
> **administrator:** account with top-level access, with the ability to change settings or add and remove users from a network
>
> **character:** single letter, digit or symbol
>
> **hacker:** somebody who tries to gain unauthorised access to a computer system or network
>
> **brute-force attack:** type of unauthorised access to a computer system that uses a large dictionary to try multiple password combinations until it is successful
>
> **biometric security:** security method that identifies people using a physical attribute (e.g. a fingerprint) or a behaviour (e.g. a hand gesture)
>
> **two-factor authentication:** method of signing into a system that requires two types of authentication (e.g. a password and a one-time SMS message code)

Biometric security requires a user to sign into systems using a biological password, such as a **fingerprint**, **facial recognition** or an iris scan. This method of **authentication** is becoming increasingly popular, with more and more devices supporting it.

Two-factor authentication can be used to authenticate a user. This is where a user is asked to confirm their identity using a second device. Often a code is sent to the second device, such as a mobile phone, which must be entered via the main computer to complete the log-in process. This adds an additional layer of security, making it harder for someone to gain unauthorised access to the system.

Biometric security and two-factor authentication are powerful policies that a network manager can put in place for certain staff, for example teachers, so that important information can be protected.

Encryption

If data is sent between devices as **plaintext**, then a hacker could intercept the data. If a teacher wanted to access details of a student from their laptop at home, if the data were not encrypted and was sent as plaintext, a hacker could intercept the data and read the contents of the data packets. Network managers can make sure that all data is encrypted using secure **protocols**, such as HTTPS.

Levels of security – a compromise!

While it would be best if all the methods above were used to keep a network secure, in reality this is not always possible. There is a fine balance between devices being usable and devices being ultra-secure.

For example, if a school has a 'no mobile phones' policy for students, then it would not be possible to ask students to use two-factor authentication every time they want to log in. Biometric scanners for all students and staff devices would be extremely expensive. Some systems within school do not hold personal data, so it is not as important for them to be secure. Imagine if you were asked to change your password every day; it would make the system very secure, but it would be extremely hard to remember your password!

Network managers always need to consider the cost of a security method, how easily users need to be able to access systems and how securely the data needs to be stored.

Machine learning in network security

Innovative approaches to keeping networks safe have been rapidly transformed by **artificial intelligence** and **machine learning**. Newer cloud

> **KEYWORDS**
>
> **fingerprint recognition:** system that matches a real-time image of a human fingerprint with a database of saved fingerprint representations to allow a user access to a digital device
>
> **facial recognition:** system that matches a real-time image of a human face with a database of saved facial representations to allow a user access to a digital device
>
> **authenticate:** confirm a user's details to ensure that they should be allowed access to a system
>
> **plaintext:** text that has not been encrypted and can be read if it is intercepted
>
> **protocol:** agreed set of rules that computers follow to communicate with each other over a network
>
> **artificial intelligence (AI):** ability of a computer system to learn and develop its own programming from the experiences it encounters
>
> **machine learning:** ability of a computer system to learn over time

Unit 9.2 Design your own network: Shape and size

products now use machine learning to find threats. For example, if an IP address is linked to a known hacker or security risk, firewalls with machine learning enabled will use this information to look for this IP address and block it from accessing the network.

Machine learning can also detect when a login looks suspicious and block it, for example, if a user tries to log in from a location that they do not usually use.

Practise

1. When designing network security, costs need to be considered. Create a table with two columns: 'Hardware' and 'Costs'. Find the cost of each of the following pieces of network hardware, which will help you in the tasks that follow.
   a. Network switch
   b. Router
   c. Wireless access point
   d. Ethernet cable
   e. Firewall (hardware)

2. Discuss each of these scenarios with your partner.
   - How secure does the data in the scenario need to be? Would it be damaging if this data were exposed?
   - How many 'groups' of users are present in the system? (For example, Customers and Staff)
   - What security measures would you want to put in place?
   - What would be the total cost to put these security measures in place, based on the hardware costs you found in the previous task?

   a. **Scenario 1**
   You are the network administrator for a large car sales garage. Sales assistants can work remotely to access customer records, so that they can make sales calls from home. All staff in the organisation are provided with a laptop when they start working for the company. Managers in the company are given an upgraded laptop and also have access to the personal details of the sales assistants, so that they can contact them when required.

   b. **Scenario 2**
   You are the network administrator for a restaurant business. There are three Wi-Fi-connected laptops in the restaurant that the table staff use to input food orders. A dataset is used to keep track of how well each food item sells. The laptops have built-in fingerprint readers, but they are not currently being used. Staff have not changed their passwords in over five years and the network does not have a firewall in place.

> For this task, imagine that you are a network manager, responsible for keeping data safe on your network. However, you also need to make sure that data is as accessible as possible for the people who need it. Remember: hardware devices are quite expensive and can have a big impact on your budget, so you should buy network hardware only if you really need to.

CAMBRIDGE LOWER SECONDARY COMPUTING 9

c **Scenario 3**

A large bank in a city centre has hundreds of bank staff, IT specialists and managers. The bank has three confidential datasets that it needs to protect: one containing the personal details of all the staff; one containing private banking information; and one containing customer details. The bank requires the highest level of security to keep their data safe.

3 Explain to your partner how using a machine-learning security feature could improve the security of a network.

a What would happen if somebody tried to log into the system from another country?

b What would happen if somebody tried to log into the system from another device?

c If a particular IP address has been identified by cloud software as a threat, what action could it take if this device tried to access the system?

Go further

Error-checking during data transmission is all about trying to work out whether a problem has occurred when transmitting data between devices. One problem with using a parity check is that this type of check does not identify *where* the error has occurred. You just know that there is an error, which means that the data has to be transmitted again.

This is where **two-dimensional parity checks** are used instead. Two-dimensional parity checks allow you to identify exactly where the error exists in the data that has been transmitted. To do this, devices need to send a **parity byte** in addition to the bytes of data that are to be transmitted. This means that data is sent in **blocks**, rather than one byte at a time.

KEYWORDS

two-dimensional parity check: check for finding where an error exists within a parity check

parity byte: byte added to a block of data to check whether the data is valid or invalid

block: string of data (0s and 1s)

parity bit: bit added to a byte to make the total number of 1 bits either even or odd

The **parity bits** and parity byte are used to determine whether the data has been transmitted correctly using this process.

1 First, the parity bit for the byte of data in each horizontal row is identified. In this example, **even** parity is being used.

	Parity bit	Bit 1	Bit 2	Bit3	Bit 4	Bit 5	Bit 6	Bit 7	
Byte 1	0	0	1	1	1	0	0	1	EVEN
Byte 2	0	1	0	0	0	0	0	1	EVEN
Parity byte									

Step 1: Calculate the parity bit for each byte of data.

Unit 9.2 Design your own network: Shape and size

2. Then, the parity byte is worked out by looking at the bits in each vertical column and making sure that the parity bit identified is following the same **odd** or **even** rule. In this example, using **even** parity, the total number of 1s and 0s in each column should be even.

	Parity bit	Bit 1	Bit 2	Bit 3	Bit 4	Bit 5	Bit 6	Bit 7	
Byte 1	0	0	1	1	1	0	0	1	EVEN
Byte 2	0	1	0	0	0	0	0	1	EVEN
Parity byte	0	1	1	1	1	0	0	0	EVEN
	EVEN	EVEN	EVEN	EVEN	EVEN	EVEN	EVEN	EVEN	

Step 2: Calculate the parity bit for each column of data.
- The parity byte is transmitted along with the rest of the data, and each byte of main data includes a parity bit.
- The receiving device will check that each row and column of the block of data sticks to the even parity rule. If they do, then the data has been transmitted successfully.

If an error has occurred during data transmission, then using parity-checking in this way will also identify where the error has occurred.

The example below, which is a larger block of data, uses an **even** checking system, so all rows and columns should be **even**. However, you can see that the checks for byte 2 and bit 6 have failed, identifying where the error has occurred. The bit where the row and column intersect can now be flipped to fix the error.

	Parity bit	Bit 1	Bit 2	Bit 3	Bit 4	Bit 5	Bit 6	Bit 7	Odd/Even
Byte 1	0	1	0	1	1	0	0	1	EVEN
Byte 2	0	1	0	1	0	1	1	1	ODD
Byte 3	0	0	1	0	1	1	0	1	EVEN
Byte 4	0	1	1	0	1	0	1	0	EVEN
Parity byte	0	1	0	0	1	0	1	1	EVEN
Odd/Even	EVEN	EVEN	EVEN	EVEN	EVEN	EVEN	ODD	EVEN	

1. To remind yourself of how to perform a parity check, identify which of the following bytes have been transferred correctly, if **even** parity has been used.
    a 11010000
    b 01100110
    c 11110101
    d 10111001
    e 00111111

> Look back to the 'Checking for errors' section for a reminder about parity-checking.

79

2. Open the file **Calculating Parity Bits.docx** provided by your teacher. Calculate the parity bit for each question.
3. The example below (that has been received by a device) uses **odd** parity.
   a. Copy and complete the table below, identifying whether each column and row is **odd** or **even**.

	Parity bit								Odd/Even
Byte	1	0	1	1	0	0	0	1	
Parity byte	0	1	0	0	0	1	1	0	
Odd/Even	ODD								

   b. Identify which bit is incorrect.
4. Open the file **Calculating Parity Blocks.docx** provided by your teacher. Complete the questions to calculate the parity bits and parity byte to discover the errors in the transmission data.
5. In pairs, explain to each other what a parity bit is and why it is useful when checking for errors.

Challenge yourself

Network administrators often use the **command line** to manage their network, or devices on their network.

A command line is another way to access the **operating system**, without the need for a **graphical user interface (GUI)**. For expert users, common tasks can be completed more quickly using the command line, and it allows for more advanced operations, such as sharing folders across the network, analysing packets of data sent around the network, and much more.

Network administrators need to learn how to use the command line when they are training for their role.

Accessing the command line (MS-DOS)

The command line allows you to type in commands to perform actions on the computer, instead of using a GUI to perform the actions. There are a number of ways to access the MS-DOS command line in Windows. The easiest way is to go to the `Start Menu` and type in `run`, then press `Enter` on your keyboard.

> **KEYWORDS**
>
> **command line:** a way of using an operating system that is navigated by typing commands
>
> **operating system:** software that manages all the computer hardware and software; it also acts as an interface between computer hardware components and the user, and provides a platform where applications can run
>
> **graphical user interface (GUI):** way of using software that is navigated by pointing and clicking on graphics on a screen

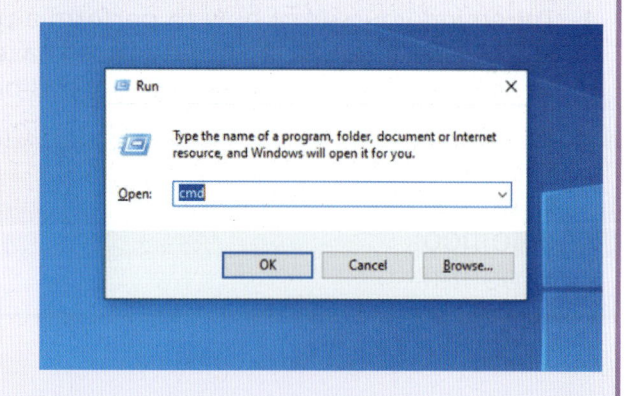

Unit 9.2 Design your own network: Shape and size

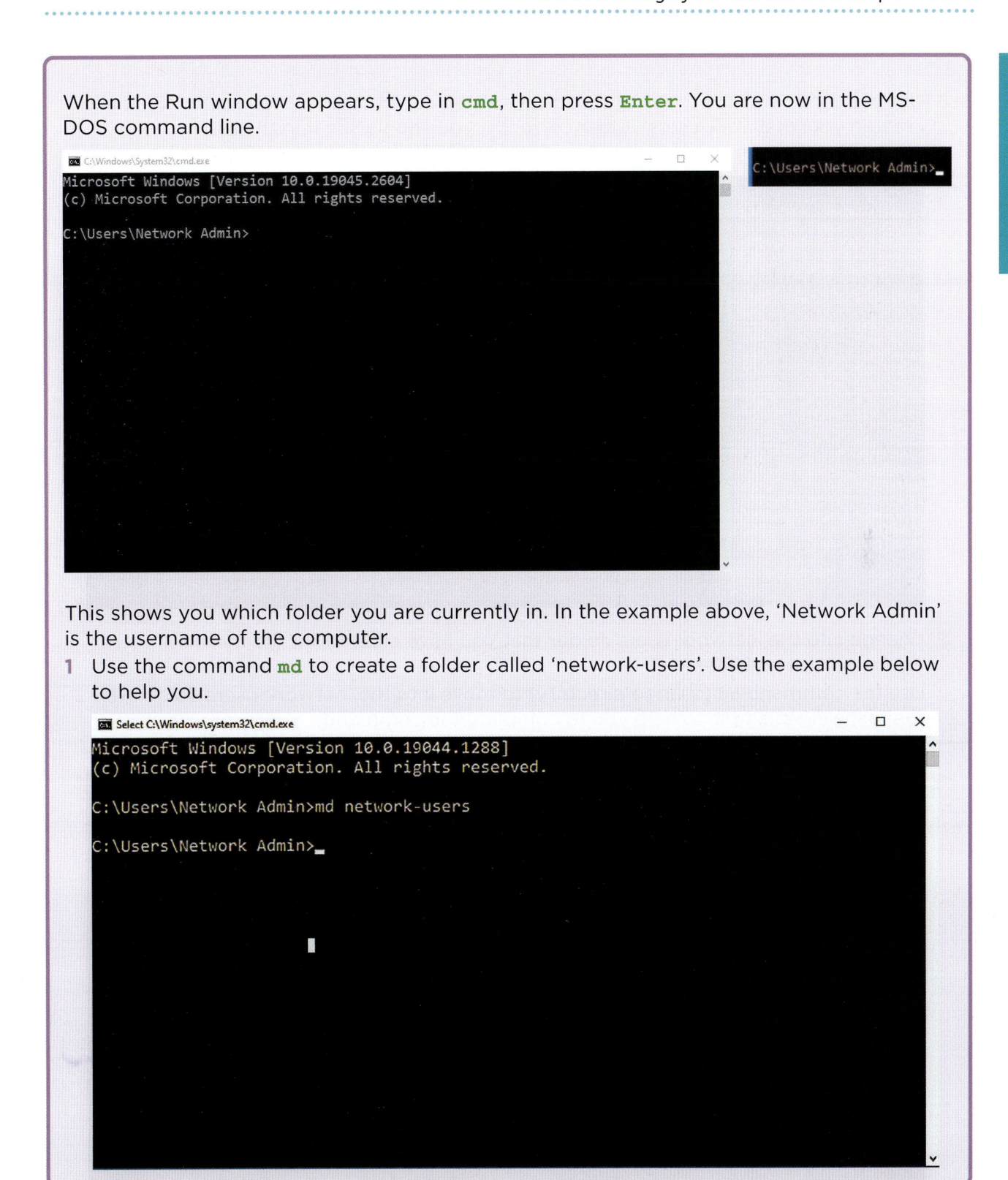

When the Run window appears, type in `cmd`, then press `Enter`. You are now in the MS-DOS command line.

```
C:\Windows\System32\cmd.exe
Microsoft Windows [Version 10.0.19045.2604]
(c) Microsoft Corporation. All rights reserved.

C:\Users\Network Admin>
```

```
C:\Users\Network Admin>
```

This shows you which folder you are currently in. In the example above, 'Network Admin' is the username of the computer.

1 Use the command `md` to create a folder called 'network-users'. Use the example below to help you.

```
Select C:\Windows\system32\cmd.exe
Microsoft Windows [Version 10.0.19044.1288]
(c) Microsoft Corporation. All rights reserved.

C:\Users\Network Admin>md network-users

C:\Users\Network Admin>
```

2 Use the command `dir` to list all the folders in the current folder that you are in. If you created your 'network-users' folder correctly, you should see it in the list.

```
C:\Windows\system32\cmd.exe

(c) Microsoft Corporation. All rights reserved.

C:\Users\Network Admin>md network-users

C:\Users\Network Admin>dir
 Volume in drive C has no label.
 Volume Serial Number is 2AE6-0115

 Directory of C:\Users\Network Admin

20/05/2022  10:56    <DIR>          .
20/05/2022  10:56    <DIR>          ..
20/05/2022  10:39    <DIR>          3D Objects
20/05/2022  10:39    <DIR>          Contacts
20/05/2022  10:39    <DIR>          Desktop
20/05/2022  10:39    <DIR>          Documents
20/05/2022  10:39    <DIR>          Downloads
20/05/2022  10:39    <DIR>          Favorites
20/05/2022  10:39    <DIR>          Links
20/05/2022  10:39    <DIR>          Music
20/05/2022  10:56    <DIR>          network-users
20/05/2022  10:49    <DIR>          OneDrive
20/05/2022  10:48    <DIR>          Pictures
20/05/2022  10:39    <DIR>          Saved Games
20/05/2022  10:39    <DIR>          Searches
20/05/2022  10:39    <DIR>          Videos
               0 File(s)              0 bytes
              16 Dir(s)   8,077,582,336 bytes free

C:\Users\Network Admin>
```

3 Change into the 'network-users' folder that you have created. At the moment, there will be no files or folders in there.

Use the command `cd` (change directory) to move into the 'network-users' folder. Use the following example to help you to complete the command.

```
C:\Windows\system32\cmd.exe

C:\Users\Network Admin>md network-users

C:\Users\Network Admin>dir
 Volume in drive C has no label.
 Volume Serial Number is 2AE6-0115

 Directory of C:\Users\Network Admin

20/05/2022  10:56    <DIR>          .
20/05/2022  10:56    <DIR>          ..
20/05/2022  10:39    <DIR>          3D Objects
20/05/2022  10:39    <DIR>          Contacts
20/05/2022  10:39    <DIR>          Desktop
20/05/2022  10:39    <DIR>          Documents
20/05/2022  10:39    <DIR>          Downloads
20/05/2022  10:39    <DIR>          Favorites
20/05/2022  10:39    <DIR>          Links
20/05/2022  10:39    <DIR>          Music
20/05/2022  10:56    <DIR>          network-users
20/05/2022  10:49    <DIR>          OneDrive
20/05/2022  10:48    <DIR>          Pictures
20/05/2022  10:39    <DIR>          Saved Games
20/05/2022  10:39    <DIR>          Searches
20/05/2022  10:39    <DIR>          Videos
               0 File(s)              0 bytes
              16 Dir(s)   8,077,582,336 bytes free

C:\Users\Network Admin>cd network-users

C:\Users\Network Admin\network-users>
```

Unit 9.2 Design your own network: Shape and size

4. You now need to create folders for five users on the network. Pick the names of five people in your class and use the example below to help you to write a command to create folders for all the users.

   You will use the `md` command, but this time you will be creating multiple folders.

```
C:\Users\Network Admin>dir
 Volume in drive C has no label.
 Volume Serial Number is 2AE6-0115

 Directory of C:\Users\Network Admin

20/05/2022  10:56    <DIR>          .
20/05/2022  10:56    <DIR>          ..
20/05/2022  10:39    <DIR>          3D Objects
20/05/2022  10:39    <DIR>          Contacts
20/05/2022  10:39    <DIR>          Desktop
20/05/2022  10:39    <DIR>          Documents
20/05/2022  10:39    <DIR>          Downloads
20/05/2022  10:39    <DIR>          Favorites
20/05/2022  10:39    <DIR>          Links
20/05/2022  10:39    <DIR>          Music
20/05/2022  10:56    <DIR>          network-users
20/05/2022  10:49    <DIR>          OneDrive
20/05/2022  10:48    <DIR>          Pictures
20/05/2022  10:39    <DIR>          Saved Games
20/05/2022  10:39    <DIR>          Searches
20/05/2022  10:39    <DIR>          Videos
               0 File(s)              0 bytes
              16 Dir(s)   8,077,582,336 bytes free

C:\Users\Network Admin>cd network-users

C:\Users\Network Admin\network-users>md mark asher safiya lauren nadia

C:\Users\Network Admin\network-users>
```

5. To check that this has worked properly, use `dir` to list the files in your 'network-users' folder.

```
20/05/2022  10:56    <DIR>          network-users
20/05/2022  10:49    <DIR>          OneDrive
20/05/2022  10:48    <DIR>          Pictures
20/05/2022  10:39    <DIR>          Saved Games
20/05/2022  10:39    <DIR>          Searches
20/05/2022  10:39    <DIR>          Videos
               0 File(s)              0 bytes
              16 Dir(s)   8,077,582,336 bytes free

C:\Users\Network Admin>cd network-users

C:\Users\Network Admin\network-users>md mark asher safiya lauren nadia

C:\Users\Network Admin\network-users>dir
 Volume in drive C has no label.
 Volume Serial Number is 2AE6-0115

 Directory of C:\Users\Network Admin\network-users

20/05/2022  11:02    <DIR>          .
20/05/2022  11:02    <DIR>          ..
20/05/2022  11:02    <DIR>          asher
20/05/2022  11:02    <DIR>          lauren
20/05/2022  11:02    <DIR>          mark
20/05/2022  11:02    <DIR>          nadia
20/05/2022  11:02    <DIR>          safiya
               0 File(s)              0 bytes
               7 Dir(s)   8,023,261,184 bytes free

C:\Users\Network Admin\network-users>
```

CAMBRIDGE LOWER SECONDARY COMPUTING 9

6 Examine the folders that you have created using Windows Explorer. Windows Explorer is the application that allows you to view your files when using the GUI version of Windows. You can access it via the Start Menu, by clicking the `Start Menu` and then clicking on `Documents` and navigating through your files.

Click on `This Computer`, then your `Hard Drive` (usually C: drive), then `Users`, then your username. In here, you should find your 'network-users' folder.

Have a look inside the 'network-users' folder to see whether your folders are there.

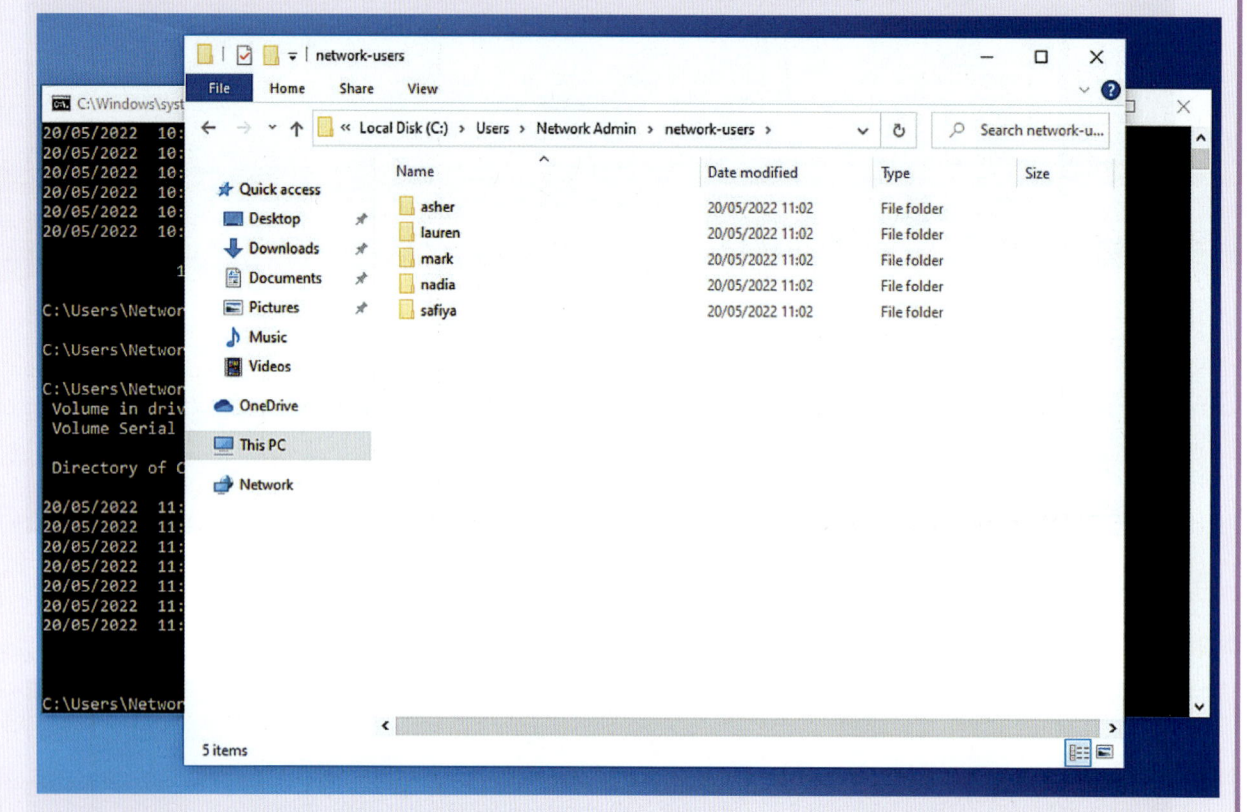

7 There are many commands that network administrators find useful to help them to manage their devices. There are too many to remember them all, but Windows has a 'help' menu built in, which lists other commands that can be used.

Go to a command line and type in `help` to investigate some of the other commands that can be run.

> It is important that you use commands only if you are sure that you know what they will do: for example, it could be easy to run a command that deleted all your files from the computer!

84

Unit 9.2 Design your own network: Shape and size

Final project

Look back to the start of this unit to remind yourself of the Scenario. Your task is to create a presentation to advise the youth centre on best practices for establishing a safe, monitored and flexible online environment.

The network must support:
- five PCs
- ten laptops
- five tablets
- fifteen smartphones
- two games consoles
- five smart watches.

Use Microsoft Word to plan the content of your presentation, and then use Microsoft PowerPoint to create your final presentation which should meet the criteria from the youth centre.

Part 1: Network topology

Make recommendations to the youth centre on the type of network topology you would recommend and the hardware you think they would need to support the setup of their local hub.

On paper, draw a network topology diagram that shows the layout of the network, with the hardware that you have chosen to include. It is important that you identify what type of topology your diagram shows (bus, ring or star).

Write notes on your Word document to include the following:
- A network hardware shopping list, with a short justification of why each item is needed.
- A list of the software tools that a network administrator might need to manage the network.
  - What are they called?
  - What would they be used for?
- Identify two protocols that your network will use.
  - What are they called?
  - Why would they be used?
- If the hub were to expand at a later date to double the number of devices it could support, what additional network hardware would you put in place and why?
  - How would this improve the scalability of your network?
  - If the youth centre were to grow the number of users, what could happen if you had not planned for it?
- Explain how parity-checking could improve the validity of data on your network.
  - How does parity-checking work? What does it help to find?
  - What is a parity bit?

- Discuss how the security needs at each level of the network may vary. The youth centre will employ management staff, network staff and teaching staff and will also have user accounts for students. There are some highly personal datasets that need to be accessed by some accounts.
    - Which accounts would you give the higher-level access to and why?
    - What would each staff member have access to?
    - What other methods could you use to secure information on the network?

Part 2: Presentation

Use your planning document to create your presentation.

Create a presentation that outlines the following:

- Slides 1–2:
    - A screenshot or picture of your network topology diagram.
    - A justification of why you have chosen to set the network out in the way that you have.
    - A list of the hardware that will be needed to set up the network.
- Slide 3:
  A list of software tools that a network administrator may need to help them to operate and maintain the network, and an explanation of what each one would be used for.
- Slide 4:
  Details about which network-security protocols will be used to keep data packets secure.
- Slide 5:
  An explanation about how using parity bits and parity blocks can check for errors, to reassure the hub staff that the network setup will be robust; assume that they do not know anything about how data is transmitted, so you will need to explain the process to them.
- Slide 6:
  Explain how you intend to:
    - secure the information on the network
    - control users' access the network, and explain why you have chosen these methods
    - keep the datasets secure.

Unit 9.2 Design your own network: Shape and size

Evaluation

1. Swap presentations with your partner or listen to each other's presentation. Make notes that comment on the following:
   a. Does it cover all the requirements?
   b. Is the content easy to understand?
   c. How could the network topology be improved?
   d. Make a list of recommendations of how they could improve their report/network topology diagram.
   e. Feed back your recommendations to your partner.
2. When you receive feedback from your partner, read the recommendations carefully. Use the feedback that you have been given to improve your presentation.

What can you do?

Read and review what you can do.
- ✔ I can explain how different network topologies (bus, ring and star) transfer information between devices.
- ✔ I can explain the role of protocols in data transmission.
- ✔ I can explain what scalability factors are and how scalability can affect a network.
- ✔ I can explain why scalability should be considered when designing networks and how networks can be designed to scale up.
- ✔ I can explain what a parity bit is and its role in error detection.
- ✔ I can perform parity-bit and parity-block calculations and identify errors in data transmission.
- ✔ I can explain the choices that must be made when securing information on a network, including cost, accessibility and the relative security requirements of different datasets.

Unit 9.3 Coding and testing: Game development for the micro:bit

Get started!

Have you ever wondered how a computer game is developed to use a **physical device** as a key component in gameplay? For example, the Nintendo Switch allows both sides to be removed and used as individual controllers within the game displayed on the screen.

Discuss with your partner:
- What computer games do you play that include a physical device?
- How is the physical device used in the game?

The micro:bit is a physical device: a small **microprocessor** that has a range of inputs and outputs. The **data** that is gathered by the micro:bit can be used in many ways: for example, pressing the A button sends data to the microprocessor and, if programmed, the micro:bit will react to this input.

In this unit, you will learn to develop a program using MicroPython for the micro:bit to create a simple game. The game will use more than one of the inputs to allow the user to interact with the game. The display and the buzzer will allow the user to see and hear the output from the game.

> **KEYWORDS**
>
> **physical computing device:** device that can be programmed using block or text-based programming languages
>
> **microprocessor:** device that has one circuit but the input, process and output functions of a computer
>
> **data:** raw facts and figures

Learning outcomes

In this unit, you will learn to:
- follow, understand, edit and correct algorithms that are presented as pseudocode
- follow flowchart or pseudocode algorithms that use loops
- create algorithms using flowcharts and pseudocode
- explain and use iteration statements with count-controlled loops in either pseudocode or flowcharts
- predict the outcome of algorithms that use iteration
- compare and contrast two algorithms for the same solution and decide which is best suited to the task
- create an algorithm as a flowchart or pseudocode using more than one construct: sequence, selection and count-controlled iteration
- identify and explain the purpose of a one-dimensional array
- identify and describe data types in MicroPython programs including integer, real, character, string and Boolean
- develop MicroPython programs with count-controlled loops
- access data from an array using MicroPython
- use iterative development on micro:bit prototypes to create solutions to problems
- develop and apply test plans that include normal, extreme and invalid data
- identify test data that covers normal, extreme and invalid data
- use a trace table to check the flow of a variable or array through an algorithm
- program a micro:bit to use data to solve a problem.

Unit 9.3 Coding and testing: Game development for the micro:bit

Warm up

1 In pairs, consider a basic game that you have played on a computing device. There are many inputs and outputs that are used to allow you to interact with a game. For example: in the game Tetris, the aim is to guide the different-shaped blocks to the bottom of the screen and position them to complete a horizontal line.

2 Discuss the game Tetris, shown here, with your partner.
   a How do you control the blocks?
   b How do you know when a game starts?
   c How do you know when a horizontal line is matched up?
   d How do you know when you win?
   e How do you know if you lose?

You can see how Tetris is played here:
https://tetris.com/play-tetris

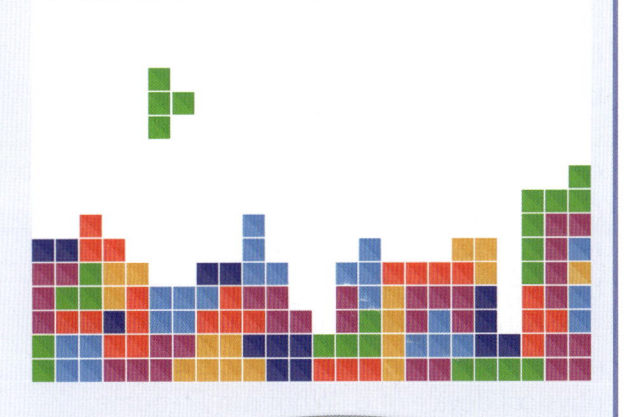

If you've never played Tetris, discuss possible answers with your partner, and then compare answers with a pair who have played the game.

DID YOU KNOW?

Computer games have developed at a fast rate, from the first simple games of Snake or Pong in the early 1970s, to the graphic-rich game environments accessible today. Pong was the first ever computer game; it allowed two players to control lines on each side of the screen to keep a ball moving between them.

Games today have graphics that are much more sophisticated than the Pong example, and allow the player to immerse themselves in a game with a story: for example, saving a character or attack scenarios.

Games on devices such as Nintendo Switch, Xbox or PlayStation have become one of the favourite pastimes of people today. In the past, games were played on desktop computers. Today, having a game that includes physical devices, for example individual handheld controllers, such as those for the Nintendo Switch, or that is played on a computing device such as the PlayStation, further increases its popularity.

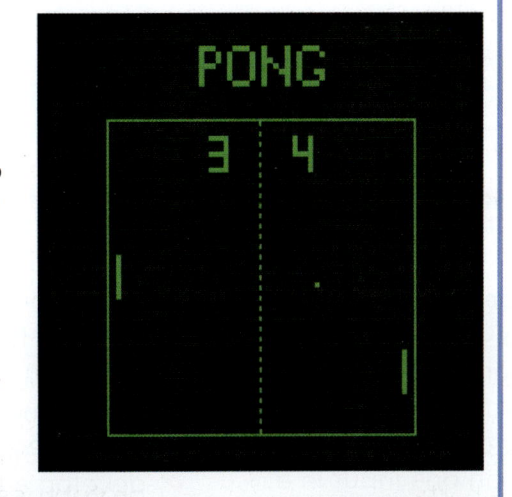

SCENARIO

You are likely to have played a computer-based game that allows you to interact with it, whether that is through the use of the keyboard or an external physical device such as a joystick. Either way, the physical device allowed you to play and experience the game.

Games have a wide range of purposes, and they can be used in an educational way, to help students to learn through games. Your school has asked you to create a prototype game on the micro:bit that acts as the physical device of a 'What am I?' game.

A 'What am I?' game allows one player to ask questions to try to discover the name of an object/animal/word. The other player can answer only 'yes' or 'no' until the first player guesses correctly. The object/animal/word can be shown on a device placed on the first player's head so that they cannot see it. Once they have guessed correctly, the player either moves the device or presses a button to access a new object/animal/word to guess.

The game should:
- display a random item from a pre-set list to the player
- use an input either through the accelerometer or a button to represent when the player has correctly guessed, and play a tune to represent a correct answer
- reset through another input, to start the game again
- create a new image to be stored in a variable
- use speech, music and images within the game
- utilise a count-controlled loop, selection, array and variables
- use a time delay to aid gameplay.

Do you remember?

Before starting this unit, you should be able to:
- ✔ create a program for the micro:bit using selection in MicroPython
- ✔ identify and use a range of inputs and outputs available on the micro:bit
- ✔ identify and use conditional operators to combine more than one input in a conditional statement
- ✔ identify and use conditional operators in a conditional statement
- ✔ send a program to the micro:bit
- ✔ create a flowchart using sequence and selection
- ✔ follow and understand an algorithm presented as a flowchart or pseudocode
- ✔ develop a test plan with a range of data inputs.

Before starting this unit, you will need to access MicroPython on a computer through online software. To access MicroPython:
1. Open your chosen web-browser software.
2. Go to https://python.microbit.org

You will also need the following physical computing devices:
- Micro:bit
- USB cable
- Optional battery pack for the micro:bit.

Unit 9.3 Coding and testing: Game development for the micro:bit

Micro:bit recap

Learn

The micro:bit is a physical computing device that can be programmed directly. You should already have used it in activities in previous stages. The **text-based programming** language that is used with the micro:bit is **MicroPython**, which is a version of the Python programming language.

The micro:bit is a **microprocessor**. It is a small device that fits in your hand and can store and run one **program** at a time. The program is downloaded from specific websites. The program can be developed as a **block-based program** on the **platform** MakeCode. The platform that uses the text-based programming language MicroPython is **https://python.microbit.org**

The micro:bit itself has a set of inputs and outputs that can be used in a program.

- The inputs are:
  - A button
  - B button
  - **accelerometer** (detects movement and direction)
  - microphone (a sound sensor)
  - light sensor (located on the display)
  - temperature sensor (located in the processor).
- The outputs are:
  - display (25 individual LED lights)
  - buzzer (located on the reverse of the micro:bit).

There are also **general-purpose input/output (GPIO)** pins at the bottom of the micro:bit that allow the micro:bit to connect to external components via **crocodile clips**.

Like any programming language, the **syntax** of MicroPython is specific and needs to be written correctly for the program to run. If a program is not written correctly, then a **syntax error** will be found. This is shown on the micro:bit as a sad face followed by the line on which the error has been found.

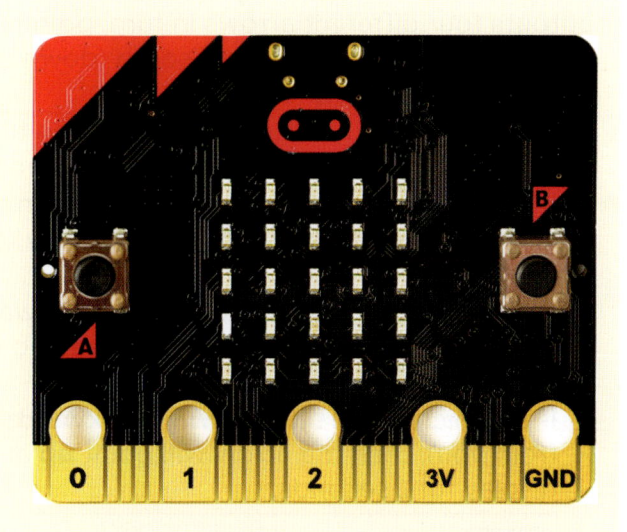

KEYWORDS

text-based programming: written lines of code using a specific programming language, e.g. Python

MicroPython: programming language used on the micro:bit

microprocessor: device that has one circuit but the input, process and output functions of a computer

program: instructions that tell a computer system how to complete a task

block-based program: individual code blocks connected together to create a program

platform: hardware and operating system that runs an application

accelerometer: detects a change in direction of a device

general-purpose input output (GPIO): pins at the bottom of the micro:bit that allow additional inputs and outputs to be added through crocodile clips

crocodile clips: cable for creating a temporary electrical connection between devices

syntax: specific rules used in a programming language

syntax error: error in program code that stops the program from running

Look at the **pseudocode** below for a micro:bit program that uses the accelerometer to detect movement. When the program starts, the micro:bit outputs four different arrows in turn, pointing north (up arrow), east (right arrow), south (down arrow) and west (left arrow).

- If the micro:bit is tilted to the **left**, then the arrow will point to the **left** and display for 2 seconds.
- If the micro:bit is tilted to the **right**, then the arrow will point to the **right** and display for 2 seconds.
- If the micro:bit is tilted **up** (forwards towards you), then the arrow will point **down** and display for 2 seconds.
- If the micro:bit is tilted **down** (backwards away from you), then the arrow will point **up** and display for 2 seconds.

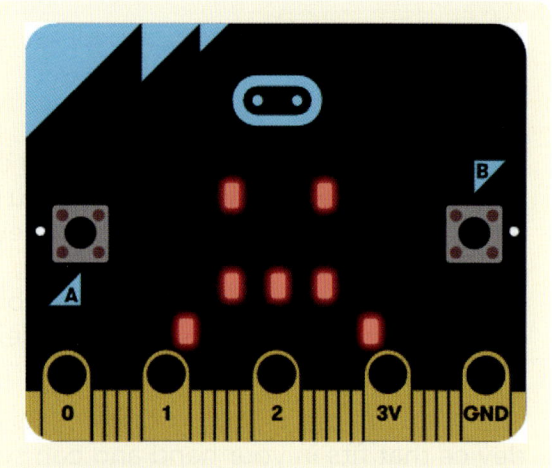

KEYWORD

pseudocode: textual representation of an algorithm

```
START
OUTPUT arrow N
DELAY 300
OUTPUT arrow E
DELAY 300
OUTPUT arrow S
DELAY 300
OUTPUT arrow W
DELAY 300

IF micro:bit moved to left THEN
    OUTPUT arrow W
    DELAY 2000
ENDIF
IF micro:bit moved to right THEN
    OUTPUT arrow E
    DELAY 2000
ENDIF
IF micro:bit moved forwards THEN
    OUTPUT arrow S
    DELAY 2000
ENDIF
IF micro:bit moved backwards THEN
    OUTPUT arrow N
    DELAY 2000
ENDIF
STOP
```

Unit 9.3 Coding and testing: Game development for the micro:bit

This program requires the use of the accelerometer built into the micro:bit. The accelerometer can detect the change in direction of the device.

The accelerometer is continuously gathering data from the movement that the micro:bit makes. This data is then used to activate an output.

In MicroPython, the code for using the accelerometer is:

```
if accelerometer.was_gesture('left'):
```

The specific test for the direction is placed in the brackets and encased in single quotation marks.

The different options include:
- up
- down
- left
- right
- face up
- face down
- freefall
- shake.

The MicroPython can be developed from the pseudocode plan by following these steps.

1 Set the program to use MicroPython. All programs must start with this code. The use of `while True` allows the program to check continuously whether an input is being used.

```
from microbit import *

while True:
```

2 Add the program code to show a changing arrow that looks like it is rotating.

OUTPUT arrow N
DELAY 300
OUTPUT arrow E
DELAY 300
OUTPUT arrow S
DELAY 300
OUTPUT arrow W
DELAY 300
	`from microbit import *`
	
	`while True:`
	`    display.show(Image.ARROW_N)`
	`    sleep(300)`
	`    display.show(Image.ARROW_E)`
	`    sleep(300)`
	`    display.show(Image.ARROW_S)`
	`    sleep(300)`
	`    display.show(Image.ARROW_W)`
	`    sleep(300)`

Remember that it is important to indent (move in) the code under the `while True` line.

`sleep(300)` is used to add a short delay between the images being displayed. A delay is required to allow each image to be seen.

Notice the code for displaying an image: `display.show(Image.ARROW_N)`. This is used for any image, with the image to be displayed in uppercase letters at the end.

3. Add the **conditional statement** to check whether the micro:bit is tilted to the left.

```
IF micro:bit moved to left THEN
    OUTPUT arrow W
    DELAY 2000
ENDIF
```

```python
from microbit import *

while True:
    display.show(Image.ARROW_N)
    sleep(300)
    display.show(Image.ARROW_E)
    sleep(300)
    display.show(Image.ARROW_S)
    sleep(300)
    display.show(Image.ARROW_W)
    sleep(300)
    if accelerometer.was_gesture('left'):
        display.show(Image.ARROW_W)
        sleep(2000)
```

Notice that:

the conditional statement (`if`) is in line with the previous line of code, and the code to be run if this is True is indented below the `if`

`sleep(2000)` is used to display the image for the specific direction for 2 seconds before the program returns to displaying the rotating arrows.

KEYWORD

conditional statement: completes a check to see whether set criteria is either True or False

4. Develop the program to add the other three conditional statements to check whether the micro:bit is being tilted in any of the other directions.

```
IF micro:bit moved to right THEN
    OUTPUT arrow E
    DELAY 2000
ENDIF
IF micro:bit moved forwards THEN
    OUTPUT arrow S
    DELAY 2000
ENDIF
IF micro:bit moved backwards THEN
    OUTPUT arrow N
    DELAY 2000
ENDIF
```

```python
from microbit import *

while True:
    display.show(Image.ARROW_N)
    sleep(300)
    display.show(Image.ARROW_E)
    sleep(300)
    display.show(Image.ARROW_S)
    sleep(300)
    display.show(Image.ARROW_W)
    sleep(300)
    if accelerometer.was_gesture('left'):
        display.show(Image.ARROW_W)
        sleep(2000)
    if accelerometer.was_gesture('right'):
        display.show(Image.ARROW_E)
        sleep(2000)
    if accelerometer.was_gesture('up'):
        display.show(Image.ARROW_S)
        sleep(2000)
    if accelerometer.was_gesture('down'):
        display.show(Image.ARROW_N)
        sleep(2000)
```

Unit 9.3 Coding and testing: Game development for the micro:bit

5 Download the program onto the micro:bit, ready for testing.
   a Connect the micro:bit to the computer through the USB cable.
 b Connect the micro:bit by clicking the **send to micro:bit** icon on the platform.
   c Select the micro:bit from the pop-up.
   d Send the program to the micro:bit.
6 Create a **test plan** to test a range of data:
- **Normal test data** is an expected input that the program should run as normal, for example a specific movement set in the program, such as tilt left.
- **Extreme test data** is something at the upper or lower boundary of what should be accepted. This is not relevant when checking the tilt of the micro:bit as the angle cannot be controlled precisely.
- **Invalid test data** is an input that will not do anything in the program. Here, another input is checked to make sure that it does not disrupt the program: for example, pressing one of the buttons as an input from these is not part of the program code.

Test	Input data	Expected outcome	Pass/fail
1 Normal	No movement	Continuous change in image from arrows pointing up, right, down and left with a very short delay between images.	Pass
2 Normal	Tilt left	Arrow to the left is displayed for 2 seconds and then returns to moving arrow.	Pass
3 Normal	Tilt right	Arrow to the right is displayed for 2 seconds and then returns to moving arrow.	Pass
4 Normal	Tilt forwards	Arrow down is displayed for 2 seconds and then returns to moving arrow.	Pass
5 Normal	Tilt backwards	Arrow up is displayed for 2 seconds and then returns to moving arrow.	Pass
6 Invalid	Press the A button	No change	Pass
7 Invalid	Press the B button	No change	Pass

The test plan above shows that the program and the use of the accelerometer works as expected.

> **KEYWORDS**
>
> **test plan:** document that details the tests to be carried out when a program is complete and whether or not they are successful
>
> **normal test data:** data of the correct type that should be accepted by a program
>
> **extreme test data:** acceptable input but at the ends of the possible input range
>
> **invalid test data:** data that should be rejected by a program

Practise

1. Discuss with your partner what the pseudocode below is designed to do.
   ```
   START
   IMPORT random library
   number = 0

   OUTPUT happy face
   DELAY 300
   OUTPUT sad face

   IF micro:bit shaken THEN
       number = random number between 1 and 2
       IF number == 1 THEN
             OUTPUT happy face
             DELAY 2000
       ELSE
             OUTPUT sad face
             DELAY 2000
       ENDIF

   STOP
   ```

2. Create a test plan using the template below, using normal and invalid test data, so that it is ready to use when the program has been created.

Test	Input data	Expected outcome	Pass/fail

3. Open the file **RandomQuestionOutput.py** provided by your teacher.
   a. Develop the MicroPython program to match the pseudocode above. To add a random number, you will need to use the following code:
   ```
   number = random.randint(1, 2)
   ```
   This will assign a **random value** between 1 and 2 to the **variable** 'number'.
   b. Connect the micro:bit and send the program to it.

4. Complete the test plan you set up in task 2 to check that the program works correctly with the normal and invalid test data.

> **DID YOU KNOW?**
> Another device that has an accelerometer in it is a smartphone. As you move the mobile phone from portrait to landscape, the display moves with it.
>
> **Accelerometer**

> **KEYWORDS**
> **random value:** randomly generated number in a program that can be set within a range
>
> **variable:** named memory location that can store a value

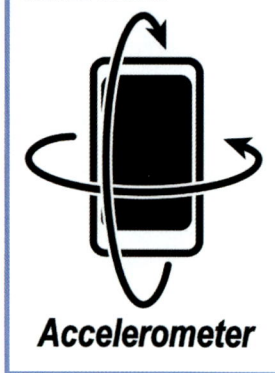

Unit 9.3 Coding and testing: Game development for the micro:bit

5 a Discuss with your partner how the program is using the accelerometer. Change the accelerometer movement that is being detected in this program and test the impact on the program by trying the original movement and the new movement.

   b

> Remember that the different accelerometer movements to be used as an input are up, down, left, right, face up, face down, freefall and shake.

Download the program to your computer and save it.
   - Select the three vertical dots next to the `Save` icon.
   - Select `Save Python Script`.
   - Move it from the 'Downloads' folder to your own folder and save it as **randomQuestionOutput.py**.

Arrays and micro:bits

Learn

In Unit 9.1, you explored how more than one item can be stored in an **array**. A variable can store only one item. An array can hold multiple items. The micro:bit can work with an array.

To set up an array in MicroPython, at the start of the program you need to use the syntax `arrayName = [ ]`. The **naming convention** for an array is the same as you would use for a variable:

- **camelCase** – no spaces, and from the second word the first letter is capitalised
- **snake_case** – no spaces; spaces are replaced with underscores.

The program below shows an array that has been set up to store five **integer** values. An integer is a whole number.

```
score = [50, 25, 65, 90, 33]
```

If the **data items** were **strings**, they would each be placed inside quotation marks:

```
score = ["50", "25", "65", "90", "33"]
```

KEYWORDS

array: data structure in a program that can store more than one item of data of the same data type under a single identifier; data items can be changed

naming convention: the way a variable or array is named in programming

camelCase: all lowercase, and from the second word the first letter is capitalised

snake_case: all lowercase, and spaces are replaced with underscores (_)

integer: whole number

data item: piece of information that represents part of the data that makes up a person, place or thing, e.g. some of the data items that represent a person are their first name and second name

string: sequence of characters that can be text, numbers or symbols; quotation marks around the characters define it as a string

Every item in the array is assigned a position, or **index**. The first position is always '0' and they increase by 1.

Position	0	1	2	3	4
Array item	50	25	65	90	33

> **KEYWORD**
> **index:** numerical reference for a location of a piece of data stored in an array

These index positions can help to identify the specific item to be used or output to the micro:bit display. To output the item that is stored in position 2, you need to use the syntax to display something on the screen: `display.scroll()`. The array details are placed inside the brackets. The format for this is the name of the array followed by the position you want to output in square brackets:

```
score = ["50", "25", "65", "90", "33"]
display.scroll(score[2])
```

This would output the value 65 for the array above.

Sometimes, you may want to add a new item to the array while the program is running. This is done using `append()`, which adds the item to the end of the list. In the example below, the number 12 will be added at index position 5:

```
score = [50, 25, 65, 90, 33]
score.append(12)
```

The table below shows the array used in the program code above and the different positions the items are in.

Position	0	1	2	3	4	5
Array item	50	25	65	90	33	12

You can check that 12 has been added correctly by outputting the contents stored at position 5 of the array. You can do this by:
- using the MicroPython code to output to the display: `display.scroll()`
- adding the name of the array inside the brackets: `display.scroll(score)`
- adding the position of the item you want to output in square brackets after the array name: `display.scroll(score[5])`.

```
score = [50, 25, 65, 90, 33]
score.append(12)
display.scroll(score[5])
```

Unit 9.3 Coding and testing: Game development for the micro:bit

The position in the array can be used in a program to output a **random value**. You have generated a random number in the previous section. In the pseudocode below, the micro:bit will generate a random selection from a list of six numbers.

```
START
IMPORT random library

ARRAY numbers = [1, 2, 3, 4, 5, 6]

IF micro:bit is shaken THEN
    OUTPUT a random item from numbers
    DELAY 500
    OUTPUT clear screen
ENDIF
STOP
```

> **KEYWORD**
>
> **random value:** randomly generated number in a program that can be set within a range

The program can be completed by following these steps.

1. After the main micro:bit library has been imported, the random library must also be imported so that the extra code to generate random elements is available to use.

    ```
    from microbit import *
    import random
    ```

2. Create the array containing the numbers 1 to 6. The numbers are stored as integers.

    ```
    from microbit import *
    import random

    numbers = [1,2,3,4,5,6]
    ```

3. Set the input for the program to be when the micro:bit is shaken.

    ```
    from microbit import *
    import random

    numbers = [1,2,3,4,5,6]

    while True:
        if accelerometer.was_gesture('shake'):
    ```

    > The input is indented beneath the `while True` code. This is to ensure that the micro:bit will react continuously to the shake movement as an input.

4. The next step is to output a randomly generated item from the array to the micro:bit display. There are two ways in which something can be displayed using the micro:bit LEDs:
   - `display.show()` is used for an integer, letter or image; if there is more than one digit or image, they will be shown in sequence with a delay between each one
   - `display.scroll()` is used for a string; the text will scroll across the screen.

   When using `display.show()`, place the array name inside the brackets:

   ```
   display.show(numbers[0])
   ```

   However, instead of a set index position being used inside the square brackets, a random position needs to be generated. The array has six items, which means that the positions are within a range of 0 to 5.

Position	0	1	2	3	4	5
Array item	1	2	3	4	5	6

   The code to randomly generate a value between 0 and 5 - the known positions in this array - is:

   ```
   random.randint(0,5)
   ```

   This is placed inside the square brackets to replace the position number:

   ```
   display.show(numbers[random.randint(0,5)])
   ```

5. To finish the program, a short delay is added to allow the number to be shown before the display is cleared:

   ```python
   from microbit import *
   import random

   numbers = [1,2,3,4,5,6]

   while True:
       if accelerometer.was_gesture('shake'):
           display.show(numbers[random.randint(0,5)])
           sleep(2000)
           display.clear()
   ```

   The program can now be sent to the micro:bit, and every time the micro:bit is shaken, a random number between 1 and 6 is displayed.

Unit 9.3 Coding and testing: Game development for the micro:bit

To test that a random number is being generated, you can create a test table to document the output after each shake. An example is shown below.

Test number	Output
1	5
2	1
3	5
4	3
5	4
6	2
7	4
8	6
9	4
10	6

Practise

1 A game such as a quiz requires the players to be placed in a group or team. Look at the pseudocode below.

```
START
IMPORT random library

ARRAY groups = [Group 1, Group 2, Group 3, Group 4]

IF micro:bit is shaken THEN
    OUTPUT a random item from groups
    DELAY 500
    OUTPUT clear screen
ENDIF
STOP
```

a How could this pseudocode help in selecting the group each person is in?

b Discuss with your partner what is different about the pseudocode above compared with the pseudocode below.

```
START
IMPORT random library

ARRAY numbers = 1, 2, 3, 4, 5, 6

IF micro:bit is shaken THEN
   OUTPUT a random item from numbers
   DELAY 500
ENDIF
STOP
```

2 Copy and complete this table to identify the item stored at each position of the array.

Position	0	1	2	3
Array item				

3 Create a test plan for the pseudocode above using normal and invalid test data.

Test	Input data	Expected outcome	Pass/fail
1 Normal			
2			

4 a Write the program code to match the pseudocode.
   b Connect the micro:bit and send the program.
   c Use your test plan from task 3 to make sure that your program is working correctly.

5 Create a table to test that the values generated are random, and use this to check the outputs from your program.

Test number	Output
1	
2	

6 Download the program to your computer and save it.
   - Select the three vertical dots next to the `Save` icon.
   - Select `Save Python Script`.
   - Move it from the 'Downloads' folder to your own folder and save it as **randomGroupGenerator.py**.

7 Discuss with your partner:
   a where data is being stored and gathered in this program
   b how a program to choose a random element from an array could be used in a game.

Count-controlled loops and the micro:bit

Learn

Look at this program. It has been created to output a section of a times table using the micro:bit to display the answer. This example outputs the answer to 1 × 2, 2 × 2 and 3 × 2.

```
1   from microbit import *
2
3   number = 1
4   times_table = 2
5   answer = 0
6
7   answer = number * times_table
8   display.show(answer)
9   sleep(500)
10
11  number = number + 1
12  answer = number * times_table
13  display.show(answer)
14  sleep(500)
15
16  number = number + 1
17  answer = number * times_table
18  display.show(answer)
19  sleep(500)
```

> **KEYWORD**
>
> **trace table:** technique for predicting step by step what will happen as each line of an algorithm or program is run, and to identify errors

The program code above is repeated each time.
The program can be decomposed using a **trace table**.

- **Lines 3, 4 and 5** – three variables are set up:
  - 'number' storing the value 1
  - 'times_table' storing the value 2
  - 'answer' storing the value 0.

> You explored trace tables in Unit 9.1. Refer back to that unit to recap how a trace table is structured.

Line	Variable	Variable	Variable	Output
	number	times_table	answer	
3	1			
4		2		
5			0	

- **Line 7** – an equation (`number * times_table`) updates the value stored in the variable 'answer'; the values stored in the variables make this equation 1 × 2, so the answer 2 is stored in the variable 'answer'.

Line	Variable number	Variable times_table	Variable answer	Output
3	1			
4		2		
5			0	
7			2	

- **Line 8** – the value stored in the variable 'answer' is displayed on the micro:bit.

Line	Variable number	Variable times_table	Variable answer	Output
3	1			
4		2		
5			0	
7			2	
8				2

- **Line 11** – the value stored in the variable 'number' is increased by 1.

Line	Variable number	Variable times_table	Variable answer	Output
3	1			
4		2		
5			0	
7			2	
8				2
11	2			

- **Line 12** – an equation (`number * times_table`) updates the value stored in the variable 'answer'; the values stored in the variables make this equation 2 × 2, so the answer 4 is stored in the variable 'answer'.

Line	Variable number	Variable times_table	Variable answer	Output
3	1			
4		2		
5			0	
7			2	
8				2
11	2			
12			4	

Unit 9.3 Coding and testing: Game development for the micro:bit

- **Line 13** – the value stored in the variable 'answer' is displayed on the micro:bit.

Line	Variable number	Variable times_table	Variable answer	Output
3	1			
4		2		
5			0	
7			2	
8				2
11	2			
12			4	
13				4

- **Line 16** – the value stored in the variable 'number' is increased by 1.

Line	Variable number	Variable times_table	Variable answer	Output
3	1			
4		2		
5			0	
7			2	
8				2
11	2			
12			4	
13				4
16	3			

- **Line 17** – an equation (`number * times_table`) updates the value stored in the variable 'answer'; the values stored in the variables make this equation 3 × 2, so the answer 6 is stored in the variable 'answer'.

Line	Variable number	Variable times_table	Variable answer	Output
3	1			
4		2		
5			0	
7			2	
8				2
11	2			
12			4	
13				4
16	3			
17			6	

- **Line 18** – the value stored in the variable 'answer' is displayed on the micro:bit.

Line	Variable number	Variable times_table	Variable answer	Output
3	1			
4		2		
5			0	
7			2	
8				2
11	2			
12			4	
13				4
16	3			
17			6	
18				6

The program allows the micro:bit to output the answers to 1 × 2, 2 × 2 and 3 × 2. The program code is long, and sections are repeated. If you wanted to extend the program to output more of the times table, you would need to repeat the lines of code below the others. However, the program code can be reduced greatly by using a **count-controlled loop**.

A count-controlled loop is a set of instructions or program code that is repeated a set number of times. In programming, a count-controlled loop is written as a **for loop**. It repeats a set of instructions *for* a set number of times.

The pseudocode below shows how a count-controlled loop, a for loop, can be used. In this example, 'number' is a variable that keeps track of how many times the code has repeated. This is known as the **counter variable**, and can be set to any variable name you choose. Each run of the instructions inside the loop is called an **iteration**. The counter variable begins with a value of 0 and increases by 1 every time the loop iterates over the instructions. The end value is the number of times the loop needs to run.

```
1    START
2    answer = 0
3    times_table = 2
4
5    FOR number = 0 to 3
6        answer = number * times_table
7        OUTPUT answer
8        DELAY 500
9    ENDFOR
10   STOP
```

KEYWORDS

count-controlled loop: set of instructions repeated a set number of times

for loop: the Python or MicroPython loop for a count-controlled loop

counter variable: variable that stores the number of times an iteration has iterated

iterate/iterative/iteration: repeat/repeated/repetition

This can be seen in the trace table below. The yellow and green shading highlights each iteration of the loop. The line numbers are revisited with each iteration (lines 5, 6 and 7) and there are four iterations of the indented instructions.

Line	Variable number	Variable times_table	Variable answer	Output
2			0	
3		2		
5	0			
6			0	
7				0
5	1			
6			2	
7				2
5	2			
6			4	
7				4
5	3			
6			6	
7				6

> If you want to increase the output to include additional numbers in the 2 times table, you just need to adjust the end value of the for loop.

This pseudocode above is then developed in MicroPython for the micro:bit. In MicroPython (and Python), `range()` is used to state how many times the code needs to be repeated, which is four times in this example:

```python
from microbit import *

answer = 0
times_table = 2

for number in range(4):
    answer = number * times_table
    display.show(answer)
    sleep(500)
```

A count-controlled loop can be used creatively on the micro:bit to output a countdown. The micro:bit has a built-in buzzer that acts as a speaker for sounds that have been programmed to be output. It can be used to generate music, sounds and speech.

In the pseudocode below, speech is used to output a countdown from 3 to 1 and then 'Go'.

```
START
IMPORT speech library

FOR number = 3 to 1
    OUTPUT speech number
    DELAY 1000
ENDFOR
OUTPUT speech "Go"
STOP
```

To generate a verbal countdown, follow these steps.
1 First, import the 'speech' library:

```
from microbit import *
import speech
```

2 So far, you have used a for loop that counts up to a set value. To count backwards, the range needs to have a start and end point and be told to reduce the number by 1 each time.

> Remember that Python will exit the loop when the count variable matches the value for the end of the range.

The table below breaks down the program code in **range()**.

range	(	3	0	–1	)
		Start of range	End of range	Reduce by 1 on each iteration	

```
for number in range(3,0,-1):
```

3 In this program, the speech function of the buzzer is used to output the number for each iteration. The speech aspect on the micro:bit can output only a string. The value stored in the variable 'number' must therefore be converted, or **cast**, to a string for it to be output.
- The structure of the code for the speech function is `speech.say()`.
- The words to be displayed are placed inside the brackets.

KEYWORD
cast: change the data type of a variable

Unit 9.3 Coding and testing: Game development for the micro:bit

- To output the contents of the variable and convert it to a string, the code `str(number)` is placed inside the brackets:

  ```
  speech.say(str(number))
  ```

  This will now take the value stored in the variable 'number', convert it from an integer to a string and output it through the buzzer as speech.
- This code must be indented inside the for loop:

  ```
  from microbit import *
  import speech

  for number in range(3,0,-1):
      speech.say(str(number))
  ```

4 A delay is added after the speech to leave a gap of 1 second before the next number. 1 second is 1000 milliseconds and so this is the value added in the brackets of the sleep function:

  ```
  from microbit import *
  import speech

  for number in range(3,0,-1):
      speech.say(str(number))
      sleep(1000)
  ```

5 The final speech output will be 'Go'. This is not part of the for loop and therefore it should not be indented. It will be the next instruction to run once the iterations of the count-controlled loop are completed:

  ```
  from microbit import *
  import speech

  for number in range(3,0,-1):
      speech.say(str(number))
      sleep(1000)
  speech.say("Go")
  ```

CAMBRIDGE LOWER SECONDARY COMPUTING 9

Practise

```
1  START
2  IMPORT speech library
3
4  ARRAY shoppingList = [bread, milk, chocolate]
5
6  OUTPUT speech "You need to buy"
7  DELAY 1000
8
9  FOR each item in ARRAY shoppingList
10     OUTPUT speech item
11     DELAY 1000
12 ENDFOR
13 STOP
```

> **KEYWORD**
>
> **algorithm:** step-by-step instructions to solve a particular problem

1 a With your partner, predict the outcome of the pseudocode above.
   b Explain how iteration has been used in this pseudocode.
   c Copy and complete the trace table below to follow the variable and array outputs through the **algorithm**.

Line	Array	Variable	Output
	shoppingList	item	
4			
6			
9			
10			
9			
10			
9			
10			

   d Discuss with your partner how using a trace table can help to identify how data is used in a program.

2 a Create the MicroPython program to match the pseudocode using a count-controlled loop.
   b Connect the micro:bit to the computer and send the program to the micro:bit.
   c Test the program to make sure that the output is what you expected.
   d Download the program to your computer and save it.
      - Select the three vertical dots next to the `Save` icon.
      - Select `Save Python Script`.
      - Move it from the 'Downloads' folder to your own folder and save it as **shoppingList.py'**.

Unit 9.3 Coding and testing: Game development for the micro:bit

3   a   Create a pseudocode algorithm containing a count-controlled loop to output an array containing three words that could be used in a 'What am I?' game: for example, 'pilot', 'chef' and 'teacher'.
    b   Create the trace table to test your algorithm.
    c   Create the program code to match your pseudocode to include a count-controlled loop and the use of speech on the micro:bit.
    d   Connect the micro:bit to the computer and send the program to the micro:bit.
    e   Save as **professionsList.py**.
    f   Test that your program works as expected by repeating the trace table you created in task 3b.
    g   Compare and contrast programs with your partner. Discuss any differences and, if there are any, which program is better suited to the task and why.

Creating a musical output

Learn

A lot of computer games have a musical element to them. This can act as an introduction or be used to highlight when something has happened in the game, such as *game over*. Music adds another layer to a game and provides the player with more of an interactive experience.

The micro:bit has a built-in buzzer that acts as a speaker for sounds that have been programmed to be output. It can accept individual musical notes that can be output to produce a musical sequence.

In the 'Arrays and micro:bits' section, you explored how an array can be used to store more than one item. The stored items can be used to represent the notes of a musical sequence. Each note is represented as a sequence of **characters**.

C	4	:	4
Note	Octave		Duration
The musical note	How high or low the musical note is played; 0 is the lowest and 8 is the highest		How long the note is held for; the higher the number, the longer the note

For example, these steps create an array to output the musical sequence for the traditional song 'Frère Jacques'.

1   The first line of notes is: C D E C. The octave remains the same at 4, a midpoint note. The length of each note is also 4. This needs only to be set on the first note and the program remembers this for each note that follows until it is told to change:
    ```
    C4:4, D4, E4, C4
    ```
2   Each of these notes now needs to be placed inside quotation marks:
    ```
    "C4:4", "D4", "E4", "C4"
    ```
3   This line of notes can now be placed inside the square brackets with the name of the array:
    ```
    line1 = ["C4:4", "D4", "E4", "C4"]
    ```

KEYWORD

character: single letter, digit or symbol

4 Follow these steps to output this array using the buzzer on the micro:bit.
   a First you need to ensure that you have imported the music library. You must do this at the start of the program, after the importing the micro:bit library:

   ```
   from microbit import *
   import music
   ```

   b Add the code to program an output to the buzzer:

   ```
   music.play()
   ```

   c Add the name of the array inside the brackets. This now says to run the contents of the array through the buzzer:

   ```
   music.play(line1)
   ```

   ```
   from microbit import *
   import music
   
   line1 = ["C4:4", "D4", "E4", "C4"]
   
   music.play(line1)
   ```

   d This will output the line once. However, the line is repeated in the song. You could write this by adding the same line again:

   ```
   from microbit import *
   import music
   
   line1 = ["C4:4", "D4", "E4", "C4"]
   
   music.play(line1)
   music.play(line1)
   ```

   e But this is not an efficient way of adding and running code. You can use a count-controlled loop to repeat the same line a set number of times:

   ```
   1  from microbit import *
   2  import music
   3
   4  line1 = ["C4:4", "D4", "E4", "C4"]
   5
   6  for counter in range(2):
   7      music.play(line1)
   ```

5   You can use a trace table to see how this program is using the array when it is run. The counter variable will start at 0 and will change to 1 for the second iteration, for example:

Line	Array	Variable	Output
	line1	counter	
4	"C4:4", "D4", "E4", "C4"		
6		0	
7			"C4:4", "D4", "E4", "C4"
6		1	
7			"C4:4", "D4", "E4", "C4"

6   You can create the next line of the song in the same way. You can use an array to store the individual notes as items. This time, the last note needs to be longer than the other two notes. Therefore, you need to add (:8) to the end of the note to tell the program to double the length of the note:

`"E4:4", "F4", "G4:8"`

7   You can then create the program in the same way as before, with the array at the start and a new for loop following the first:

```
from microbit import *
import music

line1 = ["C4:4", "D4", "E4", "C4"]
line2 = ["E4:4", "F4", "G4:8"]

for counter in range(2):
    music.play(line1)

for counter in range(2):
    music.play(line2)
```

On the next page is a trace table for the array and the two for loops. The line numbers help to identify which count-controlled loop is being run.

CAMBRIDGE LOWER SECONDARY COMPUTING 9

Line	Array line1	Array line2	Variable counter	Output
4	"C4:4", "D4", "E4", "C4"			
5		"E4:4", "F4", "G4:8"		
7			0	
8				"C4:4", "D4", "E4", "C4"
7			1	
8				"C4:4", "D4", "E4", "C4"
10			0	
11				"E4:4", "F4", "G4:8"
10			1	
11				"E4:4", "F4", "G4:8"

8 Once the program **executes** the first for loop on lines 7–8 in the code above, the program will continue to the second for loop on lines 10–11. It is important to set up the arrays at the start of the program for the musical notes and then add the sequence of for loops to represent the musical output sequence required to play the song correctly.

KEYWORD

execute: carry out the instructions described in a computer program

Practise

1 With your partner, predict the outcome of the pseudocode below. Do array 'line1' and 'line2' look familiar?

```
1   START
2
3   ARRAY line1 = [C4:4, D4, E4, C4]
4   ARRAY line2 = [E4:4, F4, G4:8]
5   ARRAY line3 = [G4:2, A4, G4, F4, E4:4, C4]
6   ARRAY line4 = [C4:4, G3, C4:8]
7
8   FOR i = 0 to 1
9       OUTPUT line1 to buzzer
10  ENDFOR
11
12  FOR i = 0 to 1
13      OUTPUT line2 to buzzer
14  ENDFOR
15
16  FOR i = 0 to 1
```

Unit 9.3 Coding and testing: Game development for the micro:bit

```
17        OUTPUT line3 to buzzer
18   ENDFOR
19
20   FOR i = 0 to 1
21        OUTPUT line4 to buzzer
22   ENDFOR
23   STOP
```

2 Create a trace table to check the flow of the variables and array outputs through the program.

3 Discuss with your partner how data is stored and used in this program.

4 a Create the MicroPython program to match the pseudocode.
  b Connect the micro:bit to the computer with the USB cable and send the program to the micro:bit.
  c Test that the program output is as expected. Does the output match the musical sequence you expect?
  d Download the program to your computer and save it.
      - Select the three vertical dots next to the **Save** icon.
      - Select **Save Python Script**.
      - Move it from the 'Downloads' folder to your own folder and save as **frereJacquesComplete.py**.

> Remember to use count-controlled loops in the right sequence to create the correct musical output.

5 a Create the pseudocode to output the tune 'Happy Birthday' twice using this musical sequence.

Happy birthday to you	G3:2, G3, A3:4, G3, C4, B3
Happy birthday to you	G3:2, G3, A3:4, G3, D4, C4
Happy birthday dear name	G3:2, G3, G4:4, E4, C4, B3, A3
Happy birthday to you	F4:2, F4, E:4, C4, D4, C4

  b Create the program code to match your pseudocode. Save as **happyBirthdayComplete.py**.
  c Connect the micro:bit to the computer and send the program to the micro:bit. Test whether the output is what you expect from your knowledge of the tune.

> Remember to use count-controlled loops to iterate over an array to repeat an array or sequence of arrays.

115

Arrays, loops and selection

Learn

In the previous themes, you explored using an array to store integers and strings. An array on the micro:bit can also store images.

There is a set of predefined images that can be used on the micro:bit. In this example, the animal ones will be used:

DUCK	TORTOISE	BUTTERFLY	GIRAFFE	SNAKE

The MicroPython syntax to display an image is:

`display.show(Image.HEART)`

To edit the image displayed, **HEART** is replaced with one of the predefined images in uppercase letters:

`display.show(Image.DUCK)`

The following example of a guess-the-animal game using images has been planned using pseudocode.

```
1   START
2   IMPORT random library
3   IMPORT music library
4
5   ARRAY images = [DUCK, TORTOISE, BUTTERFLY, GIRAFFE, SNAKE]
6   ARRAY correctTune = [G4:1, C5, E, G:2, E:1, G:3]
7
8   IF button A is pressed THEN
9       OUTPUT random image from ARRAY images
10  ENDIF
11
12  IF button B is pressed THEN
13      OUTPUT correctTune
14      DELAY 500
15      OUTPUT clear screen
16  ENDIF
17
18  STOP
```

- Two arrays have been set up: 'images' and 'correctTune'.
  - 'images' stores the list of possible images.
  - 'correctTune' stores the notes to play a tune when the user guesses correctly.
- When the A button is pressed, a random image is displayed on the micro:bit.
- When the B button is pressed, a celebration musical sequence is played, and after 500 milliseconds the display is cleared.

Unit 9.3 Coding and testing: Game development for the micro:bit

A trace table can be used to follow the data that is being used in this algorithm. It can help to find any errors that may have occurred while writing the program, for example, an incorrect or misspelt array name.

Line	Array images	Array correctTune	Condition A button = True	Condition B button = True	Output
5	DUCK, TORTOISE, BUTTERFLY, GIRAFFE, SNAKE				
6		G4:1, C5, E, G:2, E:1, G:3			
8			True		
9					One array image
12				True	
13					correctTune
15					Clear screen

The pseudocode can be used to create the program by following these steps.

1. To use 'random' and 'music' in the program, you first need to import both the 'random' and 'music' libraries:

   ```
   from microbit import *
   import random
   import music
   ```

2. You need to create the array to store the images. As the array is going to store the images that can be displayed, you need to use the correct syntax for the array items. An image is defined in the program as **Image.DUCK**, so this is the correct format to use for each list item:

   ```
   from microbit import *
   import random
   import music

   images = [Image.DUCK, Image.TORTOISE, Image.BUTTERFLY, Image.GIRAFFE, Image.SNAKE]
   ```

3. Create the array to store the celebration musical sequence. The notes and sequence have been set as **"G4:1"**, **"C5"**, **"E"**, **"G:2"**, **"E:1"**, **"G:3"**.

   ```
   from microbit import *
   import random
   import music

   images = [Image.DUCK, Image.TORTOISE, Image.BUTTERFLY, Image.GIRAFFE, Image.SNAKE]
   correctTune = ["G4:1", "C5", "E", "G:2", "E:1", "G:3"]
   ```

4 IF the A button is pressed, THEN the program should display a random image. There is a **function** that allows the program to choose an item randomly from the list: `random.choice()`. The array name is placed inside the brackets: `random.choice(images)`.

To output a random image, place this function inside the brackets of the code to output an image to the micro:bit display: `display.show(random.choice(images))`.

```python
from microbit import *
import random
import music

images = [Image.DUCK, Image.TORTOISE, Image.BUTTERFLY, Image.GIRAFFE, Image.SNAKE]
correctTune = ["G4:1", "C5", "E", "G:2", "E:1", "G:3"]

while True:
    if button_a.is_pressed():
        display.show(random.choice(images))
```

This code is indented below `while True:` to ensure that the micro:bit continuously reacts if the button is pressed.

5 IF the B button is pressed, THEN the program should play the celebration musical sequence, wait and then clear the screen.

```python
from microbit import *
import random
import music

images = [Image.DUCK, Image.TORTOISE, Image.BUTTERFLY, Image.GIRAFFE, Image.SNAKE]
correctTune = ["G4:1", "C5", "E", "G:2", "E:1", "G:3"]

while True:
    if button_a.is_pressed():
        display.show(random.choice(images))
    if button_b.is_pressed():
        music.play(correctTune)
        sleep(500)
        display.clear()
```

Once a program has been written, it is important to test it. If the program involves a random element, this should be reflected in the test plan.

The normal test data would be the expected inputs to the program. In this program, the A button is tested more than once to check that a randomly generated image is displayed each time.

The invalid test data would be any other input on the micro:bit to ensure that it does not activate any element of the program.

> **KEYWORD**
> **function:** sub-program that can exist as part of a bigger program

Unit 9.3 Coding and testing: Game development for the micro:bit

Test	Input data	Expected outcome	Pass/fail
Normal	A button pressed	Random image displayed	Pass – tortoise
Normal	A button pressed	Random image displayed	Pass – giraffe
Normal	A button pressed	Random image displayed	Pass – snake
Normal	A button pressed	Random image displayed	Pass – tortoise
Normal	A button pressed	Random image displayed	Pass – giraffe
Normal	A button pressed	Random image displayed	Pass – duck
Normal	A button pressed	Random image displayed	Pass – duck
Normal	A button pressed	Random image displayed	Pass – giraffe
Normal	A button pressed	Random image displayed	Pass – butterfly
Normal	B button pressed	Celebration musical sequence plays Wait 500 Clear screen	Pass
Invalid	Shake micro:bit	Nothing	Pass

Practise

```
1   START
2       IMPORT random library
3       IMPORT music library
4
5       ARRAY images = [CLOCK 12, CLOCK 1, CLOCK 2, CLOCK 3, CLOCK 4,
        CLOCK 5, CLOCK 6, CLOCK 7, CLOCK 8, CLOCK 9, CLOCK 10, CLOCK 11]
6       ARRAY correctTune = [G4:1, C5, E, G:2, E:1, G:3]
7
8       score = 0
9
10      IF button A is pressed THEN
11          OUTPUT random image from ARRAY images
12      ENDIF
13
14      IF button B is pressed THEN
15          OUTPUT images
16          score = score + 1
```

```
17          DELAY 500
18          OUTPUT clear screen
19      ENDIF
20
21      IF micro:bit is shaken THEN
22          OUTPUT score
23          DELAY 1000
24          score = 0
25      ENDIF
26
27      STOP
```

1 With your partner, predict what the pseudocode above will do.
2 a 'correctTune' should play if the B button is pressed. Rewrite this part of the pseudocode correctly.
  b Check the pseudocode using a new trace table.
3 Discuss with your partner how data is stored and used in this program.
4 Create a test plan using normal and invalid test data.
5 a Create the MicroPython program to match the pseudocode.
  b Connect the micro:bit to the computer with the USB cable and send the program to the micro:bit.
  c Test the program using your test plan, to make sure that the output is as expected.
  d Download the program to your computer and save it as **clockfaceGuessingGame.py**.

Go further

Remember: Development of a program is done in iterations. The program is written, tested and reviewed and, at this point, potential improvements may be identified. A new iteration of the program is then developed, tested and reviewed. It is important to save each iteration as a new version of the program. If you save over the previous version, you will not have the original to go back to if the new additions do not work. This is called **version control**. It allows the programmer to track the changes that have been made through the different development iterations.

In the previous section, you created a program that used the predefined images available on the micro:bit. You can also create your own images. Each individual LED light on the micro:bit can be used to create a unique image. You can switch a light on using the number 9 and off with the number 0.

KEYWORD

version control: saving each development iteration as a new filename to track changes

Unit 9.3 Coding and testing: Game development for the micro:bit

For example, you can create a question mark and add this to the array, using a 5 × 5 grid to plan the image. Each square on the grid represents an individual LED light on the micro:bit.

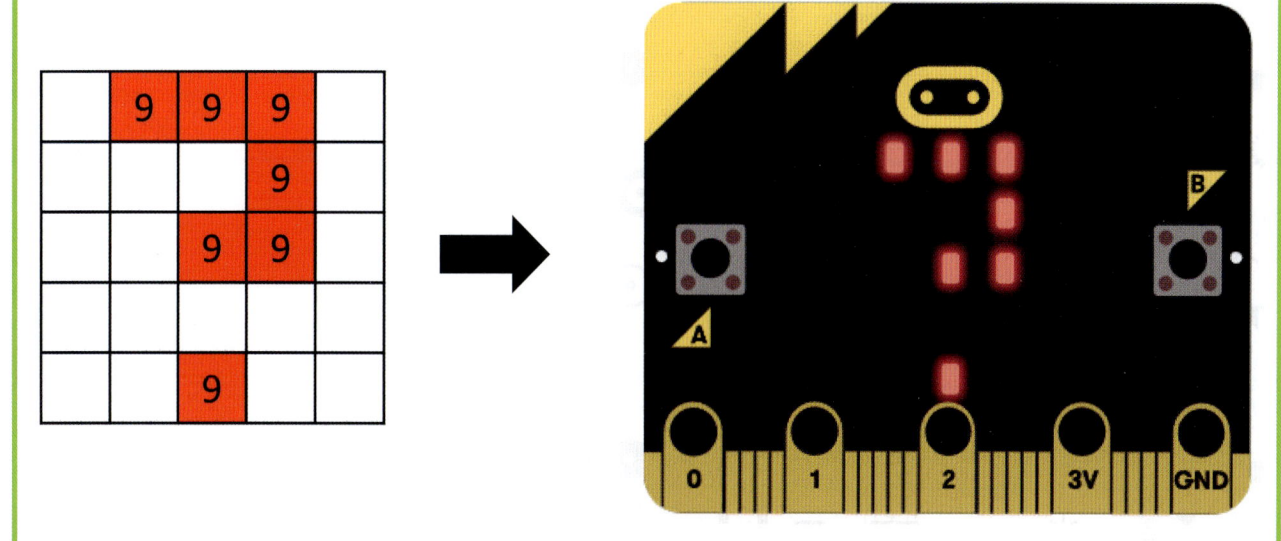

You must place the code for the new image near the top of the program, after the arrays have been created. The pseudocode below shows that the numbers for the image are placed in a grid style too. This is to ensure that the right numbers are added in the correct positions. You can enter them on a single line with each number separated by a comma, but this makes it harder to check the image layout.

```
START
IMPORT random library
IMPORT music library

ARRAY images = [DUCK, TORTOISE, BUTTERFLY, GIRAFFE, SNAKE]
ARRAY correctTune = [G4:1, C5, E, G:2, E:1, G:3]

questionMark =    09990
                  00090
                  00990
                  00000
                  00900

ADD questionMark to ARRAY images
```

```
IF button A is pressed THEN
        OUTPUT random image from ARRAY images
ENDIF

IF button B is pressed THEN
        OUTPUT correctTune
        DELAY 500
        OUTPUT clear screen
ENDIF

STOP
```

A new image can be created by following these steps.
1   a Create a variable to store the new image: `questionMark =`
    b `Image()` is required after the equals sign (`=`) to tell the program that the data that follows is a new image.
    c Each LED in the line is represented using a 0 or 9: for example, the first line of the question mark image would be `"09990:"`. The quotation marks and colon are important aspects of the syntax and must be replicated on each line:

```
questionMark = Image( "09990:"
                      "00090:"
                      "00990:"
                      "00000:"
                      "00900:")
```

2   To add this new image to the array, you need to use the `append()` function:

```
images.append(questionMark)
```

Unit 9.3 Coding and testing: Game development for the micro:bit

3 The program will now have a question mark added to the array and this will be a possible output when the A button is pressed.

```python
from microbit import *
import random
import music

images = [Image.DUCK, Image.TORTOISE, Image.BUTTERFLY, Image.GIRAFFE, Image.SNAKE]
correctTune = ["G4:1", "C5", "E", "G:2", "E:1", "G:3"]

questionMark = Image( "09990:"
                      "00090:"
                      "00990:"
                      "00000:"
                      "00900:")

images.append(questionMark)

while True:
    if button_a.is_pressed():
        display.show(random.choice(images))
    if button_b.is_pressed():
        music.play(correctTune)
        sleep(500)
        display.clear()
```

1 a Create a 5 × 5 grid and plan a new animal image.
  b Create the pseudocode for your new animal image.
2 Discuss with your partner the challenges of creating an image of an animal on the micro:bit display.
3 Create a test plan using normal and invalid test data.
  a Create the program to match the pseudocode.
  b Connect the micro:bit to the computer with the USB cable and send the program to the micro:bit.
  c Test the program using the test plan you have just set up to make sure it gives the output that you expect.
  d Download the program to your computer and save it as a new iteration.

> You will need to create a new variable to store the image and add it to the array.

Challenge yourself

A game often has a time limit. In a guessing game, the player may have 60 seconds to guess as many of the images displayed as possible. Using a second micro:bit allows a player to start a timer once the other player begins their guesses.

When you are using a count-controlled loop, you can use **selection** to check a variable each time a loop is run. The code to be run as part of the selection statement is indented another layer within the for loop. Where one programming construct, such as selection, occurs inside another construct, such as a count-controlled loop, this is known as **nesting**.

In the example below, each iteration reduces the value stored in the variable 'time' by 1. On each iteration, the value is tested to see whether it meets the conditional statement, which is to see whether it is equal to 0.

- If the outcome is False, then the next iteration continues.
- If the outcome is True, then an 'X' is displayed on the micro:bit.

```
1  from microbit import *
2
3  time = 3
4  display.scroll(time)
5
6  for i in range(3):
7      time = time -1
8      display.scroll(time)
9      if time == 0:
10         display.show(Image.NO)
```

KEYWORDS

selection: choice to be added to a program using `if… elif… else` and the next instruction executed in the program is decided by the outcome of a condition

nesting: one programming construct, e.g. selection, occurring inside another construct, e.g. a count-controlled loop

You can use a trace table to see the values of the variables and the outputs as the program iterates through each run of the code in the loop.

Line	Variable	Variable	Condition	Output
	time	i	time == 0	
3	3			
4				3
6		0		
7	2			
8				2
9			False	
6		1		
7	1			
8				1
9			False	

Unit 9.3 Coding and testing: Game development for the micro:bit

Line	Variable	Variable	Condition	Output
	time	i	time == 0	
6		2		
7	0			
8				0
9			True	
10				X displayed

The next development iteration uses a second micro:bit. The second micro:bit acts as the timer for the game. The countdown needs to go from 30 to 0, and when it gets to 0 an X should be displayed, along with a musical sequence or text output using speech to represent the end of the game.

1. Plan the algorithm for the second micro:bit program in pseudocode. Your algorithm should use speech, time, a count-controlled loop and nested selection, and you should also consider how the timer is activated.
2. Create a trace table and test the flow through the pseudocode.
3. Create a test plan using normal and invalid test data and include extreme test data to check the start and end countdown displayed.
4. a Create the program code to match the pseudocode.
   b Connect the micro:bit to the computer with the USB cable and send the program to the micro:bit.
   c Use the test plan to check that the program output is what you expected.
   d Download the program to your computer and save it as **countdownTimer.py**.

Final project

The skills you have learned in this unit are all about using arrays, count-controlled loops and new functions on the micro:bit. You have developed some of the programs iteratively to create new outputs for the micro:bit. You have learned how to trace a variable or array through pseudocode or a program using a trace table and how using music and speech can enhance a game.

Look back to the start of this unit to remind yourself of the Scenario. You now have all the skills and knowledge to follow the **criteria** to create your own program for the 'What am ?' game.

KEYWORD

criteria: set of rules that must be met

The game should:
- display an item from a pre-set list to the player randomly
- use an input either through the accelerometer or a button to represent when the player has correctly guessed, and play a tune to represent a correct answer
- reset through another input, to start the game again
- use speech, music and images within the game
- utilise a count-controlled loop, selection, array and variables
- use a time delay to aid gameplay.

> **KEYWORDS**
>
> **data type:** classification applied to a data item specifying which type of data that item represents, e.g. in a spreadsheet some of the data types available include currency, text and number
>
> **prototype:** initial product created for testing and reviewing, before a final product is released

Complete the tasks below.

Part 1: Planning

Before you start to write the code:
1. Using a table, plan the variables, arrays and **data types** you are going to use in your program.
2. Identify the micro:bit inputs and outputs you are going to use in the game.
3. Identify the libraries you need to import at the start of the program.
4. Plan the algorithm by creating the pseudocode to match the Scenario.
5. Create a trace table to follow the flow of the arrays and variables you use.
6. If necessary, iteratively develop and test the pseudocode until it is ready for you to develop into program code.
7. Make a note of any changes you have made through iterative development of the pseudocode.

Part 2: Development

When you are sure that the pseudocode algorithm is complete and correct, start the development of the MicroPython code.
1. Create a test plan to use at different stages of development, and consider normal and invalid test data.
2. Continuously develop, test, debug and improve your **prototype** program code.
3. Save each development as a new iteration of the prototype program.

Part 3: Project summary

Once you have created, tested and evaluated your program solution:
1. List the different development iterations that the program has gone through to develop your final program code.
2. Use word-processing software to write a paragraph evaluating the process of iteratively developing the program code and saving each iteration.
3. Write a short report to describe how the game is played and how the micro:bit enhances the gameplay.

Evaluation

Part 1: Planning
Swap planning documents (planning table, pseudocode and trace table) with your partner. Discuss the following:
1. Are all variables and arrays planned using a structured table?
2. Does the pseudocode use a count-controlled loop, array, speech, micro:bit inputs and musical and image outputs?
3. Does the pseudocode show the use of a time delay?
4. Does the trace table show the correct flow of the array outputs and variables through the algorithm?

Part 2: Development
Swap programs with your partner. Discuss the following:
1. Does the program randomly generate an item from the array?
2. Does the program use a count-controlled loop?
3. Does the program use speech, music and images?

Part 3: Project summary
Swap reports with your partner. Discuss the following:
1. Are the program development iterations listed?
2. Has your partner evaluated the process of developing a program iteratively to show what is good and what is not so good?
3. Does the report include a how-to guide to help a player play the game using the micro:bit?
4. a Open your own program and look at the code. Reflect on what could be improved in your own program following your partner's feedback.
   b Based on the evaluations, make the changes to improve your final program.

What can you do?

Read and review what you can do.
- ✓ I can follow, understand, edit and correct algorithms that are presented as pseudocode.
- ✓ I can follow flowchart or pseudocode algorithms that use loops.
- ✓ I can create algorithms using flowcharts and pseudocode.
- ✓ I can explain and use iteration statements with count-controlled loops in either pseudocode or flowcharts.
- ✓ I can predict the outcome of algorithms that use iteration.
- ✓ I can compare and contrast two algorithms for the same solution and decide which is best suited to a task.
- ✓ I can create an algorithm as a flowchart or pseudocode using more than one construct: sequence, selection and count-controlled iteration.

- ✓ I can identify and explain the purpose of a one-dimensional array.
- ✓ I can identify and describe data types in MicroPython programs, including integer, real, character, string and Boolean.
- ✓ I can develop MicroPython programs with count-controlled loops.
- ✓ I can access data from an array using MicroPython.
- ✓ I can use iterative development on micro:bit prototypes to create solutions to problems.
- ✓ I can evaluate the processes that are followed to develop programs.
- ✓ I can develop and apply test plans that include normal, extreme and invalid data.
- ✓ I can identify test data that covers normal, extreme and invalid data.
- ✓ I can use a trace table to check the flow of a variable or array through an algorithm.
- ✓ I can program a micro:bit to use data to solve a problem.

Unit 9.4 Drilling down: How the processor handles instructions

Get started!

Have you ever thought about the different ways in which we, as users, are able to gain access to the many digital devices we use in our daily lives?

Discuss the following with your partner:
- How do you gain access to a digital device to be able to start using it?
- What do you need to do to complete a task using the device, for example sending a message or an email to a friend?
- How does the device know what to do when you click on a particular icon or select an option on screen?

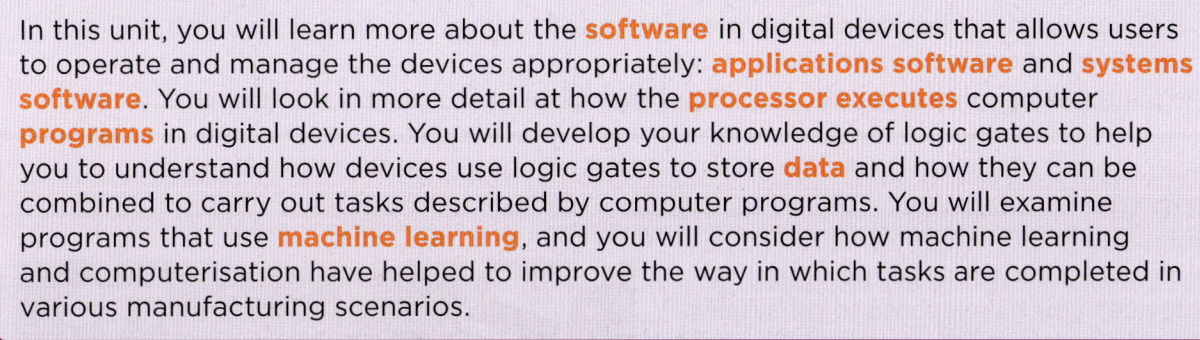

In this unit, you will learn more about the **software** in digital devices that allows users to operate and manage the devices appropriately: **applications software** and **systems software**. You will look in more detail at how the **processor executes** computer **programs** in digital devices. You will develop your knowledge of logic gates to help you to understand how devices use logic gates to store **data** and how they can be combined to carry out tasks described by computer programs. You will examine programs that use **machine learning**, and you will consider how machine learning and computerisation have helped to improve the way in which tasks are completed in various manufacturing scenarios.

KEYWORDS

software: program or set of instructions that tell a computer what to do to complete a task; aspects of a device you *cannot* touch

applications software: software designed to do a particular task, e.g. a word processor, spreadsheet, web browser, mobile-phone app

systems software: software that helps a user run a computer

processor: electronic circuitry that executes the instructions described in a computer program; often called the *central processor* or *central processing unit*

execute: carry out the instructions described in a computer program

program: instructions that tell a computer system how to complete a task

data: raw facts and figures

machine learning: ability of a computer system to learn over time

CAMBRIDGE LOWER SECONDARY COMPUTING 9

Learning outcomes

In this unit, you will learn to:
- identify improvements to the design of digital devices based on prototypes
- explain why factors such as user experience, accessibility, ergonomics and emerging technologies are important to the design of digital devices
- explain which tasks an operating system carries out
- describe examples of utility programs, including drivers, security software and defragmentation
- explain the different types of translator
- describe the main characteristics of compilers and interpreters
- explain how analogue sound is digitised
- explain how to convert between storage units
- draw logic circuits for Boolean expressions
- explain how computers store lists of instructions to be run one at a time
- explain the fetch-decode-execute cycle
- describe what is meant by *machine learning* and identify a range of applications and scenarios where machine learning is used
- explain the benefits and risks of computerising tasks in industry and manufacturing.

Warm up

1. In pairs, think about all the digital devices you have access to on a daily basis.
2. Write down the names of some of the software you use on each device. Most devices may have more than one piece of software installed. Beside each piece of software, write down the task you use it for.
3. Review your list of software and think about all the tasks you complete using the device. Have you included all tasks, such as logging on to the device, organising files on the device, creating new accounts on the device?

SCENARIO

A new computing technology company promoting student interest in the computing industry is delivering a workshop for Stage 9 students to increase understanding of how computing technology and machine learning are used in industry and home technologies.

Your task is to help the company to prepare for the workshop. You will need to create resources (a presentation, worksheets, a poster and a **prototype** design) that can be used to explain the technologies to students.

Unit 9.4 Drilling down: How the processor handles instructions

The resources you are tasked with developing need to cover the following areas:
- Information about how an **operating system** carries out tasks
- Examples of utility programs, including **drivers**, **security software** and **defragmentation**
- Why different types of **translators** are needed to convert computer programs into a form the processor can understand
- A description of the main characteristics of **compilers** and **interpreters**
- How **analogue** sound is **digitised**
- How to **convert** between **storage units** used to measure the size of data files
- How to draw **logic circuits** for Boolean expressions
- How computers store **lists** of instructions to be run one at a time
- What the fetch–decode–execute cycle does
- The meaning of *machine learning* and a range of scenarios where machine learning is used
- The benefits and risks of the computerisation of **traditional manufacturing** and industrial practices
- How prototypes can be used to identify areas where the design of digital devices can be improved.

KEYWORDS

prototype: initial product created for testing and reviewing, before a final product is released

operating system: software that manages all the computer hardware and software; it also acts as an interface between computer hardware components and the user, and provides a platform where applications can run

device driver: software program that operates a hardware device connected to a computer

security software: any type of software that secures and protects a digital device

defragmentation: reorganising files stored on a hard drive to ensure that all parts of the same file are located one after the other on the drive

translator: converts program instructions into machine-code format so the processor can carry out the instructions

compiler: translates an entire computer program into machine code and creates a file containing machine code for the entire program

interpreter: translates each line of high-level language code into machine code

analogue: continually varying signal, e.g. a sound signal

digitise: convert into digital format, i.e. into 1s and 0s

convert: change from one unit to another, e.g. storage units (e.g. bits/bytes/kilobytes)

storage units: number of bits used to store a data item in a digital device

logic circuit: combination of logic gates for solving a problem in a digital device

list: data structure in Python that can store multiple items of data of mixed data types under a single identifier; data items can be changed

traditional manufacturing: the making of products before computerisation; it often relied on human production lines, where people completed individual tasks, which were passed along the production line until the final product was complete

Do you remember?

Before starting this unit, you should be able to:
- ✔ describe the differences between applications software and systems software
- ✔ explain that the operating system is an example of systems software
- ✔ explain the role of utility programs in a computer system
- ✔ explain that data and programs that are to be reused are stored in secondary storage devices such as a hard disc drive
- ✔ explain that ASCII is a set of binary codes that can represent the character set of a digital device
- ✔ explain that data such as sound can be represented in digital format
- ✔ explain the role of logic gates in circuits, including AND, OR and NOT gates
- ✔ draw the symbols that represent AND, OR and NOT gates in a logic circuit
- ✔ describe how AND, OR and NOT gates operate
- ✔ identify text-based programming languages, such as Python
- ✔ explain what is meant by the term machine learning and identify applications where machine learning is used.

Understanding software

Learn

Digital devices use a number of different types of software to complete a task. To recap, the software available on any digital device can be divided into two broad categories: **applications software** and **systems software**; systems software in turn can be broken down into the **operating system** and **utilities software**.

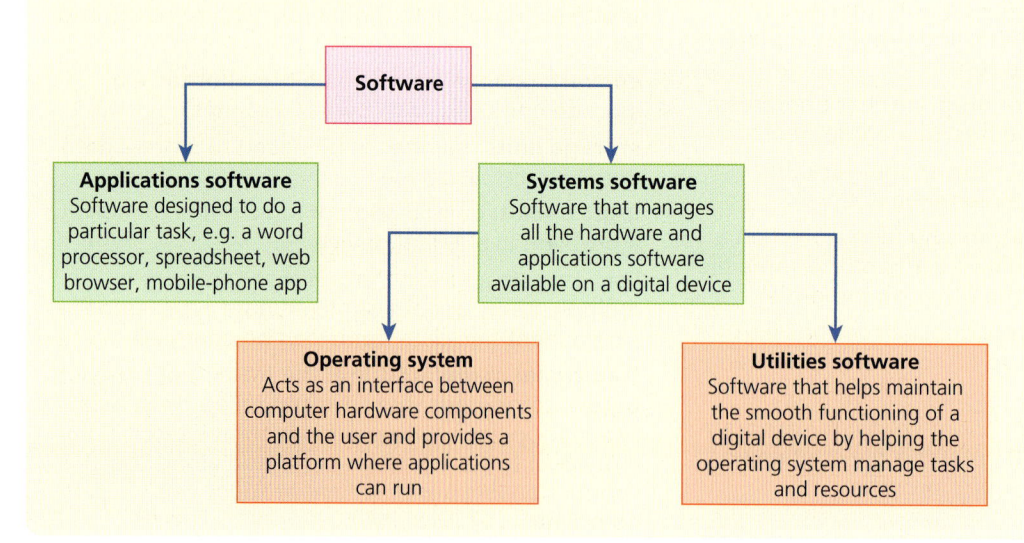

```
                        Software
                       /        \
         Applications software   Systems software
         Software designed to    Software that manages
         do a particular task,   all the hardware and
         e.g. a word processor,  applications software
         spreadsheet, web        available on a digital device
         browser, mobile-phone app
                                  /              \
                        Operating system    Utilities software
                        Acts as an interface    Software that helps maintain
                        between computer        the smooth functioning of a
                        hardware components     digital device by helping the
                        and the user and        operating system manage tasks
                        provides a platform     and resources
                        where applications
                        can run
```

The operating system is a key part of any digital device. Without the operating system, the user would not be able to interact with the device and other programs could not run on the device. The operating system has a number of key tasks. It:
- manages the **hardware** of the device, including the processor
- runs applications
- provides an interface for the user to interact with the device
- manages the storage and retrieval of files.

The operating system cannot guarantee the smooth operation of a digital device on its own. Utility programs also have an important role to play. Some examples of important utility programs (sometimes known as tools) include: **device drivers**, **security software** and **defragmentation** programs.

Device driver
This is a software program that operates a hardware device connected to a computer. Device drivers are essential for a computer to work properly. Many devices are now known as **plug-and-play devices**. This means that the device is automatically detected and set up correctly for use by the operating system. No human intervention is needed.

Security software
When considering security software, most people think about the software used to limit access to digital devices: for example, the use of **passwords** or **personal identification numbers (PINs)**. Some devices even use **biometric security** methods such as **facial recognition**, **fingerprint recognition** or **voice-pattern recognition**.

In fact, any type of software that secures and protects a digital device is an example of security software, including:
- **firewalls**
- antivirus
- anti-spyware
- anti-malware.

All these features and all the tasks you carry out using a digital device are possible only because of the software you have installed on the device.

Disc defragmenter
When you save a file on your digital device, you should give the file a relevant filename. The operating system uses an **algorithm** to decide where on the **hard drive** the file is to be saved. This can lead to pieces of files being stored in different places on the hard drive, which is called **fragmentation**. It means that when you try to open that file, the operating system has to spend a lot of time locating all the parts of the file and reassembling them correctly in **Random Access Memory (RAM)**.

You can use the defragmentation utility tool to reorganise the data on the disc so that all parts of the same file are stored together. The diagram below shows what the surface of a disc looks like before defragmentation takes place. A file may be stored in different portions of a hard disc surface. After defragmentation, the disc surface is reorganised so that all the data relating to a file is stored beside each other on the disc surface. This makes the data easier to access.

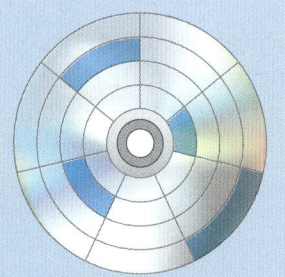

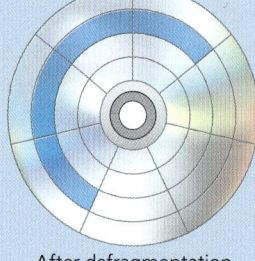

Before defragmentation   After defragmentation

> Before defragmentation, a file may be stored in different portions of a hard disc surface. After defragmentation, the disc surface is reorganised so that all the data relating to a file is stored beside each other on the disc surface. This makes the data easier to access.

KEYWORDS

applications software: software designed to do a particular task, e.g. a word processor, spreadsheet, web browser, mobile-phone app

systems software: software that helps a user run a computer

operating system: software that manages all the computer hardware and software; it also acts as an interface between computer hardware components and the user, and provides a platform where applications can run

utilities software: software that helps maintain the smooth functioning of a digital device by helping the operating system manage tasks and resources

hardware: physical parts of a computer that you *can* touch and see, e.g. the processor, storage devices, input devices, output devices

device driver: software program that operates a hardware device connected to a computer

security software: any type of software that secures and protects a digital device

defragmentation: reorganising files stored on a hard drive to ensure that all parts of the same file are located one after the other on the drive

plug-and-play device: device that is detected automatically and set up correctly for use by the operating system; no human intervention is needed

personal identification number (PIN): sometimes called a *PIN number* or *PIN code*; a numerical passcode that allows a user access to a digital device

password: code made up of numbers or numbers and letters and other characters (depending on the device), which allows a user access to a digital device

biometric security: security method that identifies people using a physical attribute (e.g. a fingerprint) or a behaviour (e.g. a hand gesture)

facial recognition: system that matches a real-time image of a human face with a database of saved facial representations to allow a user access to a digital device

fingerprint recognition: system that matches a real-time image of a human fingerprint with a database of saved fingerprint representations to allow a user access to a digital device

voice-pattern recognition: software that can understand and carry out spoken instructions

algorithm: step-by-step instructions to solve a particular problem

hard disc drive: removable disc in computers for storing large amounts of data, typically measured in gigabytes or terabytes

fragmentation: situation that occurs when pieces of files are scattered across the surface of a hard disc when the operating system is storing the file

Random Access Memory (RAM): memory used to store programs and data currently being used by the processor

Unit 9.4 Drilling down: How the processor handles instructions

Practise

Your teacher may provide you with a file called **Systems Software Presentation.pptx** to help you complete the following tasks.

1. List three examples of operating systems.
2. List five examples of applications software.
3. Use the internet to research the tasks that the following utility programs carry out.
   a Disc management tools
   b Compression tools
   c Disc clean-up tools
   d File-management systems
   e Backup utilities
4. Research the roles played by the following examples of security software.
   a Firewalls
   b Antivirus
   c Anti-spyware
   d Anti-malware
5. Summarise your findings from tasks 3 and 4 in a short report or presentation.
6. Discuss with your partner the meaning of the term *fragmentation* and explain the role of disc-defragmentation programs. Make short notes on the outcome of your discussion. You may wish to record your notes on a new slide in your copy of the file **Systems Software Presentation.pptx**.

> Remember to describe the role of each utility program and security software tool you have researched.

Digitising sound

Learn

All programs and data stored inside a digital device are stored in binary format; this includes the operating system and utility programs. Security programs, such as the biometric login security applications on digital devices, store details about users' facial representations or fingerprints, or even voice patterns, in digital formats. You have previously considered how images can be digitised, but what about applications that need to store sound in digital format?

Today, most digital devices accept input from users via microphones in the form of spoken words. Sound waves create what is called an **analogue** sound wave, such as the one shown on the right.

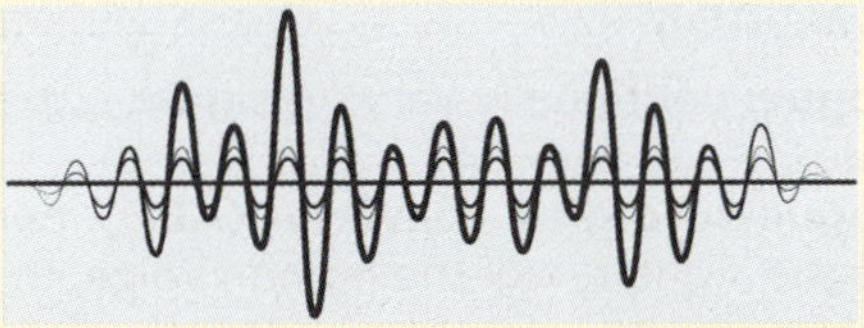

Computers do not store data in analogue format so the sound wave must be converted into digital format. Converting analogue signals into digital is carried out by a device called an **analogue-to-digital convertor (ADC)**.

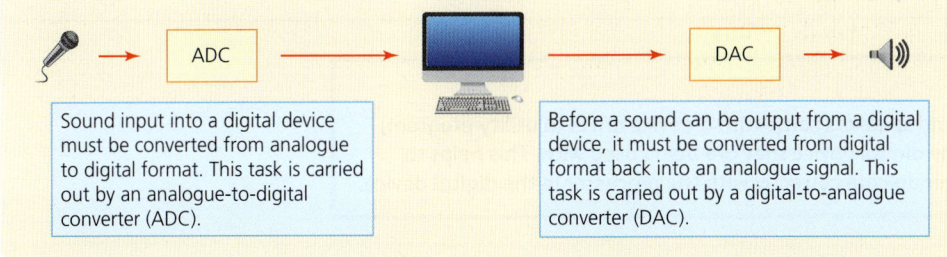

Sound input into a digital device must be converted from analogue to digital format. This task is carried out by an analogue-to-digital converter (ADC).

Before a sound can be output from a digital device, it must be converted from digital format back into an analogue signal. This task is carried out by a digital-to-analogue converter (DAC).

135

ADCs take samples of the sound wave at fixed intervals in time; this process is called **sampling**. The number of samples taken each second is called the **sample rate**. The sample rate is measured in *number of times per second*, which is known as **hertz (Hz)**. So, for example, if the sample rate were 1Hz, this would mean that only one sample was taken per second. The diagram below shows an analogue sound wave that has been sampled twenty times in 1 second.

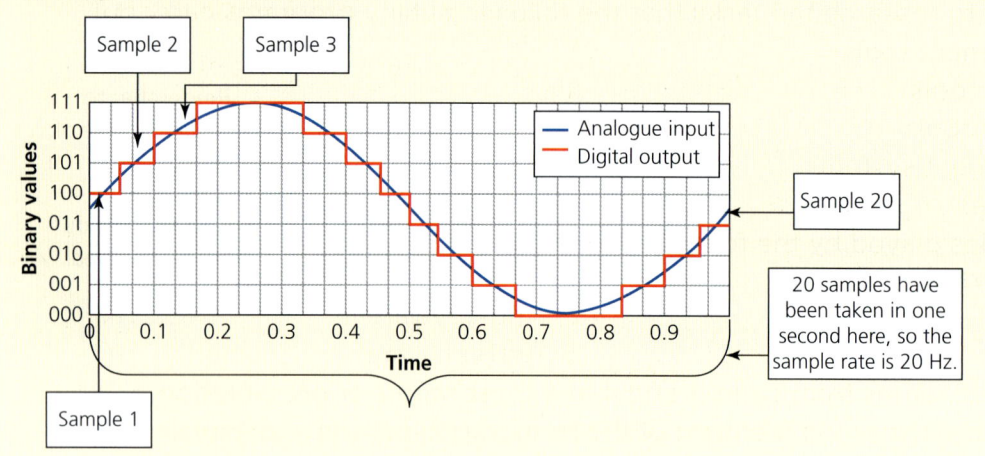

Each sample is represented by **binary digits** (in this case three) using the values on the *y*-axis of the graph ('Binary values'), for example:
- Sample 1 = 100
- Sample 2 = 101
- Sample 3 = 110

... and so on, up to:
- Sample 20 = 011.

In the example above, 3 **bits** are used to store each sound sample. The number of bits used to store each sound sample is called the **bit depth**. The more samples taken, and the more bits used to record each sound sample, the better the quality of the digital sound file.

KEYWORDS

analogue: continually varying signal, e.g. a sound signal

analogue-to-digital converter (ADC): converts analogue signals, e.g. the human voice, to digital signals

sampling: taking samples of a sound wave at fixed intervals

sample rate: number of sound samples taken each second

hertz (Hz): unit of measurement of how many sound samples are taken in 1 second

binary digit: 0 or 1; the smallest unit of binary data represented on a digital device

bit: short for 'binary digit': 0 or 1

bit depth: the number of bits used to store a single sound sample

DID YOU KNOW?

Devices such as microphones and speakers come with a device driver (a utility program) that has to be installed onto the digital device they are being used with. This helps to ensure that the device can communicate correctly with the processor in the digital device.

Unit 9.4 Drilling down: How the processor handles instructions

Practise

1. Write a short paragraph explaining how analogue sound is converted into digital format.

2. Use sampling to convert the sound wave below into digital format. The sample rate is 10 Hz.

   For example, look at the sample taken at time 0 = 10, the sample taken at time 0.1 = 10 and the sample taken at time 0.2 = 11. Where would the red line that represents the binary sound sample be at time 0.3, 0.4, 0.5?

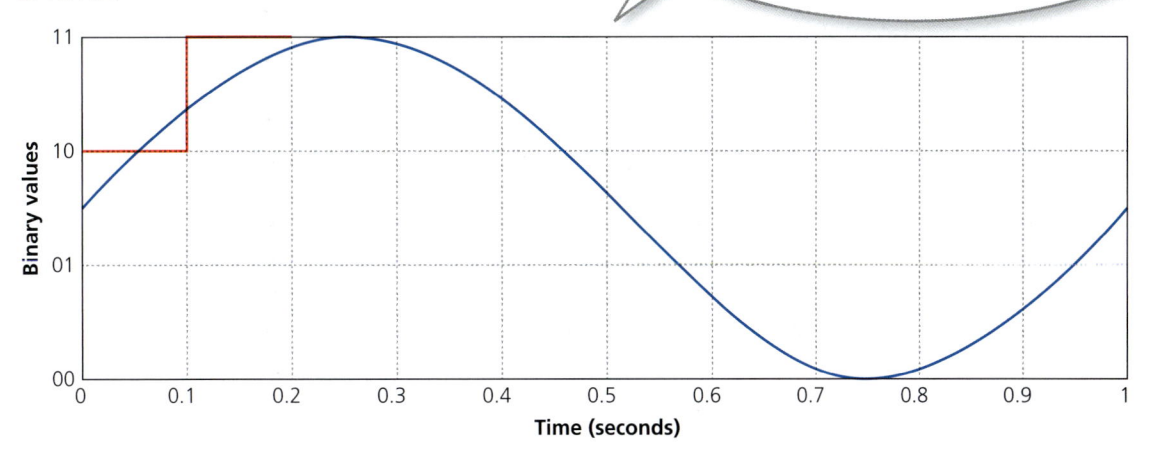

3. The sample above was recorded using only 2 bits (a bit depth of 2).
   a. Try sampling the same sound wave using 4 bits (a bit depth of 4).

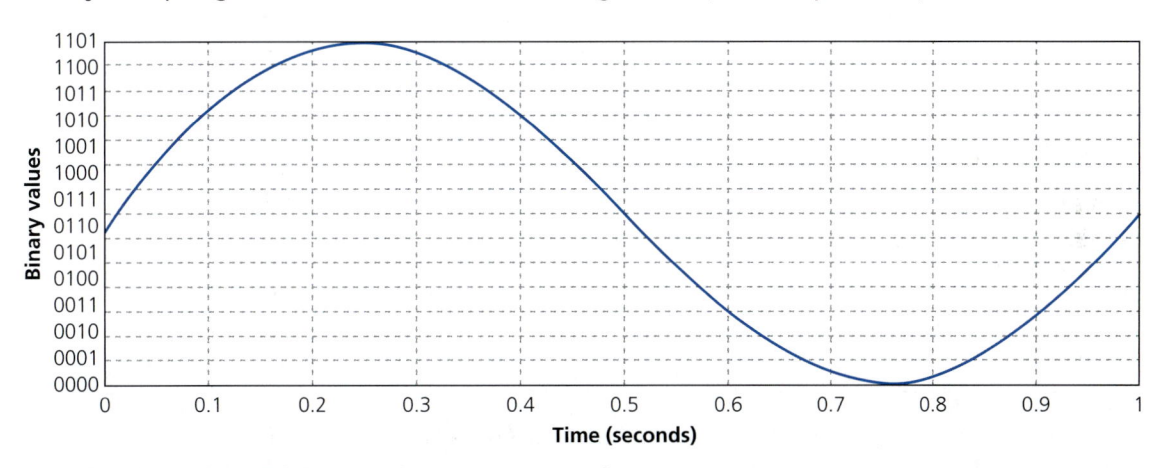

   For example, the sample at time 0 = 0110, the sample taken at time 0.1 = 1010. Complete the sample by noting the binary pattern used and writing down the sound sample at the remaining time intervals shown in the diagram.

   b. How does this 4-bit sample compare with the previous 2-bit sample?

4. a. Which sound sample would create the best-quality sound file?
   b. Which bit depth would you recommend and why?
   c. Which sound sample would create the largest file? Give a reason for your answer.

Data storage

Learn

All programs and data stored inside a digital device are stored in binary format; this includes the operating system, utility programs and even data that is associated with a biometric security system, for example, the sound pattern represented in the previous 'Learn' box.

A single **binary digit** (1 or 0) stored inside a digital device is known as a **bit**. In Stage 8, you learned that special switches called **transistors** are used to represent each binary digit inside a digital device. When data is stored inside a computer, the bits used to represent the data can be grouped together and **processed** in larger units, shown in the diagram below.

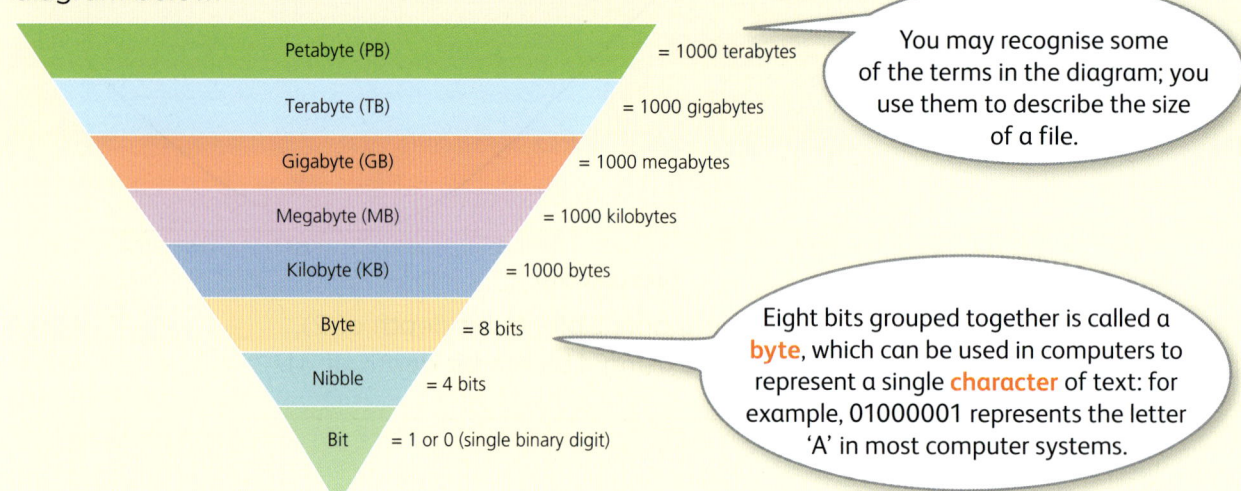

Petabyte (PB)	= 1000 terabytes
Terabyte (TB)	= 1000 gigabytes
Gigabyte (GB)	= 1000 megabytes
Megabyte (MB)	= 1000 kilobytes
Kilobyte (KB)	= 1000 bytes
Byte	= 8 bits
Nibble	= 4 bits
Bit	= 1 or 0 (single binary digit)

You may recognise some of the terms in the diagram; you use them to describe the size of a file.

*Eight bits grouped together is called a **byte**, which can be used in computers to represent a single **character** of text: for example, 01000001 represents the letter 'A' in most computer systems.*

When saving a file, it is important to know whether there is enough space in an area of memory or on the storage device to store the file. To do this, you need to be able to **convert** between one **storage unit** and another.

To help you to complete this task, it is important that you remember the name of each unit and the order in which the units appear. By multiplying or dividing repeatedly by 1000, it is easy to convert a file size from one unit into another, as shown below.

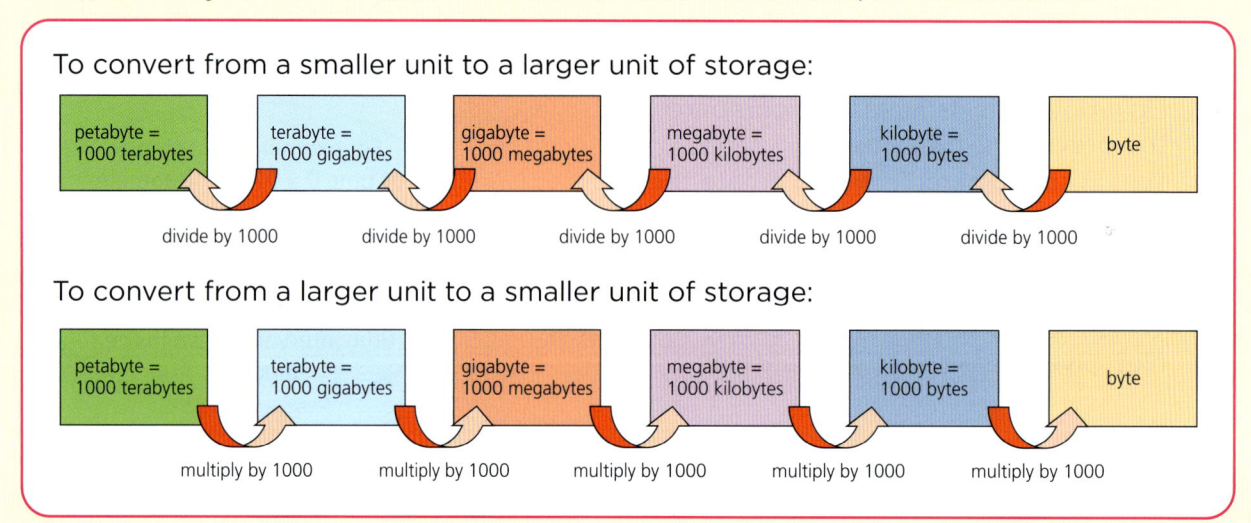

To convert from a smaller unit to a larger unit of storage:

petabyte = 1000 terabytes ← divide by 1000 ← terabyte = 1000 gigabytes ← divide by 1000 ← gigabyte = 1000 megabytes ← divide by 1000 ← megabyte = 1000 kilobytes ← divide by 1000 ← kilobyte = 1000 bytes ← divide by 1000 ← byte

To convert from a larger unit to a smaller unit of storage:

petabyte = 1000 terabytes → multiply by 1000 → terabyte = 1000 gigabytes → multiply by 1000 → gigabyte = 1000 megabytes → multiply by 1000 → megabyte = 1000 kilobytes → multiply by 1000 → kilobyte = 1000 bytes → multiply by 1000 → byte

Unit 9.4 Drilling down: How the processor handles instructions

> **KEYWORDS**
>
> **binary digit:** 0 or 1; the smallest unit of binary data represented on a digital device
>
> **bit:** short for 'binary digit': 0 or 1
>
> **transistor:** tiny switch activated by electrical signals – when the transistor is ON it represents 1; when the transistor is OFF it represents 0
>
> **process:** carrying out an operation on data, e.g. querying a database or doing a calculation using data in a spreadsheet
>
> **byte:** eight bits of data, e.g. 01010011
>
> **character:** single letter, digit or symbol
>
> **convert:** change from one unit to another, e.g. storage units (e.g. bits/bytes/kilobytes)
>
> **storage units:** number of bits used to store a data item in a digital device
>
> **backup:** copying files to another location in case the original is lost or damaged

Computational thinking – decomposition and algorithms

A word-processed document contains 300 characters, including spaces. Using this information, it is possible to work out how many bytes, kilobytes or megabytes are needed to store the file, for example:

- If each character is stored using 8 bits, that means that 300 × 8 bytes are needed to store the word-processed document. So, **300 × 8 = 2400 bytes**.
- You can work how many kilobytes are needed to store the file by dividing 2400 by 1000: **2400 ÷ 100 = 2.4 kilobytes or 2.4 KB**.

Remember: the ASCII code that represents the character set of most computers is 8 bits.

1 Another word-processed document is 6500 megabytes in size. How many characters are there in the file?
2 A utility program stored on a computer hard drive is 30 megabytes in size. What is this file size in bytes?

Practise

1 Create a rhyme or poem to help you remember the terms associated with units of storage shown in the diagram above. Use your poem or rhyme to help you learn the storage units from byte to petabyte in the correct order.
2 Explain to your partner how you can convert a file that is 2 PB in size into GB.
3 Explain to your partner how you can convert a file that is 12,000,000 bits into MB.
4 Calculate in bytes the size of each of the following programs.
  a A 2-hour movie that is 7 GB.
  b A **backup** of the contents of the school server, which is 3 petabytes.
5 Convert the following files into the most appropriate storage unit.
  a A word-processed document that contains 24,300 bytes of data.
  b A multimedia presentation that contains 2500 bytes of data.

Think about the steps you followed to convert between the storage units in the 'Learn' box. Make sure that you stop dividing or multiplying by 1000 when you have arrived at a suitable storage unit.

Computer programming languages

Learn

The instructions to be carried out by a computer are provided by a computer program. Program developers use **high-level languages (HLL)**, such as Python or Scratch, to write computer programs. These are programming languages that programmers easily understand.

However, before the processor can carry out these instructions, they need to be converted into a pattern of 1s and 0s (binary) that the **Central Processing Unit (CPU)** understands. The CPU is the part of the computer that carries out program instructions. The CPU is sometimes known simply as the *processor*. Every CPU has its own set of binary instructions it understands. This is called its **instruction set**. The instruction set of a CPU is written in binary (also known as **machine code**). Machine-code instructions are instructions that the processor understands; they are written in binary format. Instructions written in this format are known as **low-level language (LLL)** instructions.

When writing a program using an HLL, the programmer does not need to understand what is happening inside the processor; they only need to focus on writing a program to solve a problem.

> Remember: programs and data currently being used by a processor are stored in RAM while the program is being run. When you are programming, you give **data items** variable names. The **variable names** are used to identify locations in memory where the data items are being held.

The table below shows the difference between program instructions written in an HLL and an LLL.

High-level language (HLL)	Low-level language (LLL)
var1 = 0.5 if var1 > 1.3 or var1 < 0.9:	10100101010010101010101
• Easy for humans to read, write and modify • Uses variables to identify locations in memory for storing data • Portable, which means it can be run by any CPU	• More difficult for humans to read, write and modify • Identifies locations in memory using actual location addresses when storing data • Not portable, which means it can only run on a CPU with the same instruction set

> Remember: computers only understand instructions that are written in binary.

Each HLL instruction is often made up from more than one LLL instruction. Before a programmer can write a program in an LLL, they need to understand what is happening inside the processor. (You will explore this in detail in the next section.)

Low-level program instructions can be carried out by the processor easily as they are already in a format the processor understands. However, they are not easy for a programmer to understand. Programmers sometimes write instructions in a more easily understood version of machine code, called an **assembly language**.

Unit 9.4 Drilling down: How the processor handles instructions

Each assembly-language instruction corresponds to one machine-code instruction in the CPU's instruction set. However, assembly language uses a set of codes or symbols to represent each instruction, rather than a group of 1s and 0s. The assembly-language instructions are therefore easier for human programmers to understand. The example below shows how to output the word 'Hi' to a computer screen.

Assembly-language instruction	Machine-code alternative
`OUT "Hi"`	`10110101 01001000 01101001`

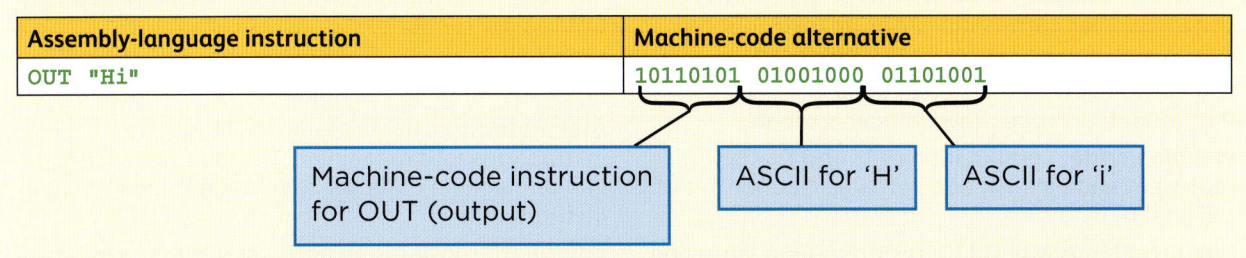

- Machine-code instruction for OUT (output)
- ASCII for 'H'
- ASCII for 'i'

The diagram below will help you to understand the link between the CPU hardware, machine code, assembly language and high-level languages.

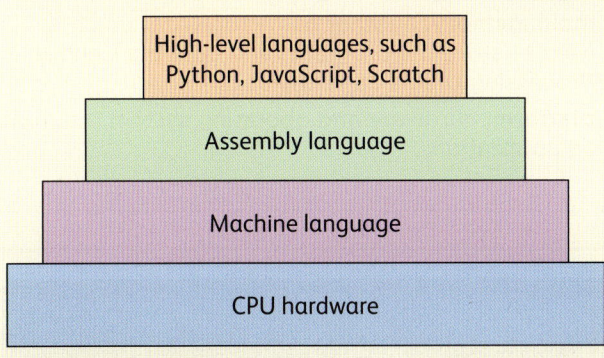

- High-level languages, such as Python, JavaScript, Scratch
- Assembly language
- Machine language
- CPU hardware

> Interpreters take each line of a computer program, translate it into machine code and execute that line of code before moving on to the next line of code. This often makes the program slow to run and may cause problems if the code makes reference to a variable that has not yet been used (declared) in the program.

Unless a computer program is written in machine-code format, it needs to be translated into machine code before the processor can execute it. A **translator** carries out this task. There are three different types of translator: **interpreters**, **assemblers** and **compilers**.

Interpreter	Assembler	Compiler
• Translates each line of HLL code into machine code • Carries out one instruction before translating the next instruction, meaning that less **main memory** is needed to run the program as the instructions are not stored for use later • Errors are displayed as soon as they are encountered • If an error is encountered, the program execution stops; this is helpful when trying to debug a program • Interprets the program each time it is run, so is useful for applications designed to run on multiple **platforms** (e.g. web-based applications written using Python)	• Converts assembly-language instructions into machine code • Creates one line of machine code for each assembly-language instruction • Does not convert the entire program into machine code in one go	• Translates the entire program into machine code • Does not run the program until all lines of code have been translated • Errors in the code are reported only at the end of the process; this can make debugging difficult • Takes a long time to compile the program • Saves a copy of the translated code so it can be used over and over again, meaning compiled programs run quickly • Useful for larger programs, e.g. computer games, which may take a long time to compile

KEYWORDS

high-level language (HLL): programming language that uses commands and terms that are linked to the words or symbols a human would use when carrying out the same task

Central Processing Unit (CPU): the part of the computer that carries out program instructions, sometimes known simply as the *processor*

instruction set: all the instructions in machine code that a Central Processing Unit can execute

machine code: combination of 1s and 0s that represent each instruction in the instruction set of a digital device

low-level language (LLL): programming language that uses commands that are similar to the type of instructions the processor understands

data item: piece of information that represents part of the data that makes up a person, place or thing, e.g. some of the data items that represent a person are their first name and second name

variable: named memory location that can store a value

assembly language: set of codes or symbols that represent each instruction, rather than a group of 1s and 0s

translator: converts program instructions into machine-code format so the processor can carry out the instructions

interpreter: translates each line of high-level language code into machine code

assembler: translates assembly-language instructions into machine code and creates one line of machine code for each assembly-language instruction

compiler: translates an entire computer program into machine code and creates a file containing machine code for the entire program

main memory: another name for RAM, which is used to store the programs and data the Central Processing Unit is currently using

platform: hardware and operating system that runs an application

DID YOU KNOW?

Programs written in a low-level programming language work only on the computer system for which they have been designed. LLLs are said to be non-portable (that is, they cannot be used on digital devices produced by other manufacturers), unlike high-level programming languages, which can be installed and executed on different computer platforms, for example, Windows or iOS, which can be used to interact with laptops, PCs, digital tablets or mobile phones.

Practise

Create a mind map that explains why program translators are needed. Your mind map should:
- show the key differences between high-level languages and low-level languages
- explain the different types of translators; make sure you list the characteristics of compilers and interpreters.

Unit 9.4 Drilling down: How the processor handles instructions

The fetch–decode–execute cycle

Learn

The main role of the **Central Processing Unit (CPU)** is to run (or execute) a set of stored instructions known as a *computer program*. The CPU coordinates all the other parts of the computer when it is executing a program.

A CPU has three main components, and it uses these components when it is carrying out (executing) the instructions in a computer program.

Arithmetic logic unit (ALU) – carries out the calculations needed during the execution of a program.

Control unit (CU) – issues commands to the other hardware components to ensure that programs are carried out correctly.

Registers – store data about memory locations, instructions and data used during execution of an instruction. The different registers are:
- **Accumulator (ACC)** – a register used by the ALU to store the results of the processing the ALU carries out
- **Program counter (PC)** – stores the address of the next instruction waiting to be executed (carried out) by the CPU
- **Current instruction register (CIR)** – stores the address of the instruction the CPU is currently executing
- **Memory address register (MAR)** – holds the address of the memory location being accessed, either to read data from or write data to
- **Memory data register (MDR)** – any data or instructions that pass into or out of **main memory** must pass through the MDR.

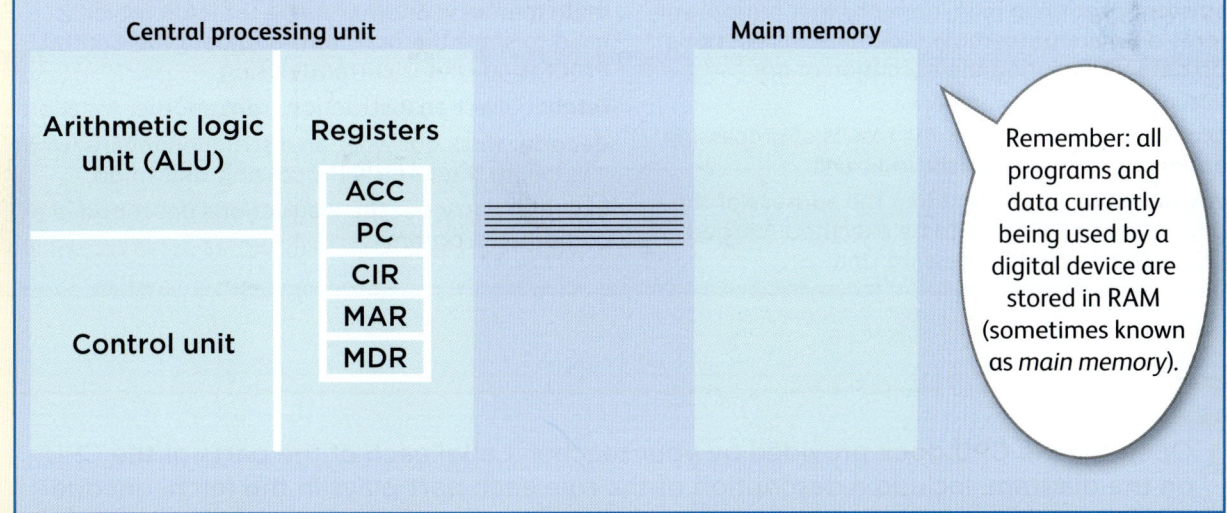

Central processing unit

Arithmetic logic unit (ALU)

Control unit

Registers
- ACC
- PC
- CIR
- MAR
- MDR

Main memory

Remember: all programs and data currently being used by a digital device are stored in RAM (sometimes known as *main memory*).

143

Fetch-decode-execute

Computer programs stored in RAM are carried out by the CPU, one instruction at a time. The CPU operates at an extremely high speed and, when it is executing a computer program, it is able to carry out many instructions every second. It does this by going through a set of steps known as the *fetch-decode-execute cycle*.

The fetch-decode-execute cycle has three stages:
1. **Fetch** – the CPU fetches an instruction from a location in memory.
2. **Decode** – the CPU works out what the instruction means, i.e. it is telling the CPU what to do.
3. **Execute** – once the CPU has figured out what it has to do, it carries out that instruction.

The processor will continually fetch instructions from memory, decode them and then execute (or carry out) those instructions.

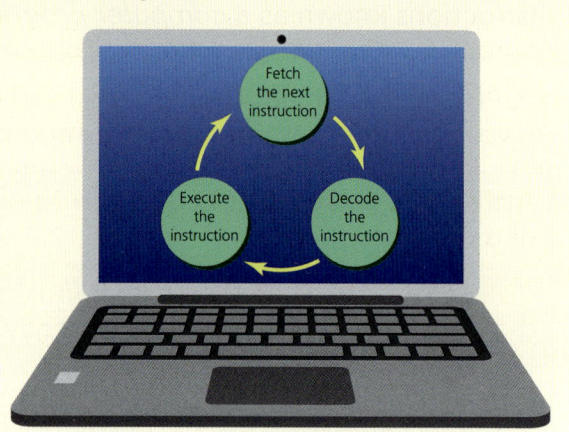

KEYWORDS

Central Processing Unit (CPU): the part of the computer that carries out program instructions, sometimes known simply as the *processor*

arithmetic logic unit (ALU): carries out the calculations needed during the execution of a program

control unit (CU): issues commands to the other hardware components to help ensure programs are carried out correctly

register: location in main memory that temporarily stores data about memory locations, instructions and data used during the execution of an instruction

accumulator (ACC): holds the results of processing carried out by the arithmetic logic unit

program counter (PC): stores the address of the next instruction waiting to be executed (carried out) by the Central Processing Unit

current instruction register (CIR): stores the address of the instruction the Central Processing Unit is currently executing

memory address register (MAR): holds the address of the memory location being accessed, either to read data from or write data to

memory data register (MDR): any data or instructions that pass into or out of main memory must pass through the MDR

main memory: another name for RAM, which is used to store the programs and data the Central Processing Unit is currently using

fetch: collect an instruction from another location

decode: work out what an instruction means/what it is telling the Central Processing Unit to do

execute: carry out the instructions described in a computer program

Practise

1. Open the file **CPU.docx** provided by your teacher. Label each of the parts of the CPU on the diagram. Include a description of the role each part plays in the fetch–decode–execute cycle.
2. When you have completed the diagram, use the keywords in the diagram to explain how computers store lists of instructions in main memory and how the processor uses the fetch–decode–execute cycle to carry out those instructions one line of code at a time.

Running the program

Learn

In the 'Learn' box in the 'Computer programming languages' section, you learned about the differences between high-level languages, assembly language and low-level programming languages. You also learned that programs must be in **machine-code** format before the processor can understand them. All programs and data stored in main memory are stored in machine-code format. Each line of code in the high-level language program may need more than one machine-code instruction to enable the processor to carry it out. This is because the processor needs to use all the registers inside the CPU correctly to help fetch and execute the instruction.

The simple high-level language instruction `answer = num1 + num2` (in Python) is a lot more complicated that you might first think. The machine-code version of the same instruction needs to tell the processor which memory locations the data is stored in, where to load the data to carry out the instruction and where to store the final result of the processing.

Below you can see how this single high-level language instruction requires the processor to carry out three additional steps.

HLL instruction	LLL instruction steps
`answer = num1 + num2`	Load the contents of location 10 into the accumulator
	Add the contents of location 11 to the contents of the accumulator
	Store the contents of the accumulator in location 12

Remember: the accumulator is a special register that stores the results of processing.

The three instructions for the processor to carry out are shown in English in the examples here, but would be in machine-code format (binary).

The machine-code instructions that the processor needs to carry out this simple Python instruction would be stored in main memory, as shown below.

Main memory	
Address	Contents
0	Load the contents of location 10 into the accumulator
1	Add the contents of location 11 to the contents of the accumulator
2	Store the contents of the accumulator in location 12
3	
4	
5	
6	
7	
8	
9	
10 (num1)	8
11 (num2)	2
12 (answer)	

The main memory locations 0, 1 and 2 would contain the machine-code instructions needed to carry out the Python instruction `answer = num1 + num2`

Memory location 10 is used to store the number stored using variable 'num1'; location 11 is used to store the number stored using variable 'num2'; and location 12 will be used to store the answer variable when the program instruction is completed.

Three fetch-decode-execute cycles are now needed for the processor to carry out this simple task.
- Cycle 1 will fetch, decode and execute the instruction stored in location 0.
- Cycle 2 will fetch, decode and execute the instruction stored in location 1.
- Cycle 3 will fetch, decode and execute the instruction stored in location 2.

> **KEYWORD**
>
> **machine code:** combination of 1s and 0s that represent each instruction in the instruction set of a digital device

Practise

1. a Copy and complete the table below to convert the high-level programming instruction into a description of the set of machine code instructions that the processor would need to carry out to complete this line of code:

   `answer = num1 - num2 + num3`

Main memory	
Address	**Contents**
0	Load the contents of location 12 into the accumulator
1	
2	
3	
4	
5	
6	
7	
8	
9	
10	
11	
12 (num1)	8
13 (num2)	2
14 (num3)	7
15 (answer)	

   b Use your machine-code instruction example to show how the processor would need four fetch-decode-execute cycles to complete this single line of code.

2. Discuss with your partner the steps a processor carries out when completing a program instruction (the fetch-decode-execute cycle). In your discussion, describe the registers the processor uses and the role each register plays during the fetch-decode-execute cycle of the instruction shown in location (memory address 0).

Unit 9.4 Drilling down: How the processor handles instructions

Logic circuits

> **Learn**

All processing inside a digital device is carried out using logic gates and logic circuits. Most logic gates, for example the AND and OR gates, accept two inputs. The exception to this rule is the NOT gate, which accepts just one input. Logic gates can be represented using the following symbols:

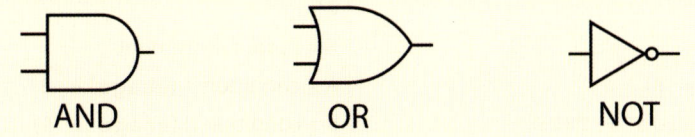

AND   OR   NOT

Logic gates can be combined to represent **conditional statements** that have two or more inputs to consider. Conditional statements use **conditional operators**. For example, consider the scenarios in the table below and the algorithms used to describe the processing required in each scenario.

You met these conditional operators in Stage 8.

Operator	Meaning
=	equal to
>	greater than
<	less than
>=	greater than or equal to
<=	less than or equal to
!=	not equal to

A local gym uses the following conditional statement to decide whether a new member is the correct age to become a junior member of the gym.
`IF age > 12 AND age < 16 then`
`    OUTPUT "This young person can become a junior member of this gym."`
`END IF`
	A computer program is helping a student to decide whether the food type they have selected is a healthy snack option.
	`IF food = "apple" OR food = "orange" then`
	`    OUTPUT "The food you have selected is a healthy snack option."`
	`END IF`

The conditional statement in this example could be described using the following **Boolean expression**: **X = A AND B** where: X = output statement A = condition 1 (`age > 12`) B = condition 2 (`age < 16`)	The conditional statement in this example could be described using the following Boolean expression: **X = A OR B** where: X = output statement A = condition 1 (`food = "apple"`) B = condition 2 (`food = "orange"`)

Some problems require more than two inputs to be processed correctly. Consider the following scenarios.

A trip is being offered to students in school. A student can attend if they are Stage 9 OR if they are Stage 8 and special permission has been given.	A fun-run event is being organised in school and students can get involved if they are Stage 8 or 9 AND they have brought in their permission forms.
`IF (stage = 8 AND permission = TRUE) OR stage = 9`	`IF (stage = 8 OR stage = 9) AND permission = TRUE`
The conditional statements in this example could be described using the following Boolean expression: X = (A AND B) OR C where: X = output statement A = condition 1 (`stage = 8`) B = condition 2 (`permission = TRUE`) C = condition 3 (`stage = 9`)	The conditional statement in this example could be described using the following Boolean expression: X = (A OR B) AND C where: X = output statement A = condition 1 (`stage = 8`) B = condition 2 (`stage = 9`) C = condition 3 (`permission = TRUE`)

When a digital device needs to consider more than two conditional statements to solve a problem, logic gates can be combined to create a **logic circuit**.

Boolean expressions, such as the examples above, can show how the logic circuit will operate. The Boolean expressions can be used to draw a diagram showing how the logic gates will combine to solve the problem.

For example, consider the logic circuit needed for the fun-run scenario above:

X = (A OR B) AND C

The following steps will help you to create a logic circuit from a Boolean expression.

1 Identify the label that represents the output from the circuit and show it at the right-hand side of your diagram.

   —— X

2 You must evaluate first any part of the expression shown inside brackets.
   Add the correct logic-gate symbol for the conditional statement and label the inputs on the left-hand side of your diagram.

   A ——⊃ P
   B ——⊃   —— X

   The output from this logic gate will be True if the student's stage = 8 OR 9.

   > You need an OR to help you with the first condition. You need to output True if the student is in Stage 8 OR Stage 9. You can label the output from this logic gate with another letter: in this example, P.

3 You can combine the True/False output from the first logic gate with the third input value to consider.
   Add a third input to your diagram to represent condition C: Permission = True.

   A ——⊃ P
   B ——⊃   —— X

   C ——

4 Add an appropriate gate to show how this third conditional statement can be combined with the output from your first logic gate to make the final decision.

Unit 9.4 Drilling down: How the processor handles instructions

Remember: a student can participate in the fun run if they are Stage 8 or Stage 9 AND they have permission to attend.

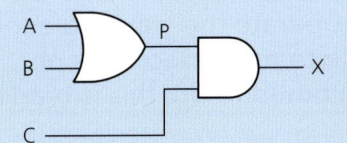

A ─┐
   ├─OR─ P ─┐
B ─┘   ├─AND─ X
C ──────────┘

Remember to show how the output from the first gate becomes an input to the second gate, along with the third input to the circuit.

KEYWORDS

conditional statement: completes a check to see whether set criteria is either True or False

conditional operator: symbol, e.g. >, < and =, used to carry out comparisons between two values

Boolean expression: expression that contains conditional operators; symbols, e.g. >, < and =, used to carry out comparisons between two values

logic circuit: combination of logic gates for solving a problem in a digital device

Practise

1. Use the steps above to create a logic circuit for the Boolean expression below.

   A trip is being offered to students in school. A student can attend if they are Stage 9 OR if they are Stage 8 and special permission has been given.

   `IF (stage = 8 AND permission = TRUE) OR stage = 9`

2. Follow the steps below to write the Boolean expression for this problem.

   A student is NOT able to participate in a school sports event if they are absent from school OR late to the track.

   In this case, there are only two inputs. X can be used to represent output from the circuit.

   A = absent

   B = late to the track

   a. Identify the correct conditional operator needed to complete the Boolean expression for this problem.
      X = NOT (A ... B)
   b. Using the completed expression and the steps outlined in the 'Learn' box, draw a logic circuit for this Boolean expression.

3. Draw logic circuits for the following Boolean expressions.
   a. X = NOT A AND (B OR C)
   b. X = (A OR B) OR NOT C

149

Machine learning and computerisation

Learn

Computer programs are needed to ensure that digital devices operate the way you expect them to when you are using them. Many digital devices are able to make decisions or perform tasks that they were not originally designed or programmed to do; this is made possible through **machine learning**.

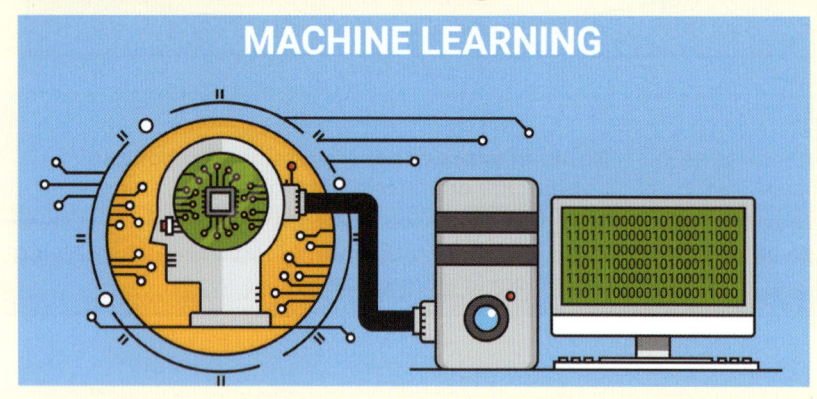

MACHINE LEARNING

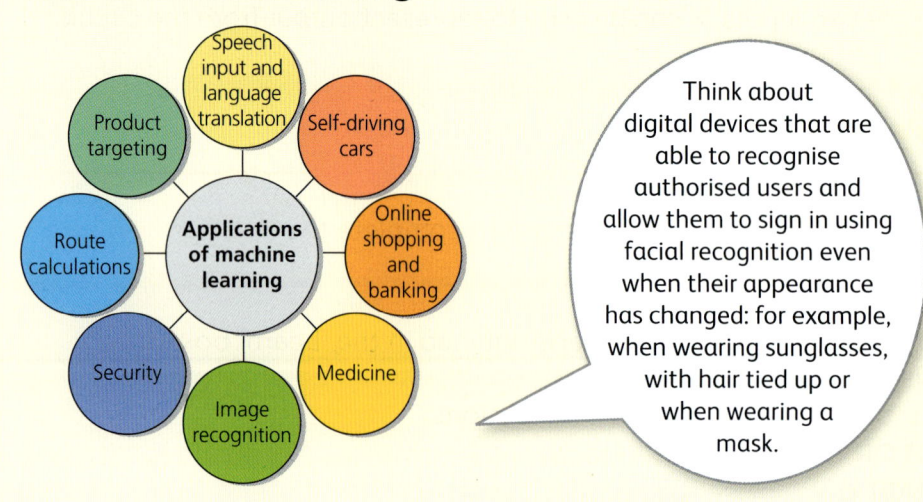

You have learned about machine learning in previous stages. Here's a recap.

> Machine learning is often confused with robotics and **artificial intelligence** (AI). Machine learning is important in helping to develop AI devices: think, for example, about how mobile phones start to understand your patterns of speech and can make recommendations for keywords in text messages you send. While it is true that some robots use machine learning to make sure that they work correctly in situations the programmer could not always anticipate (for example, some robots in industrial settings use sensors and AI to allow them to work safely in the busy environment around them), not all robots use machine learning.
>
> Machine learning is found on many of the digital applications you use on a daily basis, for example, internet search engines, email filters, online banking and biometric security systems.

Uses of machine learning

Applications of machine learning:
- Speech input and language translation
- Self-driving cars
- Online shopping and banking
- Medicine
- Image recognition
- Security
- Route calculations
- Product targeting

Think about digital devices that are able to recognise authorised users and allow them to sign in using facial recognition even when their appearance has changed: for example, when wearing sunglasses, with hair tied up or when wearing a mask.

Potential uses of machine learning include:

Speech input and language translation	Many digital assistants allow users to input instructions by speaking in normal sentences. By combining machine learning with AI, the devices are able to follow voice commands and complete tasks correctly. Communicating with other people using unfamiliar languages has been made easier using apps that automatically translate spoken, written or scanned text from one language into another.
Self-driving cars	Self-driving cars use data collected from sensors and online sources to make decisions. They use this data to select the most efficient route to take to a destination and to avoid obstacles on the journey.
Online shopping and banking	Online shopping and banking have provided criminals with opportunities to commit crimes through the creation of fake websites to steal login and bank details. Machine learning ensures that unusual online activity is quickly detected so that customers can be alerted, and unauthorised activities can be stopped quickly.
Medicine	Machine learning is often used by manufacturers of medicines to predict how an illness will respond to new medications. When diagnosing illnesses, machine learning can analyse large amounts of patient data, including images of scans, to make an accurate diagnosis and create personalised health plans for patients.
Image recognition	Used with many digital devices to allow authorised users access to the device, some software uses facial recognition to allow users to categorise photographs according to content or faces.
Security	Machine learning analyses emails and internet use and can alert authorities quickly to potential threats.
Route calculations	Satellite-navigation systems in cars use data from a range of sources, e.g. sensors in the car and real-time traffic data. This is used to choose the fastest or most economical route for a journey.
Product targeting	Many online stores and services collect data about users, including websites viewed, TV shows watched and online shopping purchases made in the past. This data can be used to make recommendations for future purchases.

Computerisation

The range of applications for machine learning and computing technology is far reaching. Many **traditional manufacturing** and industrial practices have also been computerised.

Here are some examples.
- **The manufacturing industry** was traditionally an industry that employed skilled crafts people to create new products. As technology advanced, robots that were designed to complete a single task with no input from the environment replaced human workers. When a product design changed, the robots needed to be reprogrammed to allow them to create the new design. Today, computer-aided manufacturing of new products, using computing technology to monitor and control the manufacturing process, means that products are produced to a high and consistent standard.
- **Monitoring of stock levels, using special technology known as radio frequency identification (RFID) tags.** Manufacturers are able to track the location and levels of stock and parts needed to produce products they are making. This technology is even used in checkout-free stores, where digital systems in the store track the products a customer has selected and automatically charge for them when the customer leaves the store. Previously, staff would have completed this task manually, along with counting stock levels on shop floors and warehouses. This allowed stores to decide when new products needed to be reordered, but this task is now often automated.
- **Managing communications between clients and businesses.** Computing technology is used in chatbots to troubleshoot problems. Before the introduction of chatbots, businesses would employ staff members to answer telephone calls and respond to customer queries.
- **Targeted advertising.** By collecting data about users via small programs called cookies, AI applications can send targeted advertisements to potential customers. Previously, adverts were posted publicly, for example, using large boards on roadsides, on television or on radio, in the hope that potential customers would see them.

Here are some of the benefits and risks of computerisation.

Benefits	Risks
- The products produced are a better and more consistent quality - Computers can work 24/7 - There is less chance of injury at work as fewer humans are involved in the workplace	- Technology can be expensive to purchase - Costs are unknown – computers need to be repaired if they break down - Some staff may lose their jobs

Industry 4.0

As so much manufacturing today requires the use of computers and digital technology, it is often referred to as the fourth industrial revolution or Industry 4.0.

The table below shows of the pros and cons of Industry 4.0.

Pros	Cons
- Improved security and access to data for analysis can lead to better surveillance and traffic monitoring and help businesses save money on the transportation of goods - Improved communications can reduce travel needs, make it easier to conduct business and shop online, allowing products to reach a wider market - New technologies, e.g. drones, can monitor traffic and help businesses save money on the transportation of goods	- Many people are still concerned about the security of personal data that is needed to support online activity - High reliance on technology leads to problems if the technology fails - Many of the staff normally employed in industry and manufacturing may no longer be needed, leading to job losses - Staff need to be retrained; this can be stressful for some who are not confident in the use of technology

Unit 9.4 Drilling down: How the processor handles instructions

Pros	Cons
• Increased telecommunications links mean that all areas are connected digitally, improving social links in remote areas; this can help products to be advertised and available to a wider market • Production lines are now more efficient and this can help organisations to increase their productivity • Production can easily be amended to respond to customer need • Predictive maintenance means problems with technology are anticipated and responded to quickly and this helps to limit equipment downtime • High- and consistent-quality goods are now available to customers	• Many worry about the lack of social and personal interactions, which is important to staff • Technology is expensive and a lot of investment is needed

KEYWORDS

machine learning: ability of a computer system to learn over time

artificial intelligence (AI): ability of a computer system to learn and develop its own programming from the experiences it encounters

traditional manufacturing: the making of products before computerisation; it often relied on human production lines, where people completed individual tasks, which were passed along the production line until the final product was complete

radio frequency identification (RFID) tags: technology that uses radio signals to send data to another device

chatbot: software application that uses text to ask questions to help a user

industrial revolution: rapid change in how society works following the introduction of new developments, e.g. machines, computers, robots, AI, machine learning

Industry 4.0: refers to how industry is combining electronics with new technologies, e.g. machine learning, artificial intelligence, robotics and green energy

cookies: small pieces of data, collected from websites and stored as text by web browsers

Practise

1. Write a short paragraph explaining what is meant by the term *machine learning*.
2. a Use the 'Learn' box to describe to your partner three examples where machine learning is used in today's society.
   b Use the internet to carry out research and find three additional applications or scenarios where machine learning may be useful to society.
3. Copy and complete the table below to show how machine learning has affected the scenarios you examined in task 2.

Industry	Task	How the task was completed previously	How the task is completed now	Benefits of computerising	Cons of computerising
Car manufacturing	Assembling parts to make car bodies	Previously carried out using robots designed for only one task	Robots now use sensors to ensure that movements are precise Robots are also linked to computer-aided design software	Design software can easily be altered to create custom cars Cars produced are high quality	Fewer staff are needed so some jobs are lost The software and technology needed is expensive

153

Improving technology

Learn

The way you do tasks on a day-to-day basis and the way in which tasks are completed in industry continually change as new devices and programs are developed and improvements are made to the technologies we use. Consider how mobile phone technology has changed over time.

As users' needs change, designers must consider how their digital devices operate, what they look like and how user friendly they are. When a new technology is being developed, it is common for the designers to build a **prototype** of the new product. Prototypes can be created in a variety of formats: for example, they can be a paper-based design, a computer-aided design representation, a physical model or a 3D model of the product.

Product designers and even software developers often use the prototype to help them test the product, and also use it to help make decisions about how they can improve the product before finalising the design. Sometimes, the developer may allow potential customers to use the prototype so they can get some **feedback** on possible improvements that may be needed.

As designs are reviewed, here are some of the areas that designers might consider.

- **User experience**: This refers to whether a user is able to use the product easily and confidently, no matter how familiar they are with technology. For example, if the product is for young children it should be intuitive.
- **Accessibility**: This refers to how successfully a new product or piece of software can be used by anyone. Things to consider include any physical limitations the expected user might have.
- **Ergonomics**: This is how a product or piece of software is designed or arranged so the user can use it efficiently. Examples include computer screens with swivel bases so that users can adjust the viewing angle, and computer-control devices such as mice and joysticks that are designed to fit into a user's hand so that they are comfortable to use.
- **Emerging technologies**: New technologies can be incorporated into a design to improve how the product operates.

Unit 9.4 Drilling down: How the processor handles instructions

> **KEYWORDS**
>
> **prototype:** initial product created for testing and reviewing, before a final product is released
>
> **feedback:** comments made to help improve a product
>
> **user experience:** how intuitive the product is based on the user's previous experience with digital products or applications
>
> **accessibility:** how successfully a new product or piece of software can be used by anyone
>
> **ergonomics:** how a product or piece of software is designed or arranged so that it can be used efficiently
>
> **emerging technologies:** new technologies that can be incorporated into a design to improve how the product operates

Practise

1 With your partner, identify an item of technology that you have access to at home or in school.
  a Discuss the device as though it were a prototype design. Identify what you could do to improve the 'prototype' to make the technology easier for another person to use.
  b Make a list describing how you can make the device more:
    – user friendly
    – accessible
    – ergonomic.
  c Are there any emerging technologies that you would like to include in your design?
2 Present your prototype to a small group of four. In your presentation:
  – identify improvements you made to the design based on increasing the product's user-friendliness, accessibility and ergonomic appeal to other users
  – explain why factors such as user experience, accessibility, ergonomics and emerging technologies are important.

Go further

Converting between storage units is an important part of managing memory in digital devices.

Use what you learned in the 'Data storage' section to work out the minimum amount of storage needed to store each of the files below.

> Remember: use multiply and divide by 1000 to convert between data-storage units.

	• A black and white image • The image is made up of 2000 pixels × 2000 pixels • Each pixel is represented by 1 bit
	• A black, white and grey image • The image is 20,000 pixels × 2000 pixels • Each pixel is represented by 3 bits

155

[MP3 icon]	• An MP3 sound file • The sound file contains a song that is 3 minutes long • 1 megabyte is needed to store 1 minute
[document icon]	• A word-processed document • The text in the file is represented using 8-bit ASCII • The text file contains 2500 characters
[email icon]	• An email containing a short message • The email needs 1 kilobyte of memory • The user adds the black and white image from the top of this table • The user then adds the text file from this table

Challenge yourself

Some complex logic circuits are created when processors carry out complex tasks. Creating Boolean expressions from logic circuits is an important part of understanding processing in the CPU.

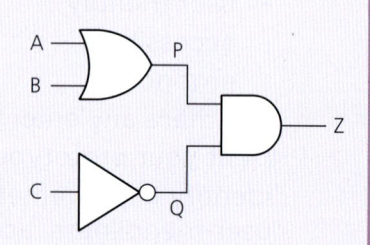

1 Copy and complete the Boolean expression below to explain how the logic circuit shown on the right operates.

   Z = (_____) AND _____

2 **Truth tables** are used to describe the operation of logic gates.
   a Do some research about truth tables using the internet.
   b Copy the truth table below. Complete it to describe the operation of the complex logic circuit shown in question **1**.

A	B	C	P = A OR B	Q = NOT C	Z = P AND Q
0	0	0			
0	0	1			
0	1	0			
0	1	1			
1	0	0			
1	0	1			
1	1	0			
1	1	1			

KEYWORD

truth table: breakdown of a logic circuit, listing all possible operations the logic circuit can carry out

Unit 9.4 Drilling down: How the processor handles instructions

Final project

Look back at the start of this unit to remind yourself of the Scenario. You now have all the skills and knowledge you need to create the resources that the computing technology company needs to deliver the workshops.

Compete the tasks below.

Part 1: Presentation

Create a presentation that explains the following.

- Slides 1–2:

  Different types of systems software, including the role played by the operating system and utility programs such as device drivers, security software and disc defragmentation.

- Slides 3–4:

  The difference between high-level languages and low-level languages and the need for language translation.
  - Include a description of why different types of translators are needed.
  - Describe the key features of a compiler and an interpreter; provide examples of when each might be used.

- Slides 5–6:

  What is meant by the fetch–decode–execute cycle and how it carries out instructions stored in memory one after another.
  - Include the registers used in the fetch–decode–execute cycle and the role they play.

- Slides 7–8:

  What is meant by *machine learning.*
  - Research and include examples of applications that use machine learning.
  - Include a short description of how at least three manufacturing or industrial practices use machine learning today.

- Slides 9–10:

  The advantages and disadvantages of computerisation.
  - Include examples of traditional manufacturing and industry areas that computerisation has affected.

Part 2: Poster

Create a poster that helps other students understand units of storage, from a single bit up to and including a petabyte. Include examples of files or applications where each unit can describe a file or a data item: for example, a bit is used to store a single binary digit (0 or 1).

Part 3: Worksheets

1. a Create a worksheet containing five questions that another student can complete to practise converting data between units of storage.
   b Create an answer sheet that allows a class teacher to mark the other student's work.
2. Create an information worksheet that includes a diagram explaining to another student how analogue sound is converted to binary format.
   - Include in your worksheet the terms *ADC*, *sampling*, *sample rate* and *bit depth*.
   - Include advice on how to increase the quality of a sound sample.

3 a Create a worksheet that asks students to convert the following Boolean expressions into logic circuits, with an explanation about how to do this.
- X = NOT A AND (B OR C)
- X = (A OR B) AND NOT C
- X = NOT A OR NOT B
- X = NOT A AND NOT B

b Create an answer sheet for the logic-circuit questions in part **a**.

Part 4: Prototype design

Produce a prototype design for a new piece of technology that allows you to complete a daily task more easily.
- Your design can be a diagram or a written description, but it should make use of a new or developing technology.
- Include ideas about how you could make your new design user friendly and accessible. Also include how you could make it more ergonomic and use emerging technologies.

Evaluation

1 Swap presentations with your partner and comment on the following:
- Is your partner's definition of *systems software* accurate? Does it include the role played by the operating system and utility programs such as device drivers, security software and disc defragmentation?
- Is it clear from your partner's presentation why language translation is needed? Have they clearly described the key features of a compiler and an interpreter?
- Has your partner clearly explained the fetch–decode–execute cycle and how it is used to carry out instructions stored in memory one after another?
- Has your partner clearly explained what is meant by *machine learning*? Have they included appropriate examples of how machine learning is used in manufacturing or industrial practices today?
- Has your partner identified the advantages and disadvantages of computerisation and included examples of traditional manufacturing and industry areas that computerisation has affected?

2 Swap posters and discuss the following:
- How clearly does your partner's poster describe the units of storage from bit to petabyte?
- How appropriate are your partner's examples of files or applications for each unit?

3 Ask your partner to complete your worksheets. Use your answer sheet to mark their work. Comment on any answers you disagreed with and discuss the differences. Make corrections as necessary.

4 Swap prototype designs. Comment on the following in your partner's design:
- How user friendly it is
- How accessible it is
- How ergonomic it is.

Suggest how your partner could improve their design.

Improve your design based on your partner's comments.

Unit 9.4 Drilling down: How the processor handles instructions

What can you do?

Read and review what you can do.
- ✔ I can identify improvements to the design of digital devices based on prototypes.
- ✔ I can explain why factors such as user experience, accessibility, ergonomics and emerging technologies are important to the design of digital devices.
- ✔ I can explain which tasks an operating system carries out.
- ✔ I can describe examples of utility programs, including drivers, security software and defragmentation.
- ✔ I can explain the different types of translator.
- ✔ I can describe the main characteristics of compilers and interpreters.
- ✔ I can explain how analogue sound is digitised.
- ✔ I can explain how to convert between storage units.
- ✔ I can draw logic circuits for Boolean expressions.
- ✔ I can explain how computers store lists of instructions to be run one at a time.
- ✔ I can explain the fetch-decode-execute cycle.
- ✔ I can describe what is meant by machine learning and identify a range of applications and scenarios that use machine learning.
- ✔ I can explain the benefits and risks of computerising tasks in industry and manufacturing.

Unit 9.5 Big Data modelling and analysis: Databases and spreadsheets

Get started!

Many organisations need huge amounts of data to operate successfully. For example, shops that sell clothing or music online store details about their customers, such as usernames and passwords, delivery addresses and payment details. They collect the data they use from many different sources, and it can be in many different formats.

Social-media applications provide users with data in the form of video, animated graphics, text and images. They also collect data about users, and this can be in many different formats. Like other organisations, social-media companies analyse the data they collect to learn more about their users. Many social-media applications collect, for example, data about users' physical location, other social-media pages they have visited or even other internet pages they have visited. Doing this allows the social-media platform to display advertisements or suggest other pages and content that might be of interest to the user.

Discuss with your partner:
- What type of data do you think organisations such as social-media providers collect when they are trying to learn more about their users?
- What do you think they use this data for?
- How do you think the organisation is able to analyse this data?

In this unit, you will learn more about the concept of 'Big Data'. You will examine the key features of Big Data and how Big Data is valuable to organisations in a range of application areas. You will also explore a range of scenarios and examples to help you to learn more about a variety of the functions in applications such as MS Access and MS Excel for modelling real-life scenarios. By exploring how a school managing a new online learning application can use both applications, you will learn how to use the MIN, MAX, IF and COUNT functions in MS Excel, in addition to learning new skills to develop and use a complex MS Access database containing more than one table of data.

KEYWORD

social-media application: web-based software that allows users to share ideas, information and thoughts in an online community

Unit 9.5 Big Data modelling and analysis: Databases and spreadsheets

Learning outcomes

In this unit, you will learn to:
- evaluate the use of models that represent real-life systems
- use functions in spreadsheets to analyse data, such as IF, MIN, MAX, COUNT
- create spreadsheets that model real-life systems
- evaluate the suitability of a spreadsheet for given purposes
- create relational databases with two or more linked tables
- create complex searches for data in databases using two or more criteria
- create complex searches in relational databases
- explain the term *Big Data* and describe its applications.

Warm up

In the last week, it is highly likely that you, or family members, have provided an organisation with some **data**. It is also highly likely that an organisation you interact with has accessed and used data it has recorded about you.

With your partner, think about organisations that hold data about you or your family members.

1. Make a list of the **data items** you think each organisation stores about you.
2. What do you think they will use that data for?
3. What software do you think they might use to help them to analyse that data?

SCENARIO

You school is introducing a new online learning tool, a **virtual learning environment (VLE)**, which teachers will use to make learning resources available to students. Teachers will post handouts, homework and assessments on the VLE, sorted by subject page. Students will use an app to access the subject pages on the VLE.

The school has collected a lot of data about the potential users of the VLE, the pages each subject department is creating on the VLE, the times and who is accessing each VLE page, and why the pages are being accessed: for example, is a teacher accessing the page to update content, or is a student viewing a page to read content?

The school have heard of the term *Big Data* and wonder whether the amount of data they need to enable them to model student and teacher use of their new VLE can be categorised as Big Data. They have asked you to help them to understand what this term means.

KEYWORDS

data: raw facts and figures

data item: piece of information that represents part of the data that makes up a person, place or thing, e.g. some of the data items that represent a person are their first name and second name

virtual learning environment (VLE): online classroom where teachers and students can share learning materials

The school has asked you to create a **relational-database** application that they could use to model student and teacher VLE access.

They've also asked you to create a **spreadsheet model** that they can use to analyse student and teacher use of the VLE pages using various **platforms**, such as a PC, mobile phone or tablet device.

> The things that the school would like to use these applications to keep track of include:
> - user login details that show how often students access pages on the VLE
> - the time of day users access the VLE
> - on average how long students or teachers view pages on the VLE
> - how many users access the VLE using platforms such as PCs, laptops, tablets or mobile phones
> - the total number of times teachers or students access specific VLE pages
> - how many times certain VLE pages are accessed
> - how often different types of users access various types of resource pages: for example, how often teachers access a **markbook** page or how often students access a multimedia tutorial page
> - time spent on specific VLE pages by all users.

Do you remember?

Before starting this unit, you should be able to:
- ✓ amend the design of a database table using MS Access
- ✓ decide on an appropriate primary key field and other field headings for a table in an MS Access database
- ✓ select data types for fields in a database model
- ✓ identify the data needed to model a real-life situation
- ✓ search a database using a single search criterion
- ✓ evaluate the suitability of a database or a spreadsheet model for a given scenario
- ✓ create spreadsheet models that use predefined functions such as SUM and AVERAGE.

Before starting this unit, you will need to install the following software on your own personal device (or use a similar database and spreadsheet software application):
- MS Access
- MS Excel

KEYWORDS

relational database: database that stores data using two or more linked tables

spreadsheet model: spreadsheet containing data that represents a real-life scenario

platform: hardware and operating system that runs an application

DID YOU KNOW?

VLEs can be used to support distance learning and also provide students with an opportunity to review content delivered in the classroom at a pace that suits their own learning.

Unit 9.5 Big Data modelling and analysis: Databases and spreadsheets

Introducing 'Big Data'

Learn

In 'Get started!' at the start of this unit, you considered the many different **types of data** made available to organisations today. Data used by organisations can be in the form of images, video, audio, animation, text or even **Global Positioning System (GPS)** data. The data can be presented in the form of 'like' or 'dislike' icons on a social-media website, live video streams or location data. Large organisations are able to use all of this data to learn more about their users and potential customers, and help them to promote their goods and services. However, for the data to be useful to the organisations, they must be able to access and analyse the data at an extremely high speed.

In the past, organisations used applications such as **databases** and **spreadsheets** to help them to make sense of data they had collected. With data now being generated in so many different formats and at such high speeds, traditional applications such as databases and spreadsheets are not always able to **process** and at such high speeds the data.

Data that cannot easily be processed using traditional applications is known as **Big Data**. Big Data can be described using **5Vs**.

Big Data

Volume — Value — Veracity — Variety — Velocity

- **Volume**: Companies collect and analyse massive amounts of data on an ongoing basis. If the volume of data is large enough, it can be considered to be Big Data.
- **Value**: This refers to how useful the data is. What can the organisation do with the data they have collected? Are they able to get useful information from the data quickly?
- **Veracity**: This refers to accuracy and quality of the data. In Big Data analysis, the applications analysing the data determine how reliable or accurate the data is. The data-analysis software tries to determine whether the data is from a reliable source or whether the data is the most up-to-date version.
- **Variety**: Data can be presented in a range of data formats and data types. Data collected and stored in databases or spreadsheets tends to be structured: for example, it may be organised under field headings. The data collected and used in Big Data applications is not easily organised in this way.
- **Velocity**: Data being collected may come from many different sources, such as other computers, smart devices or even social media. *Velocity* refers to how quickly the data is generated, processed and turned into useful information.

The analysis of Big Data sets is known as **Big Data analytics**. The analysis of Big Data sets can help organisations to use the data they have collected more efficiently and to identify new opportunities.

The following table gives some of the applications of Big Data.

Application	Example of Big Data use
Transportation	Google Maps uses Big Data analytics to plan routes that are efficient, helping drivers avoid routes affected by traffic and improving fuel consumption.
Delivery companies	UPS analyses **vehicle telematics** from cars and trucks along with advanced **algorithms** to calculate the best routes, automatically control engine idle time and predict when maintenance is needed.
Mobile-phone companies	Some mobile-phone companies combine data from a number of their customer-management, billing and social-media applications to predict when a customer might want to leave the organisation and go to another mobile-phone company.
Medicine/healthcare	Search engines such as Google work closely with health providers to track when users are inputting search terms related to, for example, flu topics. Working together, the organisations can predict which regions may experience outbreaks. Big Data analysis can also help medical professionals to predict and prevent some diseases.
Media streaming services	Media streaming services such as Netflix analyse international viewing habits before they create or buy programmes that will appeal to their audience.
Advertising and marketing	Advertising companies often buy or gather huge quantities of data to identify what consumers actually click on, search for and 'like' when they are online. This data is used to tailor advertising campaigns more effectively.
Banking	Banks make use of Big Data analytics in the speedy identification of unusual account activity. This allows them quickly to flag potential illegal use of their customers' bank details.
Meteorology	Using data collected worldwide by satellites and other sensors, Big Data analysis allows meteorologists to produce accurate weather forecasts, predict natural weather-related disasters and make predictions about the impact of issues such as global warming.

> **KEYWORDS**
>
> **data type:** classification applied to a data item specifying which type of data that item represents, e.g. in a spreadsheet some of the data types available include currency, text and number
>
> **Global Positioning System (GPS):** satellite-based system that keeps track of users' physical locations and helps with navigation
>
> **database:** application that organises data for storing, processing and accessing electronically
>
> **spreadsheet:** application that uses rows and columns to organise data and carry out calculations using that data
>
> **process:** carrying out an operation on data, e.g. querying a database or doing a calculation using data in a spreadsheet
>
> **Big Data:** datasets that are too large or complex for traditional data-processing applications, e.g. databases or spreadsheets, to process
>
> **5Vs:** the terms used to describe the concept of Big Data: volume, velocity, variety, value, veracity
>
> **volume:** the massive amounts of data collected and analysed on an ongoing basis
>
> **velocity:** how quickly data is generated, processed and turned into useful information

Unit 9.5 Big Data modelling and analysis: Databases and spreadsheets

> **KEYWORDS**
>
> **variety:** the range of data formats and data types collected
> **value:** how useful data is to an organisation
> **veracity:** accuracy and quality of data
> **Big Data analytics:** the analysis of sets of data known as *Big Data*
>
> **vehicle telematics:** information monitored and transmitted from vehicles, e.g. their location and speed, using GPS, engine diagnostics and driving style
> **algorithm:** step-by-step instructions to solve a particular problem
> **meteorology:** study of climate and the weather

Practise

1. Search the internet for more information on how Big Data is used. Write a paragraph to explain the term Big Data and describe its applications.

2. Select one of the applications of Big Data in the table in the 'Learn' box. Copy and complete the table below to include a list of pros and cons of using Big Data analytics in the application area you have selected.

Pros of Big Data in [add your application here]	Cons of Big Data in [add your application here]

3. With your partner, describe an example of an organisation you are familiar with that uses Big Data. Tell your partner how the organisation uses Big Data and the advantages to that organisation of using Big Data.

Introducing relational databases

Learn

Organisations use databases to help them to manage large quantities of data. The simplest databases look more like large **tables** of information organised under a set of headings.

The data on the next page is taken from a database that has only one table of information; this is known as a **flat-file database**.

You can see in this database extract that the continent of Asia is referenced a number of times.

For example, the table, **country_continentTBL**, shows an extract from a database that records the details of some countries around the world. Some of the data in the table appears multiple times: for example, the data related to the continent of Asia. This data is repeated unnecessarily. Having data that is repeated unnecessarily can sometimes lead to the introduction of errors in the data.

country_continentTBL

Unnecessary repetition of data.

Country name	Capital city	Country population	Continent	Size of continent (square miles)	Continent population
India	New Delhi	1,420,062,022	Asia	17,139,445	4,436,224,000
Brazil	Brasilia	209,737,513	South America	6,880,706	442,535,000
Nigeria	Abuja	200,962,417	Africa	11,677,239	1,216,130,000
Philippines	Manila	108,106,310	Asia	17,139,445	4,436,224,000
Vietnam	Hanoi	97,429,061	Asia	17,139,445	4,436,224,000
Germany	Berlin	82,438,639	Europe	3,997,929	738,849,000
France	Paris	67,480,710	Europe	3,997,929	738,849,000
UK	London	66,959,016	Europe	3,997,929	738,849,000
Canada	Ottawa	37,279,636	North America	9,361,791	579,024,000
Saudi Arabia	Riyadh	34,140,662	Asia	17,139,445	4,436,224,000
Peru	Lima	32,933,835	South America	6,880,706	442,535,000
Australia	Canberra	25,088,636	Australasia	2,697,909	34,601,860
Taiwan	Taipei	23,758,247	Asia	17,139,445	4,436,224,0

Compare the population of Asia in the last row of this database with the other references to Asia. An error has been made when the value was entered for the final record in this database table.

When the same piece of data is held in two separate places in a database, it is known as **data redundancy**. Data redundancy can increase the chance of **data-entry errors** occurring when a new record is added.

Relational databases can help to prevent this type of error occurring by removing data redundancy. Relational databases use additional tables to store the data relating to each **entity** in the database. An entity is an individual person, place or object. In this example, there are two entities: country and continent. Therefore, you should create two tables, and use one of the tables to record the repeating data items. The headings used to organise data in a relational-database table are known as **attributes**: for example, **continentTBL** on the next page has three attributes.

A single entry is made in this table for each data item being recorded.

> Look carefully at the value for the Continent population of Asia in the last row of this flat-file database example. Can you detect an error in the data?

> Look carefully at the flat-file database example above. Can you identify other places where data is repeated unnecessarily?

> This means that the data relating to the fields 'Continent', 'Size of continent' and 'Continent population' need only be entered once into the database.

Unit 9.5 Big Data modelling and analysis: Databases and spreadsheets

continentTBL

Continent	Size of continent (square miles)	Continent population
Asia	17,139,445	4,436,224,000
Africa	11,677,239	1,216,130,000
Australasia	2,697,909	34,601,860
Europe	3,997,929	738,849,000
North America	9,361,791	579,024,000
South America	6,880,706	442,535,000

The database now consists of two tables, as shown below: **countryTBL** and **continentTBL**. **countryTBL** can use **continentTBL** to look up additional details for each country.

countryTBL

Country name	Capital city	Country population	Continent
India	New Delhi	1,420,062,022	Asia
Brazil	Brasilia	209,737,513	South America
Nigeria	Abuja	200,962,417	Africa
Philippines	Manila	108,106,310	Asia
Vietnam	Hanoi	97,429,061	Asia
Germany	Berlin	82,438,639	Europe
France	Paris	67,480,710	Europe
UK	London	66,959,016	Europe
Canada	Ottawa	37,279,636	North America
Saudi Arabia	Riyadh	34,140,662	Asia
Peru	Lima	32,933,835	South America
Australia	Canberra	25,088,636	Australasia
Taiwan	Taipei	23,758,247	Asia

continentTBL

Continent	Size of continent (square miles)	Continent population
Asia	17,139,445	4,436,224,000
Africa	11,677,239	1,216,130,000
Australasia	2,697,909	34,601,860
Europe	3,997,929	738,849,000
North America	9,361,791	579,024,000
South America	6,880,706	442,535,000

In this example, 'Continent' is the **primary key** for **continentTBL** but it also appears in **countryTBL** to create a link between the two tables. When the primary key from one table appears in another table to create a link, it is known as a **foreign key**. 'Continent' is a foreign key in **countryTBL**.

Notice that the attribute 'Continent' appears in both tables. The 'Continent' field provides a link between **countryTBL** and **continentTBL**.

When a continent name appears in **countryTBL**, the database will access **continentTBL** to look up the remaining information.

'Country name' is unique for each record in countryTBL so it can be used as the **primary key** in countryTBL. 'Continent' can be used as the primary key in continentTBL.

CAMBRIDGE LOWER SECONDARY COMPUTING 9

> **KEYWORDS**
> **table:** set of facts or figures that are set out in a column and row structure
> **flat-file database:** database that stores all data items using one table
> **data redundancy:** when data is unnecessarily repeated in a database
> **data-entry error:** error that occurs when data is being entered into a database
> **relational database:** database that stores data using two or more linked tables
> **entity:** person, place or object represented in a table in a relational database
> **attribute:** heading for organising data in a relational database
> **primary key:** field in a database table that provides a unique identifier for a record/entity
> **foreign key:** when the primary key from one table appears in another table to establish a link between two entities

Practise

1 The flat-file database below stores data about students' scores in examinations they have taken at school this year.

StudentID	Name	Class	Exam	ExamScore	ExamGrade
1001	A Student	9X2	Mathematics	89	B
1002	M Student	9X3	Mathematics	92	A
1003	P Student	9Y7	Mathematics	77	C
1001	A Student	9X4	Art	90	A
1002	M Student	9X3	Art	84	B
1003	P Student	9Y10	Art	87	B
1001	A Student	9X2	Science	71	C
1002	N Student	9X3	Science	75	C
1003	P Student	9Y7	Science	88	B

  a Identify the data items that have been unnecessarily repeated in this flat-file database.
  b Identify two examples where unnecessary repetition of data has led to data-entry errors in this table.

  The fields that are unnecessarily repeated may not always be the last fields in the table.

  c List two attributes that appear in this flat-file database table.
  d Name two entities represented in this flat-file database table.
2 a Copy and complete the following to show how you could split this flat-file database into two tables to create a relational database and remove data redundancy.

Add your table name here
List the table attributes here

Add your table name here
List the table attributes here

168

Unit 9.5 Big Data modelling and analysis: Databases and spreadsheets

b Place an * beside the primary key field in each of your tables.
c Circle the field that will be used to link the two tables together.
3 Relational databases can sometimes contain more than two entities. This means that the database needs more than two data tables. The flat-file table below keeps track of students' book loans from the school library. Identify the three entities represented in this table.

Student ID	Student Name	Class	LoanID	DateOut	DateBack	BookID	BookTitle	BookAuthor
1001	A Student	9X2	L1	21 Jan	30 Jan	B9865	Learn Programming	P Author
1002	M Student	9X3	L2	22 Jan	31 Jan	B8856	AI Today	Q Writer
1003	P Student	9Y7	L3	22 Jan	31 Jan	B7787	Python Programs	L Expert
1001	A Student	9X2	L4	1 Feb	10 Feb	B5654	Relational Databases	P Creator
1002	M Student	9X3	L5	3 Feb	13 Feb	B7231	Spreadsheet Modelling	J Modeller
1001	A Student	9X2	L6	12 Feb	22 Feb	B5541	Database Queries	S Story
1001	A Student	9X2	L7	12 Feb	22 Feb	B6632	Big Data	B Article

4 Copy and complete the following to show the attributes needed for each table to convert this flat-file database into a relational-database model.
Remember to * the primary keys in each table.

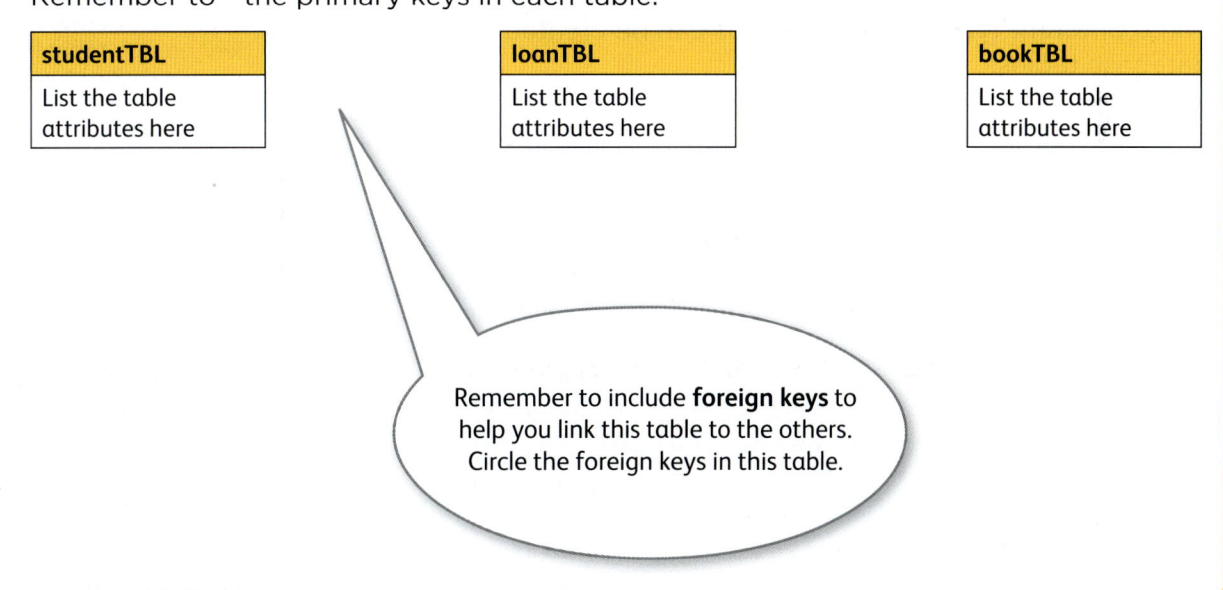

studentTBL
List the table attributes here

loanTBL
List the table attributes here

bookTBL
List the table attributes here

Remember to include **foreign keys** to help you link this table to the others. Circle the foreign keys in this table.

169

Creating relational databases

Learn

In the previous section, you learned that a common field is needed to link together tables in a relational database. Remember how the 'Continent' field was used to link **continentTBL** and **countryTBL**. Remember: this common field will be a *primary key* in one table, which is added to another table as a foreign key.

However, just adding the fields to the tables is not enough. The tables in a relational database must also be linked using a special feature known as a *relationship*.

Each table in a relational-database model represents different *entities* that exist in the database model, for example in the school-library example from the last 'Practise' box, the data model you developed on paper had three entities: students, loans and books.

The entities in a relational database can be linked in a number of different ways. In the library database example, each student was represented only once in **studentTBL**, so their **StudentID** appeared only one time in **studentTBL**. A student's **studentID** could then appear in the **loanTBL** as a foreign key as it links the two tables together. It would be reasonable to assume that a student could borrow more than one book, so their **studentID** would appear in **loanTBL** many times. This creates what database developers call a *one-to-many relationship*.

Three different types of relationships can be created between database tables:

- **one-to-one**
- **one-to-many**
- **many-to-many**.

Database designers use a special diagram called an *entity relationship diagram (ERD)* to show how the entities in the relational database are linked.

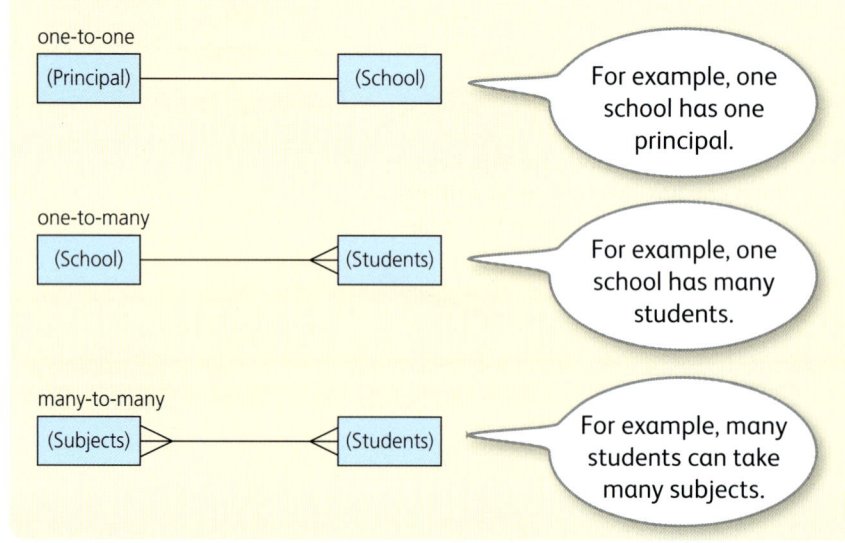

one-to-one
(Principal) ——— (School)

For example, one school has one principal.

one-to-many
(School) ——<(Students)

For example, one school has many students.

many-to-many
(Subjects) >——<(Students)

For example, many students can take many subjects.

KEYWORDS

primary key: field in a database table that provides a unique identifier for a record/entity

relationship: feature in database applications for linking tables together

entity: person, place or object represented in a table in a relational database

one-to-one relationship: a primary key can exist once as a primary key on one table in a relational database and once as a foreign key to link a second table in the relational database

one-to-many relationship: a primary key can exist once as a primary key on one table in a relational database and many times as a foreign key to link a second table in the relational database

many-to-many relationship: a primary key can exist many times as a primary key on one table in a relational database and many times as a foreign key to link a second table in the relational database

entity relationship diagram (ERD): diagram that illustrates the relationships between two entities in a relational database

Unit 9.5 Big Data modelling and analysis: Databases and spreadsheets

Practise

Part 1

1 In Stage 8, you used data dictionaries to design suitable data tables for database models. The following **data dictionary** describes the tables used to create the library-book loan database in the 'Learn' box. Remember how the data dictionary includes details about **validation** methods, and how **input masks** help to reduce the chance of a user making an error when adding data to the database table. In the example below, you do not need to consider validation or input masks as they are not included in the data dictionary.

studentTBL

Field name	Data type	Field length
*studentID	Number	–
studentName	Short text	20
Class	Short text	3

loanTBL

Field name	Data type	Field length
*loanID	Short text	2
dateOut	Date/Time	–
dateBack	Date/Time	–
studentID	Number	–
bookID	Short text	6
overdue?	Yes/No	

bookTBL

Field name	Data type	Field length
*bookID	Short text	6
bookTitle	Short text	30
bookAuthor	Short text	25

> The * shows the primary keys in each of the three tables.

a Open MS Access.

b Create a database by clicking once on `Blank database`, giving the database the name **libraryDB** and clicking `Create`. A blank table will appear on screen as shown below. View the table in `Design View`.

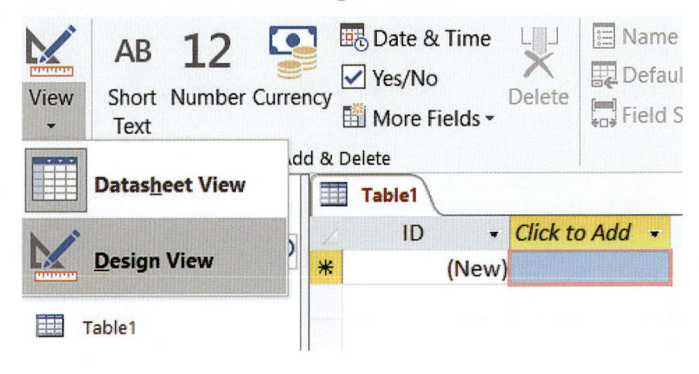

171

CAMBRIDGE LOWER SECONDARY COMPUTING 9

    c Name the table **studentTBL** and use the data dictionary on the previous page to add the appropriate fields and data types to the table design.

    d Close the table and save your changes.

2 a Click on the `Create` tab and select `Table`.

    b View the table in `Design View`. You will be asked to give the table a name. Call the table **loanTBL**.

    c Add the fields and data types shown in the data dictionary for **loanTBL**.

    d Close the table and save your changes.

3 Use the data dictionary and repeat the steps in task 2 to create the final table, called **bookTBL**.

Part 2

1 Now that there are three tables for the **loanDB** database, you can create the relationships between the tables. The following entity relationship diagram will help you with this task as it shows you the types of relationships needed between the student and loan table (one-to-many) and the book and loan table (one-to-many).

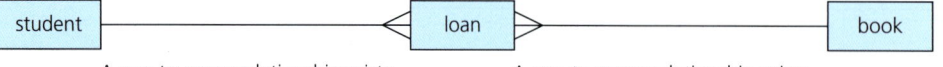

student —————⊲ loan ⊳————— book

A one-to-many relationship exists between the student and the loan tables. This tells you that each student should appear only once in **studentTBL** but they can appear many times in **loanTBL**: for example, while the student is at the school, they can have many book loans.

A one-to-many relationship exists between the book and the loan tables. This tells you that each book should appear only once in **bookTBL** but it can appear many times in **loanTBL**: for example, a book can be loaned out many different times.

KEYWORDS

data dictionary: table that represents the structure of a database table at the design stage of developing a database; often contains details, e.g. data type, field length and details about validation checks applied to data items

validation: automatic checks applied to individual fields in a database table to help reduce the chance of error when adding data to the table

input mask: control added to a field in a database table to control the format of data being added

Unit 9.5 Big Data modelling and analysis: Databases and spreadsheets

a   Click on the `Database Tools` tab and select `Relationships`.

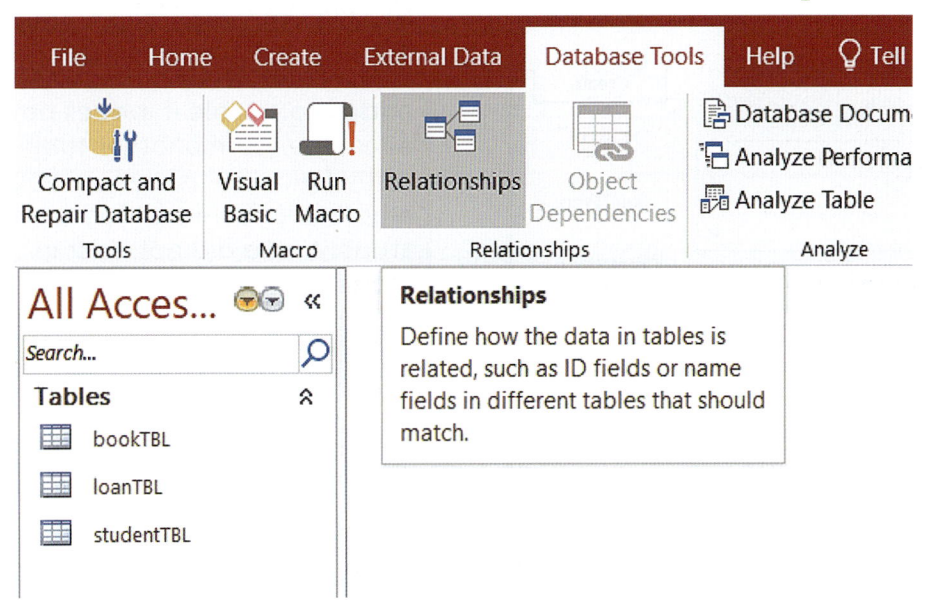

b   Add all three tables to the `Relationships` window and arrange them as shown.

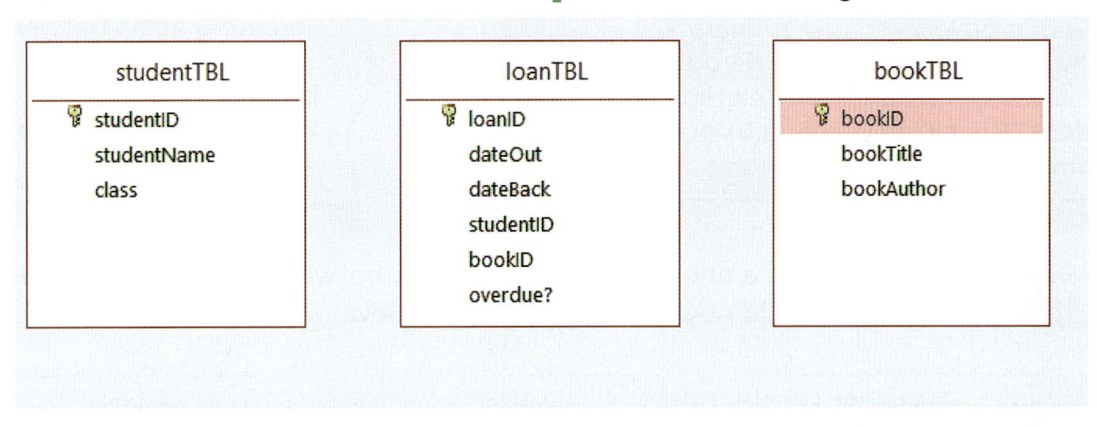

c   Click and drag from **studentID** on the **studentTBL** to **studentID** on the **loanTBL** to let MS Access know that you would like to create a link between the two fields. You will be asked to edit the relationship between the two tables. Select the following options.

CAMBRIDGE LOWER SECONDARY COMPUTING 9

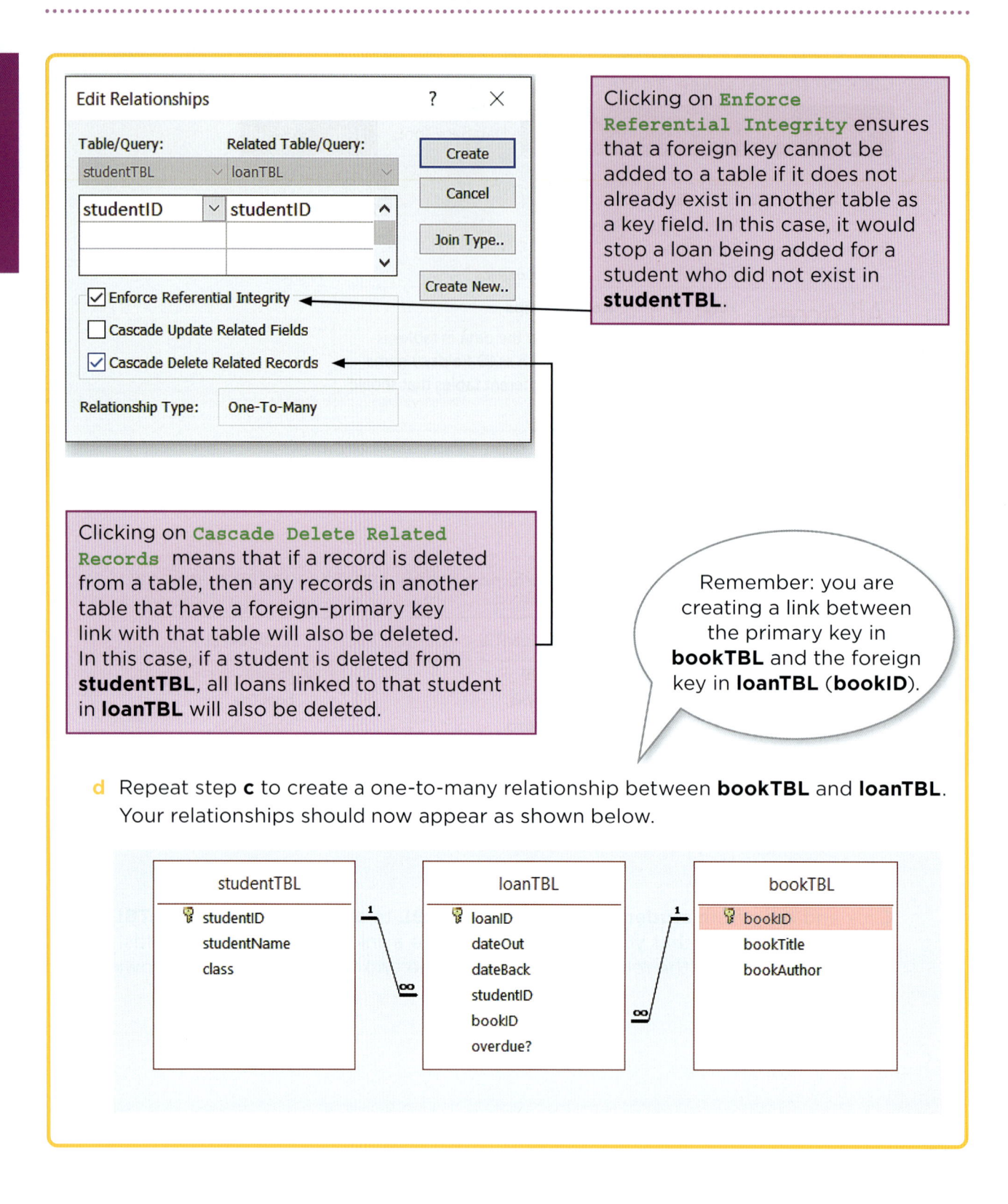

Clicking on `Enforce Referential Integrity` ensures that a foreign key cannot be added to a table if it does not already exist in another table as a key field. In this case, it would stop a loan being added for a student who did not exist in **studentTBL**.

Clicking on `Cascade Delete Related Records` means that if a record is deleted from a table, then any records in another table that have a foreign–primary key link with that table will also be deleted. In this case, if a student is deleted from **studentTBL**, all loans linked to that student in **loanTBL** will also be deleted.

Remember: you are creating a link between the primary key in **bookTBL** and the foreign key in **loanTBL** (**bookID**).

d Repeat step **c** to create a one-to-many relationship between **bookTBL** and **loanTBL**. Your relationships should now appear as shown below.

Unit 9.5 Big Data modelling and analysis: Databases and spreadsheets

2 Open each table in turn and add the appropriate data, shown below, to each table in the database.

studentTBL

studentID	studentName	class
1001	A Student	9X2
1002	M Student	9X3
1003	P Student	9Y7

bookTBL

BookID	BookTitle	BookAuthor
B9865	Learn Programming	P Author
B8856	AI Today	Q Writer
B7787	Python Programs	L Expert
B5654	Relational Databases	P Creator
B7231	Spreadsheet Modelling	J Modeller
B5541	Database Queries	S Story
B6632	Big Data	B Article

Be sure to add the student and the book data to the database before adding the loan data. loanTBL includes foreign key fields and, if they have not already been added to studentTBL and bookTBL, an error will occur when you try to include them in loanTBL.

loanTBL

loanID	dateOut	dateBack	studentID	bookID	overdue?
L1	21 Jan	30 Jan	1001	B9865	True
L2	22 Jan	31 Jan	1002	B8856	True
L3	22 Jan	31 Jan	1003	B7787	True
L4	1 Feb	10 Feb	1001	B5654	False
L5	3 Feb	13 Feb	1002	B7231	False
L6	12 Feb	22 Feb	1001	B5541	False
L7	12 Feb	22 Feb	1001	B6632	False

3 a Open **studentTBL** to check that your relationship has been created correctly. Notice the + sign to the left of each record in the table.

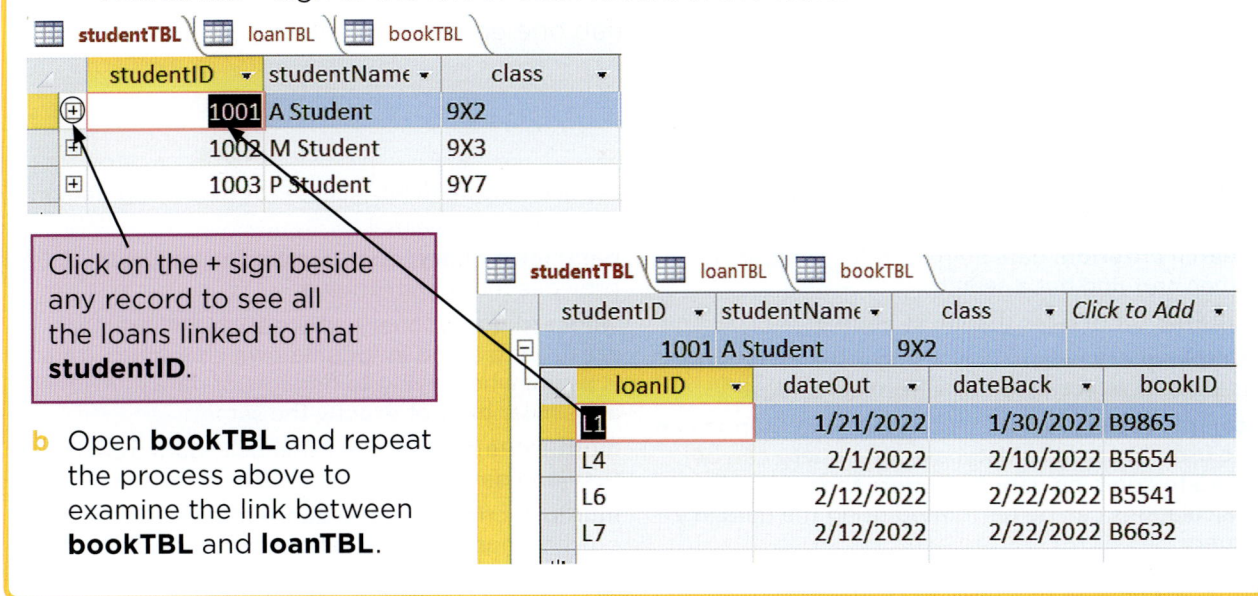

*Click on the + sign beside any record to see all the loans linked to that **studentID**.*

b Open **bookTBL** and repeat the process above to examine the link between **bookTBL** and **loanTBL**.

175

Processing data: Complex queries

Learn

Databases often contain large amounts of data. Data stored in a database can be processed and analysed much more quickly than it could be by a human processing the data by hand. One of the ways in which data in a database can be processed is using a tool called a **query**. Queries allow users to search a database for specific data based on **search criteria**.

Queries fall into two different categories:
- **Simple queries**, where only a single search criterion is used to select data items from a database: for example, searching a school database for all the students who are in Stage 9 or all the students whose age is >13.
- **Complex queries**, where more than one criterion is used to search a database, where a query is used to combine data from more than one table, or where calculations are performed using the data in a query or a **report**.

Examples of complex queries include:
- **parameter queries**: queries where the end user provides the search criteria
- **wildcard queries**: queries where special characters are used to stand in for unknown characters (this is useful when trying to find lots of data items that are similar but not exactly the same)
- **multi-table queries**, which use data from more than one data table
- **multiple-criteria queries**, which use more than one criterion to select data items from a database.

> **KEYWORDS**
>
> **query:** tool that allows users to search for data that meets specific rules or criteria
>
> **search criterion:** data item used for comparison when carrying out a search
>
> **criteria:** set of rules that must be met
>
> **simple query:** where only a single search criterion is used to select data items from a database
>
> **complex query:** where more than one criterion can be used to search a database, or a query can be used to combine data from more than one table, or calculations can be performed using the data in a query
>
> **report:** feature in MS Access for displaying data in a user-friendly format
>
> **parameter query:** query where the end user provides the search criteria
>
> **wildcard query:** query where special characters are used to stand in for unknown characters (this is useful when trying to find lots of data items that are similar but not exactly the same)
>
> **multi-table query:** query that uses data from more than one data table
>
> **multiple-criteria query:** query that uses more than one criterion to select data items from a database

Unit 9.5 Big Data modelling and analysis: Databases and spreadsheets

Practise

Parameter queries

1 Parameter queries allow the user to enter their own data items when searching for a data item: for example, a librarian may wish to search for a book with a specific title.

   a Open **LibraryDB2.accdb** provided by your teacher.

   b Click on the `Create` tab and click on `Query Design`.

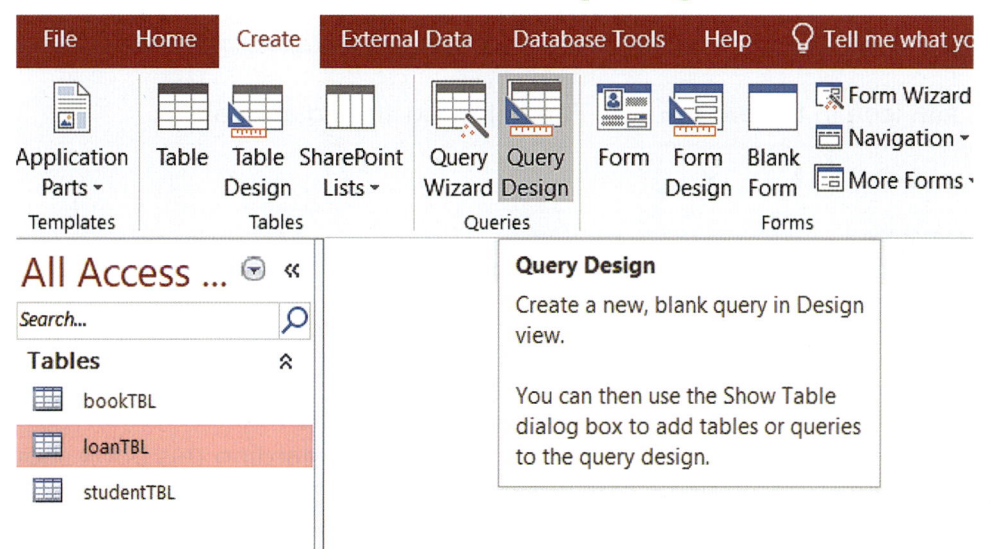

   c In the `Show Table` window that appears, double-click on **bookTBL** and then close the `Show Table` window.

   d Double-click on each field in **bookTBL** so that they appear in the query field list at the bottom of the window.

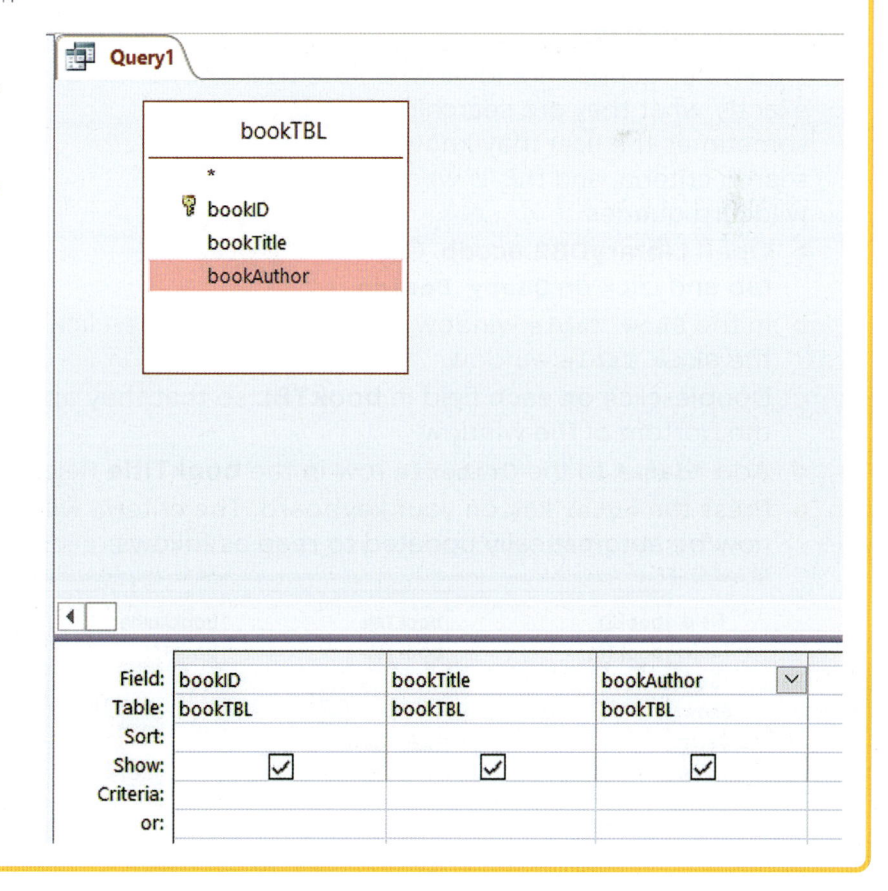

177

e Add `[Please enter book title]` to the `Criteria` row, underneath the **bookTitle** field.

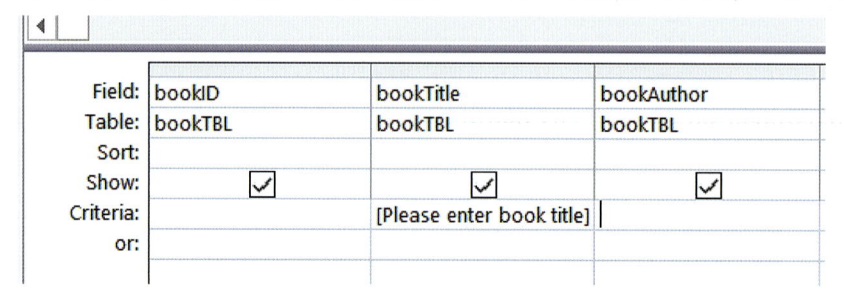

Field:	bookID	bookTitle	bookAuthor
Table:	bookTBL	bookTBL	bookTBL
Sort:			
Show:	✓	✓	✓
Criteria:		[Please enter book title]	
or:			

2 a Click the `Run` icon in the `Design` tab. The following should appear.

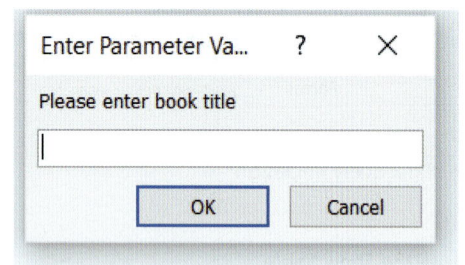

b Enter the book title `Big Data` and click `OK`. The details regarding this book should now be displayed.

c Close the query and save it as **bookTitleQRY**.

> It is good practice to include the letters QRY at the end of the name of a new query as it helps to distinguish it from other objects in the database.

Wildcard queries

1 Parameter queries are ideal when the user knows exactly what they are searching for. However, sometimes the user may know only part of the search criteria, and this is when you can use wildcard queries.

   a Open **LibraryDB2.accdb**. Click on the `Create` tab and click on `Query Design`.

   b In the `Show Table` window that appears, double-click on **bookTBL** and then close the `Show Table` window.

   c Double-click on each field in **bookTBL** so that they appear in the query field list at the bottom of the window.

   d Add `*data*` to the `Criteria` row in the **bookTitle** field.

   e Press the `enter` key on your keyboard. The criteria will now be automatically updated to read as follows:

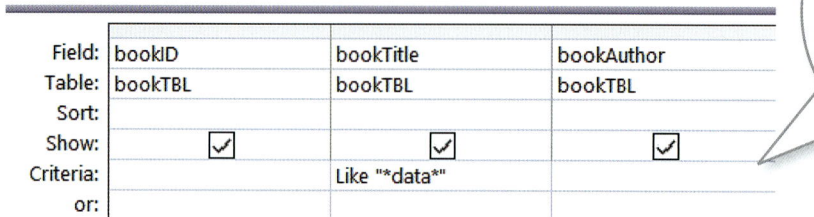

Field:	bookID	bookTitle	bookAuthor
Table:	bookTBL	bookTBL	bookTBL
Sort:			
Show:	✓	✓	✓
Criteria:		Like "*data*"	
or:			

> Using * before and after the word 'data' means that the query will return any record that has the combination of letters 'data' somewhere in the data stored in the **bookTitle** field.

Unit 9.5 Big Data modelling and analysis: Databases and spreadsheets

2 a Click the **Run** icon to test the query. The following data items should be displayed.

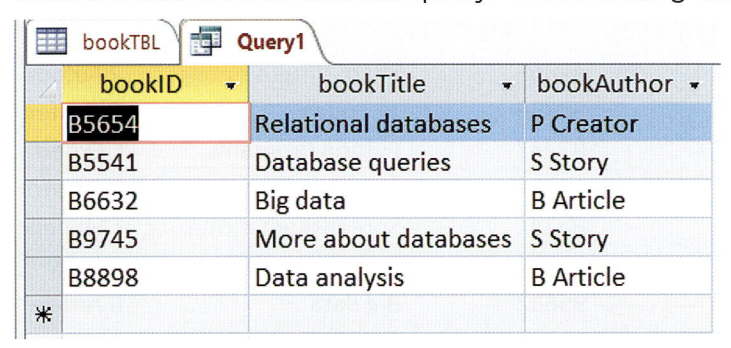

bookID	bookTitle	bookAuthor
B5654	Relational databases	P Creator
B5541	Database queries	S Story
B6632	Big data	B Article
B9745	More about databases	S Story
B8898	Data analysis	B Article

   b Close the query and save it with the name **dataTitleQRY**.

Multi-table queries

1 Sometimes it can be useful to display data from more than one table when searching a database: for example, if a librarian needs to see which books are on loan to which students at a given time.

   a Open **LibraryDB2.accdb**. Click on the `Create` tab and click on `Query Design`.

   b In the `Show Table` window that appears, double-click on **studentTBL**, **loanTBL** and **bookTBL** and then close the `Show Table` window.

   c Double-click on each field in the **studentTBL** and **bookTBL** tables so that they appear in the query field list at the bottom of the window, as shown below.

> You must include all tables in the query design in this way to ensure the foreign keys will link the data in **StudentTBL** and **bookTBL** to **loanTBL**.

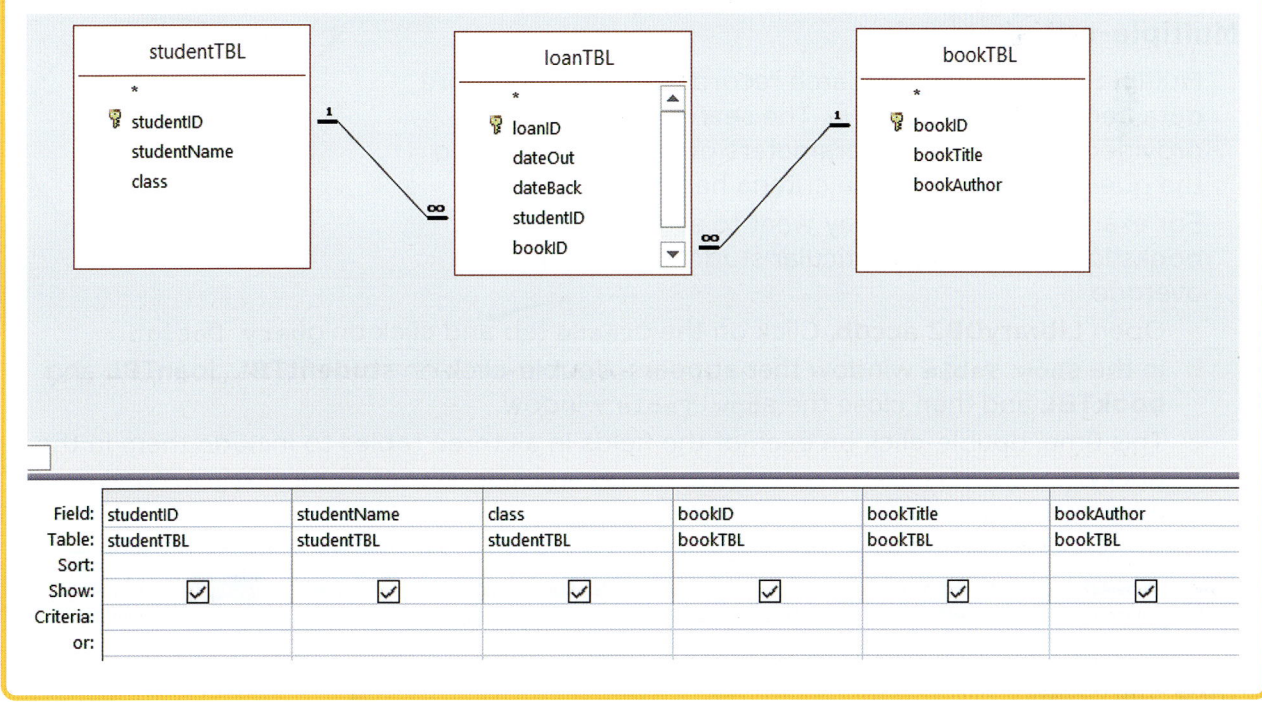

studentTBL
- studentID
- studentName
- class

loanTBL
- loanID
- dateOut
- dateBack
- studentID
- bookID

bookTBL
- bookID
- bookTitle
- bookAuthor

Field:	studentID	studentName	class	bookID	bookTitle	bookAuthor
Table:	studentTBL	studentTBL	studentTBL	bookTBL	bookTBL	bookTBL
Sort:						
Show:	✓	✓	✓	✓	✓	✓
Criteria:						
or:						

179

CAMBRIDGE LOWER SECONDARY COMPUTING 9

d Click the `Run` icon to test the query. The following data items should be displayed.

studentID	studentName	class	bookID	bookTitle	bookAuthor
1001	A Student	9X2	B9865	Learn Programming	P Author
1002	M Student	9X3	B8856	AI Today	Q Writer
1003	P Student	9Y7	B7787	Python Programs	L Expert
1001	A Student	9X2	B5654	Relational databases	P Creator
1002	M Student	9X3	B7231	Spreadsheet modelling	J Modeller
1001	A Student	9X2	B5541	Database queries	S Story
1001	A Student	9X2	B6632	Big data	B Article
1003	P Student	9Y7	B5541	Database queries	S Story
1003	P Student	9Y7	B7787	Python Programs	L Expert

2 a You can narrow down this search further by adding `[Enter StudentID]` to the criteria for **StudentID**.

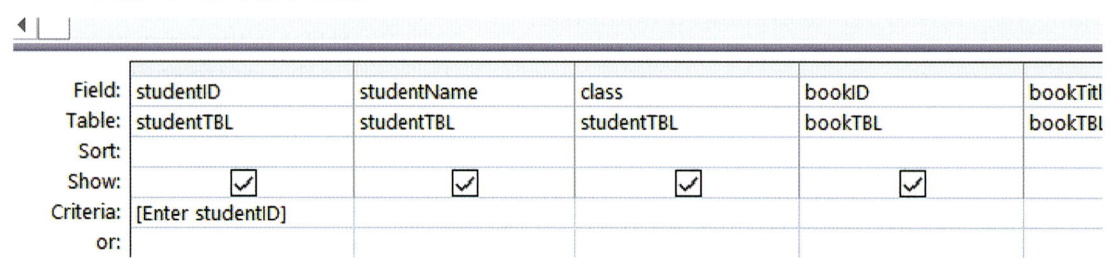

Field:	studentID	studentName	class	bookID	bookTitl
Table:	studentTBL	studentTBL	studentTBL	bookTBL	bookTBl
Sort:					
Show:	☑	☑	☑	☑	
Criteria:	[Enter studentID]				
or:					

b Click on the `Run` icon to test the query and enter a **studentID** such as **1002** when prompted. Close the query and save it as **loansByStudentIDQRY**.

Multiple-criteria queries

1 Multiple-criteria queries search records using two or more data items as search criteria. The search criteria can be provided by the user as parameters or can be added into the query design under the criteria heading.

For example, a librarian may want to search for all the books loaned out to a particular student, which are also overdue.

> You have now combined a multi-table query with a parameter query.

a Open **LibraryDB2.accdb**. Click on the `Create` tab and click on `Query Design`.

b In the `Show Table` window that appears, double-click on **studentTBL**, **loanTBL** and **bookTBL** and then close the `Show Table` window.

c This time, double-click on each of the fields in all three tables to include them in the query.

d Add the following criteria to the query design.

Field:	studentID	studentName	class	loanID	dateOut	dateBack	overdue?	bookTitle	bookAuthor
Table:	studentTBL	studentTBL	studentTBL	loanTBL	loanTBL	loanTBL	loanTBL	bookTBL	bookTBL
Sort:									
Show:	☑	☑	☑	☑	☑	☑	☑	☑	☑
Criteria:	[Enter studentID]						True		
or:									

Unit 9.5 Big Data modelling and analysis: Databases and spreadsheets

e Notice how some data items appear twice in this query. You can stop data items from displaying when you run a query by unticking **Show**. Remove the **tick** from underneath the `overdue?` field.

2 a Click on the `Run` icon to test your query. Enter the **studentID 1001** when prompted. The following results should appear.

studentID	studentName	class	loanID	dateOut	dateBack	bookTitle	bookAuthor
1001	A Student	9X2	L1	1/21/2022	1/30/2022	Learn Programming	P Author

b Close your query and save it as **overdueByStudentQRY**.

Computational thinking – abstraction

1 a Discuss with your partner how you can create a query to search **libraryDB2** for a list of books about programming taken out by student 1003 that are overdue.
  b Save your query as **programOverdueQRY**.
2 Look carefully at the book names in **bookTBL** in the file **libraryDB2.accdb**. Do the titles of all the books contain the full word 'programming' or do some titles include abbreviated terms that relate to programming (for example, the book title *Python Programs*)? How could you use a wildcard query to search the book titles?
3 Think about the criteria you need to enter to search for books that are overdue. If the term date() can be used to insert today's date as a database search criteria, how could this term be used to develop a query that produces a list of all the books that are overdue?

> You may want to use a parameter to enter **studentID** so that you can use the query again with a different **studentID** at a later stage.

Creating spreadsheet models

Learn

As you've explored in previous stages, spreadsheets can be used to analyse data and improve how it is presented. A spreadsheet can perform calculations and, if the values are changed, it can work out the new results automatically. This is an advantage because it means that you can try lots of values and see the new results. As the calculations are done so quickly, you can spend time focusing on the results and thinking about how they are affected by changes to the data values. In other words,

181

you can predict what would happen if you made certain changes. Spreadsheets can be used to collect and store large amounts of data in rows and columns.

Spreadsheet software can be used to make decisions in real life. The spreadsheet can be used to create a model of a real-life event and the relationships between different factors in that event. For example, when creating a spreadsheet model to represent the costings associated with organising a birthday party, there is a link between the overall cost of the party and the number of people invited: as the number of people attending increases, so too does the cost of the party. By changing data or a formula in the spreadsheet, it is possible to see how certain data items in the model affect other data items and the output. Spreadsheets contain a wide range of tools and special **functions** that can be used to explore the links between data items.

Some of the MS Excel functions you will already be familiar with include **SUM** and **AVERAGE**.

For example, the Geography department in school created the model below to record temperature and rainfall in a location over a period of one week. They used formulae to calculate the average temperature and rainfall over seven days and the total rainfall in that period of time.

	A	B	C
1	Day	Temperature (Centigrade)	Rainfall (mm)
2	1	23.4	5
3	2	22.2	0
4	3	21.6	0
5	4	19.5	0
6	5	23.8	0
7	6	24.4	0
8	7	21.2	2
9	Total		7	← =SUM(C2:C8)
10	Average	22.3	1	← =AVERAGE(B2:B8)
11			

Additional functions can be used to help with the analysis of data in a spreadsheet model. These include the following.

Function	Purpose	Example
MIN	Returns the lowest value in a specified range of cells	=MIN(B2:B8)
MAX	Returns the highest value in a specified range of cells	=MAX(B2:B8)
IF	Evaluates a condition and displays one value in a cell if the condition is True and an alternative output if the condition is False	=IF(C2>0,"There was rain today", "There was no rain today")
COUNT	Checks all the cells in a specified range and outputs how many contain a numerical value	=COUNT(B2:B8)

Unit 9.5 Big Data modelling and analysis: Databases and spreadsheets

> **KEYWORDS**
>
> **function:** sub-program that can exist as part of a bigger program
>
> **MIN function:** returns the lowest value in a specified range of cells in a spreadsheet
>
> **MAX function:** returns the highest value in a specified range of cells in a spreadsheet
>
> **IF statement:** in Python, this evaluates a condition which determines the path of the program depending on whether the condition is true or false
>
> **COUNT function:** checks all the cells in a specified range in a spreadsheet and outputs how many contain a numeric value

Practise

1. Expand the Geography department's weather model. This model contains the rainfall, temperature readings and estimated percentage (%) cloud coverage over a period of 28 days. Edit the formulae to calculate the highest temperature and rainfall level in a 28-day period by following these steps using the functions described in the 'Learn' box.

    a Open the file **Weather.xlsx** provided by your teacher.

    b Edit the model to add the additional label 'Highest' in cell **A30**.
     - Add the formula `=MAX(B1:B29)` to cell **B30**.
     - Press **enter** to display the highest temperature recorded in the 28-day period.

    c Copy the formula you created in part **b** into cell **C30** so that you can now also calculate the highest rainfall level in the 28-day period.

2. With your partner, work out how you can use the MIN function in cells **B31** and **C31** to calculate the lowest temperature and lowest rainfall in the 28-day period in the **Weather.xlsx** model. Add the label 'Lowest' to cell **A31** to ensure that anyone viewing the spreadsheet data can easily understand what the new data items represent.

3. In Stage 8, you were introduced to the AVERAGE spreadsheet function. Edit the formula to calculate the average temperature in a 28-day period using the AVERAGE function.
    - Add the label 'Average Temperature' to cell **A32** and then use a formula in cell **B32** to calculate the average temperature in the 28-day period.
    - Display the average temperature to 2 decimal places.

	A	B	C	D
1	Day	Temperature (Centigrade)	Rainfall (mm)	CloudCover
2	1	23.4	5	50
3	2	22.2	0	No Clouds
4	3	21.6	0	No Clouds
5	4	19.5	0	No Clouds
6	5	23.8	0	No Clouds
7	6	24.4	0	No Clouds
8	7	21.2	2	10
9	8	22.8	0	No Clouds
10	9	21.7	0	50
11	10	20.9	0	10
12	11	21.6	2	40
13	12	25.2	0	No Clouds
14	13	22.4	20	50
15	14	21.3	1	10
16	15	22.1	1	10
17	16	21.6	2	20
18	17	23.5	0	No Clouds
19	18	20.6.	2	25
20	19	20.7	0	No Clouds
21	20	21.8	0	No Clouds
22	21	19.8	0	No Clouds
23	22	23.4	1	10
24	23	21.5	3	20
25	24	21.3	2	20
26	25	22.5	1	15
27	26	22.3	2	10
28	27	21.2	1	10
29	28	22.2	0	No Clouds
30	Highest	25.2	20	
31	Lowest	19.5	0	

On days that there were no clouds in the sky, the teacher recorded 'No Clouds' in column D.

CAMBRIDGE LOWER SECONDARY COMPUTING 9

4 Edit the formula to calculate the number of cloudy days using the COUNT function.

   a In cell **A33**, add the label 'Cloudy Days'.

   b In cell **D33**, add the formula `=COUNT(D2:D29)` and press **enter**. This will display the total number of days where a numerical value was entered into a cell in the range D2 to D29; that is, the number of days when clouds were seen in the sky.

5 The Geography department have decided that if the average temperature is over 24 degrees in a 28-day period then that month can be classified as 'Very Hot'. Edit the formula to calculate temperature analysis using the IF function.

   a In cell **A34**, add the label 'Temperature Analysis'.

   Add the following IF statement to cell **B34** and then press **enter**.

   The IF statement has three main parts:

   `=IF (B32>24, "Very Hot", "Mild Temperature")`

   - The condition.
   - What happens if the condition is True.
   - What happens if the condition is False.

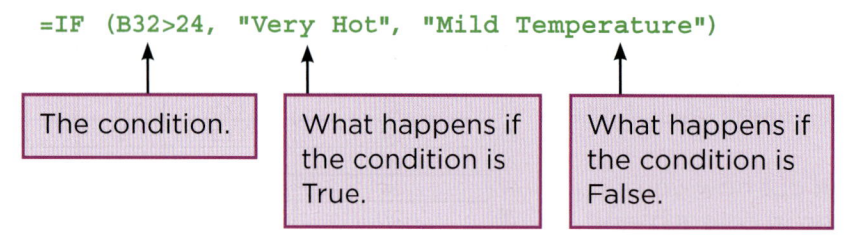

   b Save your updated spreadsheet by selecting **File** and **Save**.

	A	B	C	D
1	Day	Temperature (Centigrade)	Rainfall (mm)	CloudCover
2	1	23.4	5	50
3	2	22.2	0	No Clouds
4	3	21.6	0	No Clouds
5	4	19.5	0	No Clouds
6	5	23.8	0	No Clouds
7	6	24.4	0	No Clouds
8	7	21.2	2	10
9	8	22.8	0	No Clouds
10	9	21.7	0	50
11	10	20.9	0	10
12	11	21.6	2	40
13	12	25.2	0	No Clouds
14	13	22.4	20	50
15	14	21.3	1	10
16	15	22.1	1	10
17	16	21.6	2	20
18	17	23.5	0	No Clouds
19	18	20.6.	2	25
20	19	20.7	0	No Clouds
21	20	21.8	0	No Clouds
22	21	19.8	0	No Clouds
23	22	23.4	1	10
24	23	21.5	3	20
25	24	21.3	2	20
26	25	22.5	1	15
27	26	22.3	2	10
28	27	21.2	1	10
29	28	22.2	0	No Clouds
30	Highest	25.2	20	
31	Lowest	19.5	0	
32	AverageTemperature	22.09		
33	Cloudy Days			16

Unit 9.5 Big Data modelling and analysis: Databases and spreadsheets

Computational thinking – algorithms

1. Discuss with your partner how you could make the following changes to the model.
   - Display 'Very Hot' in cell **B34** if the temperature was 22.09 or above.
   - Display text in cell **D34** that says 'Cloudy month' if the number of Cloudy Days is 16 or above, but 'Not cloudy' if the number of Cloudy Days is <16.
2. Use the symbols below to create a flowchart that can help you to plan your Cloudy Day IF statement.

   This spreadsheet structure could also be used to illustrate the operation of the 'Very hot' IF statement already used in cell **B34**.

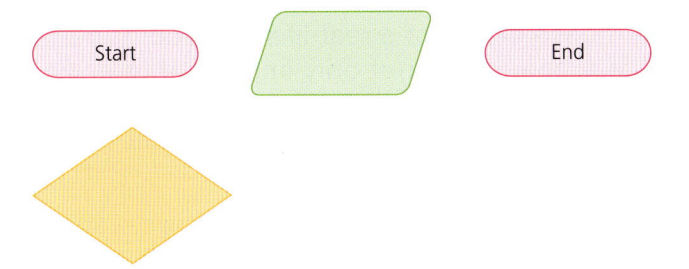

   Start   End

Evaluating models that represent real-life systems

Learn

Evaluation is an especially important part of the development of models that represent real-life systems. The process of evaluation involves checking that a solution that has been developed actually solves the problem it has been designed for, and it also involves making sure that the solution works correctly and **efficiently**.

Evaluation is something you do all the time. For example, in your day-to-day life you evaluate the movies you watch, the computer games you play, the activities you are involved in and even lessons or learning experiences in the classroom. You can think of evaluation as passing judgement at the end of a process or experience. In the digital world, however, you can think of evaluation as a continuous activity (it happens at all stages in the design, development and testing of a solution).

When developers are asked to create a new solution to a problem, they are often presented with a set of **user requirements**. User requirements are a list of the things that the new digital solution is meant to include. They can involve comments on the colour scheme for a new webpage, a list of queries that a database is expected to produce or a list of questions that need to be answered by a spreadsheet model.

Evaluation can take place at different stages in the development of a digital solution, and how the evaluation is carried out often depends on the type of solution being developed for a problem: for example, a database solution would be evaluated in a different way from a spreadsheet solution to a problem. When evaluating a database solution, it is important to ensure that queries used to extract data can successfully provide the user with the data they require from the database model of a real-life scenario. When evaluating a spreadsheet model of a real-life scenario, it is not only important to ensure that the spreadsheet is a suitable model for the real-life scenario, for example, by ensuring that it includes all the required data items, but it is also important to ensure that the results produced by formulae in the spreadsheet model are accurate.

The following table gives some of the key points to consider when evaluating database and spreadsheet models.

Evaluating solutions	
Does the solution meet all the user requirements? ✓	
Evaluating the suitability of a database model	Evaluating the suitability of a spreadsheet model
✔ Does it include all the queries needed to answer the user's questions? ✔ Do the queries produce the correct results? ✔ Does the model include all the important factors linked to the scenario it is modelling? ✔ Are all the data items in the model displayed using the correct **data type**? (This will ensure that the data is presented to the user in the correct format and that it can be processed correctly.) ✔ Can you make any improvements to the data model? ✔ Are there any easier ways of allowing the user to query the database (e.g. instead of creating a query for every title in the book database in a library, could you use a parameter query instead)?	✔ Does the spreadsheet include all the factors linked to the scenario it is modelling? ✔ Are the factors all displayed in the correct data format? ✔ Are the correct factors in the model linked by formulae? ✔ Do the formulae output the correct results? ✔ Can you make any improvements to the data model?

> **KEYWORDS**
>
> **evaluation:** checking the suitability of a solution to a problem
>
> **efficient:** the efficiency of a program can be measured by how quickly it runs
>
> **user requirements:** tasks a user expects of an application
>
> **data type:** classification applied to a data item specifying which type of data that item represents, e.g. in a spreadsheet some of the data types available include currency, text and number

Unit 9.5 Big Data modelling and analysis: Databases and spreadsheets

> **Practise**

Evaluating a database model
In this task, you will evaluate the suitability of pre-existing database and spreadsheet models of two real-life scenarios to ensure that they accurately represent the real-life systems. As part of your evaluation, you will determine whether the models are suitable for purpose in each instance.

1 Open the file **LibraryDB2Evaluate.accdb** provided by your teacher. It should cover the following user requirements.

> The database is to be used by the school librarian to help them to keep track of books on loan to students at any given time. They have said that the database model should:
> - store details about members of the library (students), so that they can be contacted if their books are overdue
> - work out how many days a book is overdue
> - allow users to create a list of all the books borrowed by a student
> - allow users to search for books by book title
> - allow users to search for books by author name.

With your partner, evaluate the database against the user requirements above. Check the following:
- That the database meets each of the user requirements. (Do the queries produce the correct results?)
- Whether the queries work in the most efficient manner. (Can you think of a better way of searching for the data?)
- Whether the database structure is correct: for example, are the correct data types assigned to all fields, and are the field lengths appropriate?

2 As you evaluate the database, make a list of any of the requirements it does not meet, and any improvements you would make to the design.

Evaluating a spreadsheet model
The Geography department have developed a spreadsheet model that shows the level of traffic on a local road.

1 Open the file **Traffic Evaluate.xlsx**. It should cover the following user requirements...

> The spreadsheet should show:
> - the total number of vehicles travelling along the road in one month
> - the average number of cars, motorcycles and lorries travelling along the road in one month
> - the total number of days each month when motorcycles travelled along the toad
> - the highest number of motorcycles and cars travelling along the road in one day
> - an alert that reads 'Busy Road' if the total number of vehicles travelling along the road in one month is greater than 1000.

CAMBRIDGE LOWER SECONDARY COMPUTING 9

2 With your partner, evaluate the spreadsheet against the user requirements.
   As you evaluate the spreadsheet model, check the following:
   - Does the model contain all the factors needed to generate a full picture of the scenario?
   - Does the model meet each of the user requirements? (As you evaluate the spreadsheet, make a list of any of the requirements it does not meet.)
   - Do the formulae produce the correct results? (Correct any formula you find to be incorrect in the model and re-save your copy of **Traffic Evaluate.xlsx**).
   - Is the data formatted in the correct manner?
3 Correct any formula you find to be incorrect in the model.
4 Remember to save your updated spreadsheet at the end of the task.

Go further

Databases

Database queries can be used to generate additional data items: for example, a librarian can compare today's date with the dateBack date in the **libraryDB** to work out how many days a library book is overdue.

1 Open **LibraryDBGF.accdb** provided by your teacher. Create a new query containing the following data items and criteria.

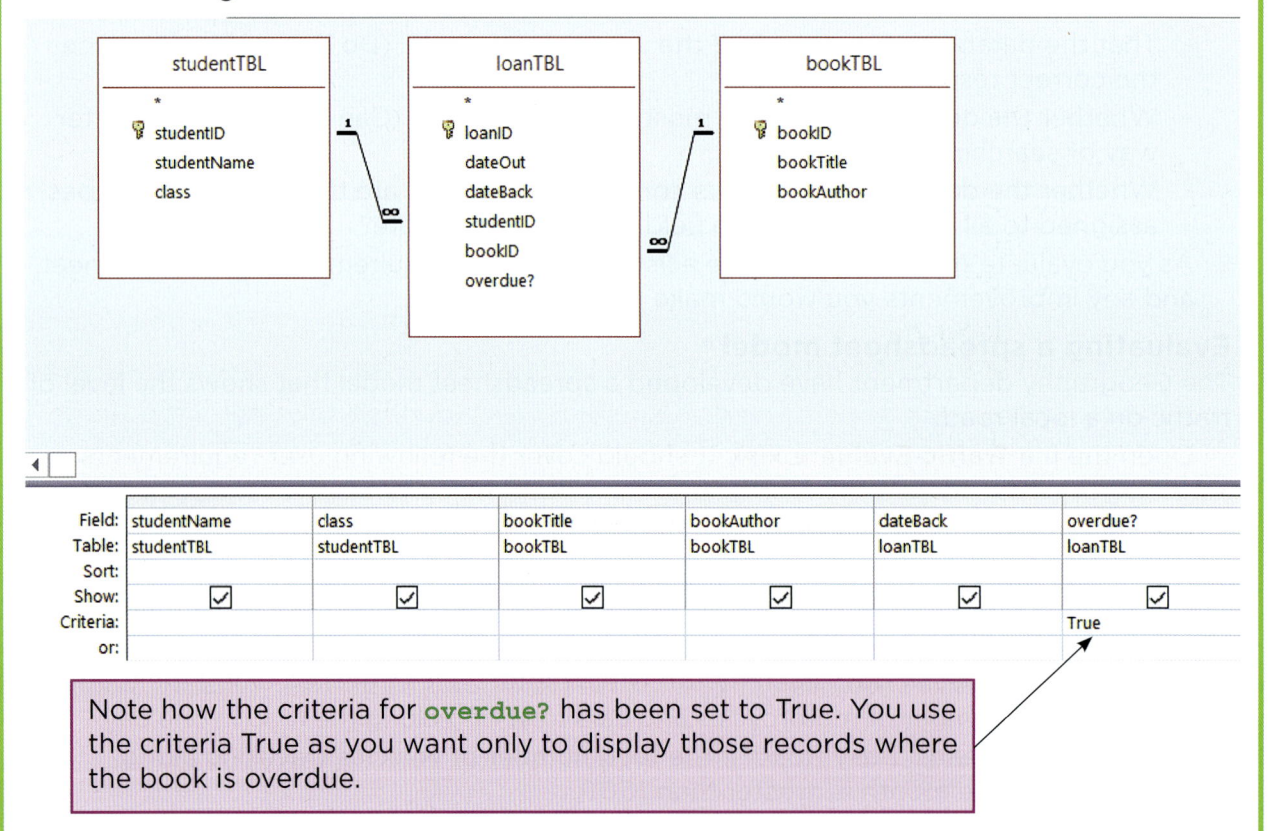

	studentName	class	bookTitle	bookAuthor	dateBack	overdue?
Field:	studentName	class	bookTitle	bookAuthor	dateBack	overdue?
Table:	studentTBL	studentTBL	bookTBL	bookTBL	loanTBL	loanTBL
Sort:						
Show:	✓	✓	✓	✓	✓	✓
Criteria:						True
or:						

Note how the criteria for `overdue?` has been set to True. You use the criteria True as you want only to display those records where the book is overdue.

2 In the `Field` row, to the right of `overdue?`, add `DaysOverDue:Date()-[dateBack]` to the next available column in the spreadsheet query.

188

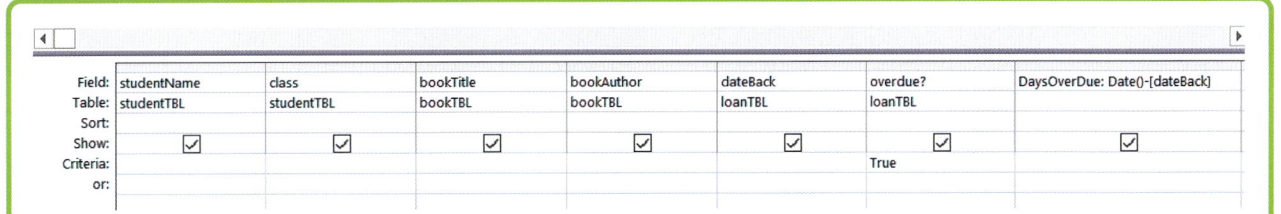

Unit 9.5 Big Data modelling and analysis: Databases and spreadsheets

Field:	studentName	class	bookTitle	bookAuthor	dateBack	overdue?	DaysOverDue: Date()-[dateBack]
Table:	studentTBL	studentTBL	bookTBL	bookTBL	loanTBL	loanTBL	
Sort:							
Show:	✓	✓	✓	✓	✓	✓	✓
Criteria:						True	
or:							

The instruction you are adding to the field row has three main parts.

`DaysOverDue:`	This is the name of the new field you are creating as part of this query
`Date()`	This is a special function that will insert today's date into the equation
`-[dateBack]`	This is an instruction that tells the query to subtract the value stored in the dateBack field in the database from today's date

3 Run your query to test that it works correctly. Results similar to the ones shown below will appear.

> Note that your days overdue will be different as the date added using `Date()` will be different.

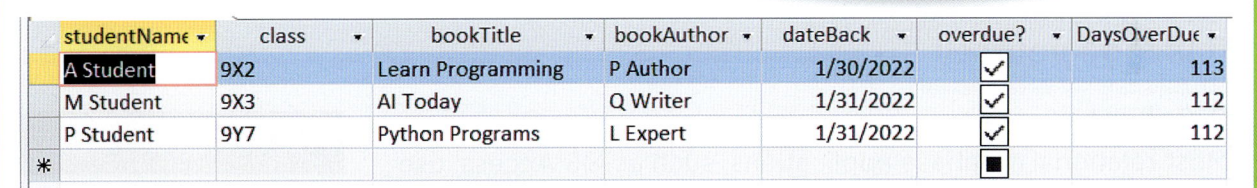

studentName	class	bookTitle	bookAuthor	dateBack	overdue?	DaysOverDue
A Student	9X2	Learn Programming	P Author	1/30/2022	✓	113
M Student	9X3	AI Today	Q Writer	1/31/2022	✓	112
P Student	9Y7	Python Programs	L Expert	1/31/2022	✓	112

4 Save your query as **daysOverdueQRY**.

Spreadsheets

In the 'Creating spreadsheet models' section, you learned how to use conditions in IF statements to determine the content of a cell in a spreadsheet model. IF functions can also be used to combine more than one condition at a time.

The Geography department would like to add a new column to the weather model from the previous section, to give advice to students about the weather.

The column will examine 'CloudCover' and 'Rainfall' each day and will display the words 'Umbrella needed' in column E if there is more than 2 mm of rainfall OR if cloud cover is 20 or higher.

1 Open **Weather GF.xlsx** provided by your teacher. Add the heading 'Weather Advice' to cell `E1`.
2 In cell `E2`, add the formula `=IF(OR(D2>=20,C2>2),"Umbrella needed","")`.

> The Boolean operator is outside the brackets.

> Notice how the two conditions are inside round brackets and separated by a comma.

CAMBRIDGE LOWER SECONDARY COMPUTING 9

> You can use "" to indicate that you do not want to display anything.

```
=IF(OR(D2>=20,C2>2),"Umbrella needed","")
```

> The structure of the rest of the IF statement remains unchanged; it is still contained inside ( ) and the two outcomes that depend on the condition are still separated by commas.

3 Press **enter** to test your formula. The words 'Umbrella needed' should appear in cell **E2**.
4 Replicate this formula to the rest of the cells in column E.
5 The Geography teacher realises that they have made a mistake with the formula and that the words 'Umbrella needed' should be displayed only if the cloud cover is >=20 AND rainfall is >=2. Amend the formula in column E to reflect this change.
6 Save your updated version of the spreadsheet as **Weather GF.xlsx**.

Challenge yourself

Databases

Most relational database applications, such as MS Access, use a special programming language called **Structured Query Language (SQL)** to access the data stored in data tables. The method you have used to create queries up until now is known as **Query by Example (QBE)**.

In exceptionally large databases, queries created using SQL are processed more rapidly than those created using the QBE method. This could be particularly important when the library database becomes larger in size and the librarian is, for example, answering queries on book availability at a time when the library is very busy.

Create a query to search **bookTBL** for all the books written by P Author.

1 Open **LibraryDBCY.accdb** provided by your teacher.
2 Click **Create** and then **Query Design**.
3 Close the **Show Table** dialogue box that appears on screen. Click **View** and then select **SQL view**.
4 Add the following statement to the **SQL** query window.

```
SELECT [bookID], [bookTitle], [bookAuthor]
FROM bookTBL
WHERE [bookAuthor] = "P Author";
```

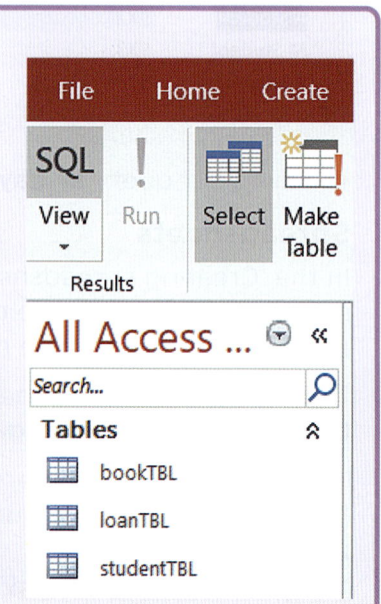

Unit 9.5 Big Data modelling and analysis: Databases and spreadsheets

```
SELECT [bookID], [bookTitle], [bookAuthor]
FROM bookTBL
WHERE [bookAuthor] = "P Author";
```

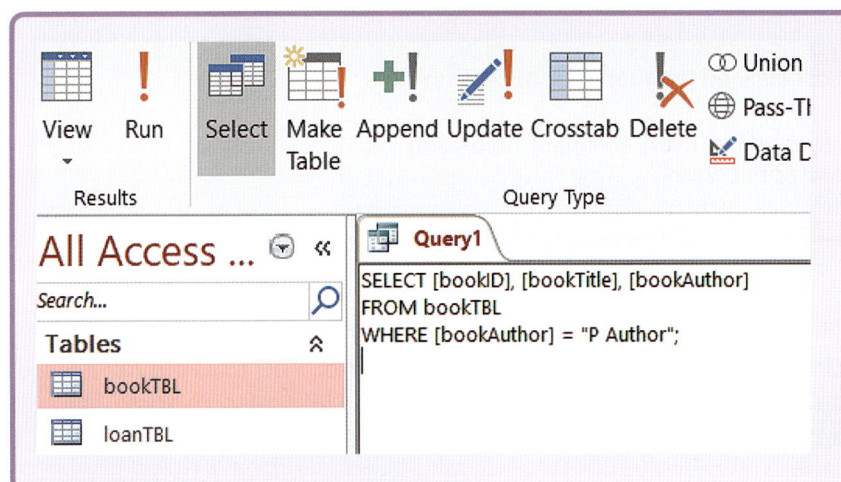

5 Click **Run** to test your query.
6 Save your query as **P AuthorQRY**.

Spreadsheets

The Geography department in your school have asked you to expand the weather model you produced in the 'Creating spreadsheet models' section.

Your teacher will provide you with a file called **Weather CY.xlsx** to allow you to complete this task, which uses a new spreadsheet function called COUNTIF.

COUNTIF can be used to extract more specific information from a spreadsheet. For example, in the weather model, it could be used to count the number of days when:

- rainfall was greater than 5 mm
- CloudCover was >15
- there were no clouds.

1 Edit the weather spreadsheet and expand the spreadsheet to contain the additional information described above. Open **Weather CY.xlsx** provided by your teacher.

> Normally, only text values need to be enclosed in double quotation marks (" "), and numbers do not, but when a logical operator is included with a number, double quotation marks are needed.

2 In cell **H3**, add **=COUNTIF(C2:C29, ">5")** and press **enter**.

H3   fx =COUNTIF(C2:C29, ">=5")

	A	B	C	D	E	F	G	H	I
1	Day	Temperature (°Celsius)	Rainfall (mm)	CloudCover					
2	1	23.4	5	50					
3	2	22.2	0	No Clouds			Rainfall >5	2	
4	3	21.6	0	No Clouds			CloudCover>15		
5	4	19.5	0	No Clouds			No Clouds		
6	5	23.8	0	No Clouds					
7	6	24.4	0	No Clouds					

3 Add a similar COUNTIF formula to cell **H4** to count the number of days when cloud cover was >15, and to cell **H5** to count the number of days there were no clouds in the sky. When you press **enter**, the following values should appear:
   - Cell H4 = 9
   - Cell H5 = 12
4 Resave your updated spreadsheet.

191

CAMBRIDGE LOWER SECONDARY COMPUTING 9

> **KEYWORDS**
>
> **Structured Query Language (SQL):** specialised language for accessing data in relational databases
>
> **Query by Example (QBE):** interface that allows users to select fields and criteria for use in a query in a database application

Final project

Look back to the start of this unit to remind yourself of the Scenario. You now have all the skills and knowledge you need to create a spreadsheet and database model that can help the school to create and evaluate models that represent students' and teachers' use of the new VLE.

Compete the tasks below.

Part 1: Big Data

After hearing about the term *Big Data*, the school are worried that the data generated by the new VLE will be too complex to be analysed.

1. Produce a report that explains what is meant by the term *Big Data*.
2. In your report, explain what is meant by *Big Data* in terms of the 5Vs; also provide examples to illustrate how Big Data is used in some real-life applications.
3. At the end of the report, comment on whether the VLE data can be considered an example of Big Data; also explain why you think this is the case.

Part 2: The database

> The school have asked you to help them create a relational database that will keep track of information such as:
> - a list of all the pages accessed using any of the following devices: PC, laptop, mobile phone, tablet
> - a list of all student logins and passwords
> - a list of all teacher logins and passwords
> - a list of all teachers and the subjects they teach
> - a list of all user logins and the times they have accessed any page from a selected subject
> - a list of all the pages accessed by a teacher for updating; the list should include information about when and on what type of device the page was accessed.

Your teacher will provide the file **FinalProject.accdb** for these tasks. The file contains three tables and some of the data used to create a real-life model of teacher and student use and access of the VLE. The tables contain:
- a list of users and details about the users
- a list of pages and information about the pages
- a list of times each page is accessed and information about who accessed the page and why they accessed it.

Unit 9.5 Big Data modelling and analysis: Databases and spreadsheets

1. Open the file **FinalProject.accdb**.
   a. Open each table in the database and identify the primary key in each table (make a note of the primary keys in writing).
   b. Look carefully at each table and identify any primary keys used as foreign keys in another table (make a note of the foreign keys in writing).
2. a. Click on the `Database Tools` tab in the database and click on `Relationships`.
   b. Use your notes on primary and foreign keys to create relationships between the three tables in the database.
   c. Save your updated copy of **FinalProject.accdb**.
3. Use your relational database to create queries to enable the school to find the following information.
   a. A list containing the pageTitle, subjectName, pageType and dates and times when any History pages were accessed; save this as **query3a**.
   b. A list containing the pageTitle, subjectName, pageType and dates and times when any History pages were accessed on a laptop; save this as **query3b**.
   c. A list containing the userLogin, userType, pageTitle and subject of any Stage 7 pages that have been updated; save this as **query3c**.
   d. A list of all the data from pageAccessTable that shows when teacher3 accessed the VLE to update pages; save this as **query3d**.
   e. A parameter query that will allow the school to search for the date, time and page title of the pages accessed by a userLogin; save this as **query3e**.
   f. A list of dates and times when teachers have accessed a **markbook** page on the VLE ; save this as **query3f**.
   g. A list of all the dates and times when times students have accessed a multimedia tutorial page on the VLE; save this as **query3g**.
   h. Save your updated copy of the database.
4. The school would also like to use the relational database model **FinalProject.accdb** to keep track of how well the school VLE is being used by teachers and students. Create queries in your database model that will also allow the school to do the following (assign appropriate names to each query).
   a. Create a list of all the pages accessed using a mobile phone or tablet.
   b. Produce a list of all student logins and passwords.
   c. Produce a list of all teacher logins and passwords.
   d. Create a list of all teachers and the subjects they teach. (Think carefully about this query; does the database contain enough information about each teacher to allow you to create this query?)
   e. Produce a list of all user logins and the times when they accessed VLE pages that relate to a subject which is specified by the user.
   f. Create a list of all the pages accessed by a teacher for updating, including information about when and on what type of device the page was accessed.

   Remember to save your updated database.
5. a. Evaluate the database model **FinalProject.accdb**, including the queries you created in tasks 3 and 4. Produce a word-processed report that comments on the following.
   - How complete is the data model? (Does it include all the data needed to allow the school to generate the new lists described above?)

- Are there any improvements to be made to the designs of any of the queries completed in Part 3?
- Review each of your queries in design view and look for any data items that are not needed according to the query description provided in the task.
- Are there any queries that could be reused if a parameter query were used instead of providing the data in the query design?

b Make the appropriate changes to your query design and save your updated version of **FinalProject.accdb**.

Comment on the changes you have made in your report.

In your report, suggest three more possible queries that could be created using the data available in the current model. List the field headings and the criteria needed in each query.

Part 3: The spreadsheet

Your teacher will provide the file **FinalProject.xlsx** for these tasks. This spreadsheet contains two worksheets:

- The first is a copy of some of the data exported from **FinalProject.accdb** and relates to teacher and student access to the VLE pages (`AccessData` tab).
- The second is to help the school understand how some of the VLE pages are being used by teachers and students (`Dept Summary Spreadsheet` tab).

1 a Examine the `Dept Summary Spreadsheet` tab in **FinalProject.xlsx**. Comment on how effective this model is in helping the school model the VLE access so that they can answer the following questions:
- What is the most popular time of day for students to access a VLE page?
- How long, on average, do teachers spend updating the VLE pages?
- What is the longest period of time spent on a Drama VLE page?
- How many minutes in total were spent on a Drama VLE page?
- How many times were the Computing VLE pages accessed in total?
- What is the average length of time spent on the Computing VLE pages?
- How many hours in total were spent on the Computing and Drama VLE pages?
- What was the shortest length of time spent on the Computing and Drama VLE pages?

b Write a short report that comments on the effectiveness of the model in addressing each of these questions. Comment on:
- any changes you think need to be made to formulae
- any additional formulae that need to be added
- any additional data items needed to answer the questions.

c Make any necessary changes to the spreadsheet formulae to ensure that the data output is correct.

2 a Create a new sheet in **FinalProject.xlsx**. Do this by clicking on the + sign at the bottom of the existing worksheet in your spreadsheet. Double-click on the new tab and rename it 'Teacher Student Access Summary'.

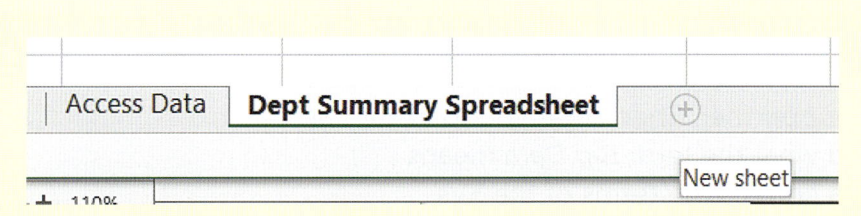

Unit 9.5 Big Data modelling and analysis: Databases and spreadsheets

   b Copy and paste the data from the `Access Data` tab into `Teacher Student Access Summary`.
   c Sort the data in the spreadsheet so that it is displayed in order of userType.
      i Click on the first label in the spreadsheet.
      ii Select the `Data` tab and click on `Sort`.
      iii Select `Sort by userType` and click on `OK`.

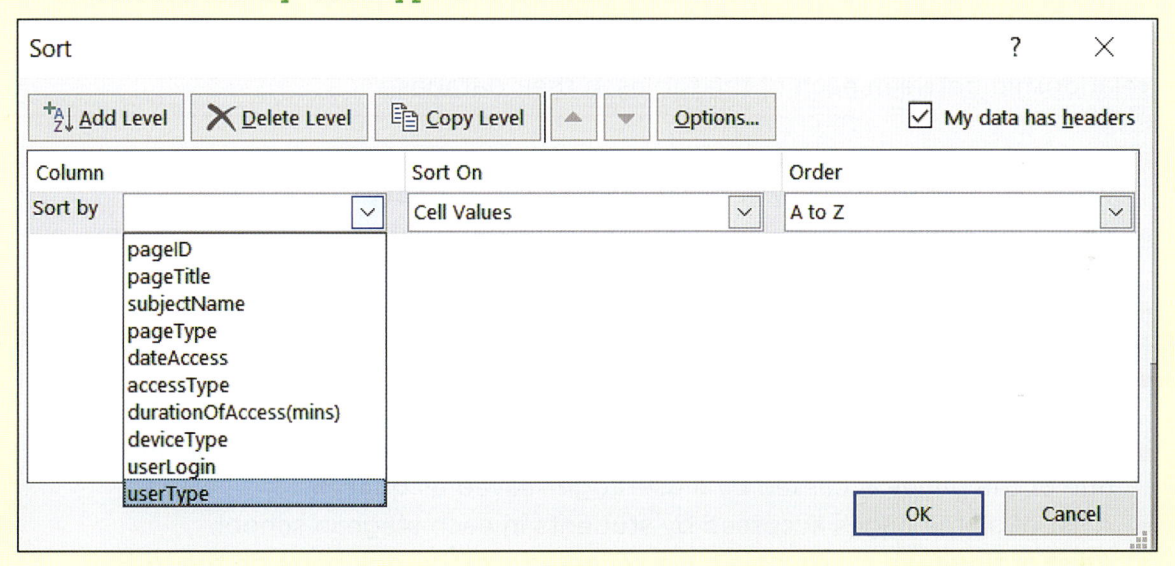

3 Add appropriate formulae to your spreadsheet to allow the school to extract the following data from your model:
   - The average number of minutes spent on the VLE by students
   - The average number of minutes spent on the VLE by teachers
   - The number of minutes spent accessing the VLE in total by both students and teachers
   - The total number of times the VLE was accessed by students
   - The total number of times the VLE was accessed by teachers
   - The longest period of time spent on any VLE page by a student
   - The longest period of time spent on any VLE page by a teacher
   - The longest period of time spent on any VLE page by either a student or a teacher
   - The shortest period of time spent accessing a VLE page by either a student or a teacher
   - An output message that states 'High Level of Use' if the total time spent accessing the VLE is over 200 minutes, or outputs the message 'We need to encourage more use' if total access time is 200 minutes or less.

4 Save your updated version of **FinalProject.xlsx**.

195

CAMBRIDGE LOWER SECONDARY COMPUTING 9

Evaluation

Part 1: Big Data

1 Swap reports with your partner. Check that your partner has:
   a correctly explained what the term *Big Data* means
   b described Big Data correctly in terms of the 5Vs
   c provided examples of how Big Data is used in a number of real-life applications
   d commented on whether the data used by the school in developing real-life models of their VLE scenario would be an example of Big Data.
2 Make changes to your report following your partner's feedback.

Part 2: The database

1 Swap **FinalProject.accdb** with your partner.
   Use this list to check that your partner has correctly created an appropriate relationship between each of the tables in their database.

   - A list containing the pageTitle, subjectName, pageType and dates and times when any History pages were accessed; saved as **query1**.
   - A list containing the pageTitle, subjectName, pageType and dates and times when any History pages were accessed on a laptop; saved as **query2**.
   - A list containing the userLogin, userType, pageTitle and subject of any Stage 7 pages that have been updated; saved as **query3**.
   - A list of all the data from pageAccessTable that shows when teacher3 accessed the VLE to update pages; saved as **query4**.
   - A parameter query that allows the school to search for the date, time and page title of the pages accessed by a userLogin; saved as **query5**.
   - A list of all the pages accessed by students in each stage in school.
   - A list of times when teachers have accessed a markbook page on the VLE.
   - A list of all the times when students have accessed a multimedia tutorial page on the VLE.

2 Check that your partner has also:
   – created a list of all the pages accessed using any of the following devices: PC, laptop, mobile, tablet
   – produced a list of all student logins and passwords
   – produced a list of all teacher logins and passwords
   – created a list of all teachers and the subjects they teach
   – produced a list of all user logins and the times when they accessed any page from a selected subject
   – created a list of all the pages accessed by a teacher for updating.
3 Update your copy of **FinalProject.accdb** based on your partner's feedback.

Unit 9.5 Big Data modelling and analysis: Databases and spreadsheets

Part 3: The spreadsheet

1 Swap **FinalProject.xlsx** with your partner.
   a Evaluate the Dept Summary Spreadsheet worksheet to ensure that it can be used to produce the following data correctly:
   – How long, on average, do teachers spend updating the VLE pages?
   – What is the longest period of time spent on a Drama VLE page?
   – How many minutes in total were spent on a Drama VLE page?
   – How many times were the Computing VLE pages accessed in total?
   – What is the average length of time spent on the Computing VLE pages?
   – How many hours in total were spent on the Computing and Drama VLE pages?
   – What was the shortest length of time spent on the Computing and Drama VLE pages?
   b Evaluate the Teacher Student Access Summary tab to ensure that it can be used to produce the following data correctly:
   – The average number of minutes spent on the VLE by students
   – The average number of minutes spent on the VLE by teachers
   – The number of minutes spent accessing the VLE in total by both students and teachers
   – The total number of times the VLE was accessed by students
   – The total number of times the VLE was accessed by teachers
   – The longest period of time spent on any VLE page by a student
   – The longest period of time spent on any VLE page by a teacher
   – The longest period of time spent on any VLE page by either a student or a teacher
   – The shortest period of time spent accessing a VLE page by either a student or a teacher
   – An output message that states 'High Level of Use' if the total time spent accessing the VLE is over 200 minutes, or outputs the message 'We need to encourage more use' if total access time is 200 minutes or less.
2 Update your copy of **FinalProject.xlsx** based on feedback provided by your partner.

What can you do?

Read and review what you can do:
- ✔ I can evaluate the use of models that represent real-life systems.
- ✔ I can use functions in spreadsheets to analyse data, such as IF, MIN, MAX, COUNT.
- ✔ I can create spreadsheets that model real-life systems.
- ✔ I can evaluate the suitability of a spreadsheet for given purposes.
- ✔ I can create relational databases with two or more linked tables.
- ✔ I can create complex searches for data in databases using two or more criteria.
- ✔ I can create complex searches in relational databases.
- ✔ I can explain the term Big Data and describe its applications.

Unit 9.6 An array of skills

Get started!

Consider a very simple game that requires you to navigate a player from one place to another to collect an item. In the example below, the smiley face needs to move from its current position to collect the apple.

The smiley face can understand only the commands:

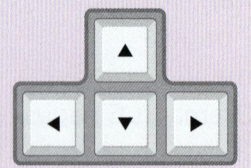

The first command would be:

Discuss the following with your partner:
- What commands are needed to get the smiley face from its starting point to the apple?
- Are there patterns in your solution?
- How could you group some of the similar commands together to make your program more efficient?

Identifying patterns in solutions allows you to make programming code more efficient and to reuse code when needed in other parts of your programs.

In this unit, you will build on your Python programming skills, using iteration and arrays to store, find and retrieve data to create solutions to problems. You will continue to develop your knowledge and skills of coding in Python to create programs that use sequence, selection and iteration to solve a variety of problems.

Unit 9.6 An array of skills

Learning outcomes

In this unit, you will learn to:
- identify and explain the purpose of a one-dimensional array
- develop a Python program with count-controlled loops
- access data from an array using Python
- develop Python programs using string manipulation, including length, uppercase and lowercase
- use iterative development on Python prototypes to create solutions to problems
- develop and apply test plans using test data that is normal, extreme and invalid
- identify and describe a range of errors, including syntax, logic and runtime errors
- use a trace table to debug a Python program
- follow, understand, edit and correct algorithms that are presented as pseudocode
- use a sub-routine in flowcharts or pseudocode
- explain and use iteration statements with count-controlled loops in either pseudocode or flowcharts
- predict the outcome of algorithms that use iteration.

Warm up

In pairs, consider the following list of numbers:

7, 19, 3, 11, 20, 65, 2, 34, 41, 14

How would you find out whether the number 34 is in this list? Think about the following questions:
- Which number would you check first?
- What would you do if the first number that you check is not the number you are looking for?

Now consider the same set of numbers, but ordered from smallest to largest:

2, 3, 7, 11, 14, 19, 20, 34, 41, 65

How would you find out whether the number 41 is in this list?
- Would you use the same method as you used for the list above?
- Can you think of another way to check for the number?

To complete these tasks, you have used data that is stored in a list. In this unit, you will learn how to search through lists to retrieve data to use in your programs.

SCENARIO

A local primary school has asked you to develop a game that can be used to teach younger students their times tables. They want the program to be an adventure-style game that asks the students questions based on a scenario to help their problem-solving skills. The game should follow these criteria:

- When the game starts, the player will need to log in using their name, and input their age as they must be between 7 and 10 years old to play the game.
- They will then pick the character they want to play as and choose the times table that they want to practise.
- The game will need to ask the player five multiplication questions that are phrased as sentences. For example, instead of 2 × 5 it would ask questions such as 'In the cave you see 2 chests each containing 5 coins. How many coins do you have?'
- The player will get two attempts to answer each question. If they get it right first time, they will receive 2 points. If they get it right second time, they will receive 1 point. Otherwise, they will receive 0 points.
- After the five questions have been asked, users will be given a score to indicate how well they have done, including how many correct answers they got and how many they got right at the first attempt.

As you work through this unit, you will be given flowchart and pseudocode algorithms and examples of Python code to enable you to complete the tasks. You will also create new code, edit code, design solutions using algorithms and test the program to make sure that it works correctly.

Do you remember?

Before starting this unit, you should be able to:
- ✔ identify and describe different data types that are used in Python
- ✔ predict and test the outcome of different algorithms
- ✔ break problems down into smaller sub-problems
- ✔ use program libraries to add additional functionality to programs
- ✔ develop programs that make use of selection
- ✔ develop programs that use different data types
- ✔ develop programs that use different Boolean operators
- ✔ refine and develop programs using iterative processes
- ✔ identify appropriate test data to ensure that programs work as expected.

In this unit, you will use the Python programming language.

Python's Integrated Development and Learning Environment (IDLE) provides features for creating, editing and running programs. Before using Python, you will need to install IDLE on your own personal device.

1. Go to **www.python.org/downloads**
2. Select `Download Python`.
3. Once downloaded, double-click on the file to open it and then choose `Install Now`.
4. Once IDLE has installed, it should appear in your Start Menu.

Breaking it down: decomposition and sub-programs

Learn

In previous units, you recapped the different stages of an **iterative** development process and used repeated cycles to develop **programs**. Here's an overview of the process.

> The first stage is **planning**, where the problem is **decomposed** into the different sub-problems that need to be solved and the **requirements** of the finished product are identified.
>
> The **algorithms** are then **designed**, and the program is **developed** and **tested**. At the end of the cycle the work is **reviewed** and **evaluated** before the next cycle begins.

In Stage 8, you also learned how to use **sub-programs** in Python, so that each sub-problem could be written as a mini-program. The sub-programs were combined to make the finished program.

Here's a recap.

> In Python, a sub-program is created, or defined, by writing the keyword `def` followed by the name you want to call the sub-program, followed by parentheses and a colon. All sub-programs are written before the main program, for example:
>
> ```
> #Sub-program
> def welcome():
>     print("Welcome to my program.")
>
> #Main program
> welcome()
> ```
>
> To run the sub-program, it is **called** by writing its name followed by parentheses in the main program. The main program is written below all the sub-programs.

You will be using sub-programs and an iterative process throughout this unit to develop your program code.

KEYWORDS

iterate/iterative/iteration: repeat/repeated/repetition
program: instructions that tell a computer system how to complete a task
user requirements: tasks a user expects of an application
algorithm: step-by-step instructions to solve a particular problem
sub-program: small program that can be called from the main program to run at any time

> **Practise**
>
> 1. Decompose the problem presented in the Scenario at the start of this unit to identify the different sub-programs that will be needed.
> 2. Write a list of the requirements for each sub-program.
> 3. Evaluate and compare your list with your partner.
>   a. Have you broken down the problem into similar sub-programs that will need writing?
>   b. Are your program requirements the same?
> 4. What are the benefits of developing a program using decomposition and iterative development?
> 5. Discuss with your partner:
>   a. What is the next stage in the program development process?
>   b. How will you know if your program code is working correctly?
>   c. What is the final stage in the program development process?

An example of a sub-program that will be needed is the process of generating the question to be asked.

Think about the size of the problems once they have been decomposed and the complexity of them compared with one single program

User login: it's all in the loops

> **Learn**
>
> The first sub-task that you should have identified (in the previous 'Practise' tasks) is the need for the player to log in.
>
> A **login system** is a common type of program that makes use of **iteration**. A user is normally allowed a set number of attempts to log in before they are locked out or prevented from trying again for a period of time.
>
> To allow a user to have repeated attempts to log in to a system, the program code needs to use iteration to run the block of code several times. To do this, the program uses a **count-controlled loop**.
>
> As you've explored in previous units, a count-controlled loop allows a block of code to be repeated a set number of times. Remember that, in Python, these are often referred to as *for loops* as they begin with the keyword `for`.

Unit 9.6 An array of skills

The `range()` states the number of times that the indented code below will be repeated. The following program loops three times.

```
for counter in range (3):
    print('Hello')
```

The word 'Hello' is printed to the screen each time the code repeats.

```
Hello
Hello
Hello
```

In the example above, 'counter' is a **variable** that keeps track of how many times the code has repeated. It starts with the value 0 and is increased by 1 each time the code is run. The loop ends when its value matches the number set in the range. The **loop variable** can have any name you choose, and it is sensible to use a name that relates to the **data** that it is storing.

The following program prints out the value of the loop variable; in this case, 'number'.

```
for number in range (4):
    print(number)
```

The output shows that the loop variable starts at 0.

```
0
1
2
3
```

However, you can add another **parameter** if you want to specify the starting value for the count: for example, `range(11, 16)` means values from 11 to 16 (but not including 16), so the program below will print out the numbers from 11 to 15.

```
for number in range (11,16):
    print(number)
```

```
11
12
13
14
15
```

Remember: writing count-controlled loops in **pseudocode** is very similar to writing the actual program code in Python. You use the keyword **for**, and then put how many times you want the code to be repeated. This example would repeat the code ten times.

```
FOR count = 1 to 10
    OUTPUT count
ENDFOR
```

If you want to show a count-controlled loop in a **flowchart**, you need to include the loop variable and show where it is **incremented**. The flowchart algorithm shown here does the same as the pseudocode algorithm above.

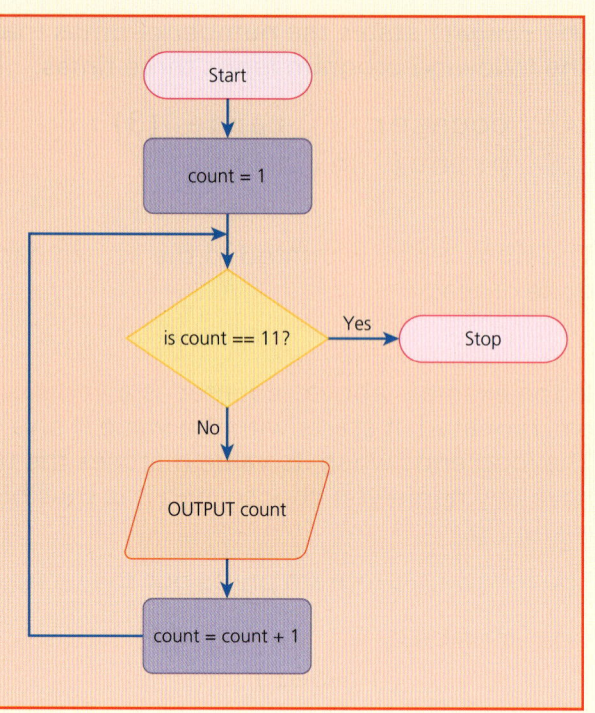

The pseudocode below shows the algorithm for a login system. The user is given three attempts to log in, and to access the game they must enter the name 'Superstar'.

```
SUBPROGRAM login ()

username = "Superstar"
entry = ""
count = 0

FOR attempt = 1 to 3
    entry = INPUT
    count = count + 1
    IF entry == username THEN
        PRINT "Welcome to the game"
        BREAK
    ELSEIF count < 3 THEN
        PRINT "Try again"
    ELSEIF count == 3 THEN
        PRINT "3 incorrect attempts. You are locked out."
        EXIT()
    ENDIF
ENDFOR

ENDSUBPROGRAM
```

Key elements of the pseudocode include the following.
- **count:** This keeps track of how many times a username has been entered. It is used to give appropriate feedback after each incorrect attempt.
- **BREAK:** This breaks out of the loop. It is used when the correct username has been entered to prevent the player from being asked to enter it again. In Python, you add the keyword `break` as a single line of code at the point where you want to exit the loop.
- **EXIT():** This code indicates that the program should stop running at this point. It is used here because the game should not continue if the username has been entered incorrectly three times. In Python, you use the **function** `exit()` at the point in the program where you want it to finish.

> **KEYWORDS**
> **login system:** method of accessing different systems using a username and/or password
> **iterate/iterative/iteration:** repeat/repeated/repetition
> **count-controlled loop:** set of instructions repeated a set number of times
> **variable:** named memory location that can store a value
> **loop variable:** variable that counts the number of times code has been repeated in a count-controlled loop
> **data:** raw facts and figures
> **parameter:** value that is passed into a function to be used as part of a sub-program
> **pseudocode:** textual representation of an algorithm
> **flowchart:** visual representation of an algorithm
> **incremented:** when the value of a variable is increased by 1
> **function:** sub-program that can exist as part of a bigger program

Practise

1. Write a flowchart algorithm for a program to do the following.
   - Ask the user to enter their name and store it in a variable 'name'.
   - Ask the user to enter their age and store it in a variable 'age'.
   - Use a count-controlled loop to print out five times a sentence that includes the user's name and age.
2. Open a new program file in Python. Create the code for your flowchart. Use two variables to store your name and age. Use a count-controlled loop to print out a sentence five times that includes your name and age.
3. Using the pseudocode in the 'Learn' box, create the login system for the **prototype** Times Table Adventure game. Write the login system as a sub-program called `login()`. The sub-program should:
   - allow the player to enter a username
   - check whether the username entered matches the one stored in the program
   - give the user three attempts to enter the correct username
   - give appropriate feedback after each attempt
   - use `break` to exit the loop if the user enters the correct username
   - use `exit()` to stop the program running if the username is entered incorrectly three times.

4. Add code to your main program, below the sub-program, to call `login( )`. Save the completed program as **TimesTableGameV1.py**.

5. Copy and complete the table below to develop a **test plan** that uses normal, extreme and invalid data to check the different pathways through your sub-program. An example test has been included to get you started.

Test number	Data entered	Expected outcome	Pass/fail
1 Correct feedback given when the correct username is entered	`username = "Superstar"`	Welcome to the game	
2			
3			
4			

> Think back to Unit 9.1, when you were introduced to normal, extreme and invalid data. Ensure that you test data that should be accepted, data that should be rejected and data that is on the boundaries of what is acceptable.

6. Apply your test plan to your program to make sure that it works correctly.

7. Identify the different variables used in your program for the login system and their data types, and explain why these are the most appropriate data types to use, by completing the table below.

Variable name	Data type	Justification

> **KEYWORDS**
>
> **prototype:** initial product created for testing and reviewing, before a final product is released
>
> **test plan:** document that details the tests to be carried out when a program is complete and whether or not they are successful

Unit 9.6 An array of skills

String manipulation

> **Learn**
>
> When a user enters data into a system, they may use a number of different **data types**. A reminder of the key data types is shown below.
>
> | Data type | Explanation |
> |---|---|
> | String | A combination of letters, numbers or symbols |
> | Character | A single letter, number or symbol |
> | Integer | A whole number, negative or positive |
> | Real | A number with decimal places, negative or positive |
> | Boolean | Two possible values: True or False |
>
> *Remember: Python does not have a specific data type for an individual character. A single character is simply stored as a string with a length of 1.*
>
> As you've explored in previous units, when developing programs you need to consider how the user might enter data, as it might not always be as you expect. You have already used **casting** to change the data type of an input, for example, using `int` to store input data as an integer. Remember that you can also use **string manipulation** to ensure that the data is input in the correct format. Here's a recap.
>
> > Imagine that you are developing a game that requires the user to enter their answer to a multiple-choice question as a letter: for example, A, B, C or D.
> >
> > ```python
> > answer = input("Enter your answer (A, B, C or D): ")
> > if answer == "A":
> >     print("Correct")
> > else:
> >     print("Incorrect")
> > ```
> >
> > If the user entered 'a' rather than 'A', they would be told that their answer is incorrect, as Python treats 'A' and 'a' as different characters.
> >
> > One solution to this problem would be to edit the program code using a Boolean operator to check for alternative inputs.
> >
> > *Think back to Unit 9.4. ASCII assigns each character that a computer can represent a unique binary code, and this includes upper and lowercase characters.*
> >
> > ```python
> > answer = input("Enter your answer (A, B, C or D): ")
> > if answer == "A" or answer == "a":
> >     print("Correct")
> > else:
> >     print("Incorrect")
> > ```
> >
> > However, there are also a range of different string manipulation techniques that can be used to return new values where the contents of a string have been altered.

207

The `upper()` method converts all the characters of a string to uppercase.

```
answer = input("Enter your answer (A, B, C or D): ")
answer = answer.upper()
print(answer)
```

When the program is run and the user enters 'a', it is changed to 'A'.

```
Enter your answer (A, B, C or D): a
A
```

The `lower()` method converts all the characters of a string to lowercase.

```
username = input("Enter your username: ")
username = username.lower()
print(username)
```

In both of the examples below, the alphabetical characters have been changed to lowercase. The numbers are ignored and remain the same.

```
Enter your username: TESTING123        Enter your username: TeStIng123
testing123                              testing123
```

The `capitalize()` method converts the first character of a string to uppercase and all the rest of the characters to lowercase.

```
name = input("Enter your name: ")       Enter your name: akil
name = name.capitalize()                Akil
print(name)
```

Note that all the characters input by the user are stored as a single string. Therefore, if there is more than one word separated by a space, only the very first letter of the first word is in uppercase.

```
Enter your name: AKIL HUSSAIN
Akil hussain
```

Unit 9.6 An array of skills

Another useful function that can be used with strings is `len()`:

```
name = input("Enter your name: ")
length = len(name)
print(length)
```

This tells you the number of characters in a string:

```
Enter your name: Akil
4
```

It can be used to check whether anything has been input, as the length of the string is 0 if nothing is stored in it:

```
Enter your name:
0
```

> **KEYWORDS**
>
> **data type:** classification applied to a data item specifying which type of data that item represents, e.g. in a spreadsheet some of the data types available include currency, text and number
>
> **cast:** change the data type of a variable
>
> **string manipulation:** process of changing the format of a variable/string to allow it to be analysed

Practise

1 Open the file **StringManipulation.py** provided by your teacher.
   a Add code where the comments are so that the program completes the following string manipulation:
   - 'first' is capitalised
   - 'middle' is changed to uppercase
   - 'last' is changed to lowercase.
   b Test your program using the following inputs:
   - `first = sanya`
   - `middle = ali`
   - `last = ABBAS`

2. Open your file **TimesTableGameV1.py** from the previous section. You are going to use iterative development processes to add further functionality to what you have created previously.

   a. Edit the sub-program `login()` so that the program capitalises the username entered by the user.

   b. Develop the sub-program further to add a check to make sure that a username has been entered. To do this, you need to use a **conditional statement** to check the length of the username the player has entered. If it has a length of 0, your program should tell the player 'You did not enter a username'.

   c. Save the updated program as **TimesTableGameV2.py**.

3. Test your code to make sure that the username entered by the player is capitalised, and that a suitable message is output if no username has been entered.

4. Use the flowchart below to add a new sub-program `age()` to your times-table game to check that the user is the correct age to play the game.

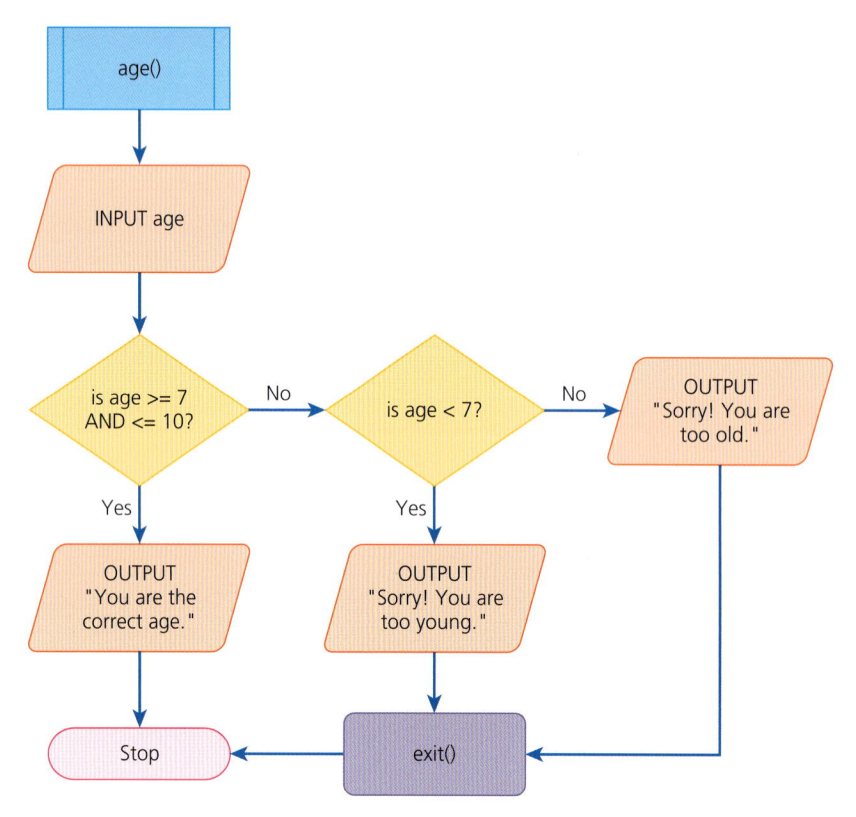

```
age()
  │
  ▼
INPUT age
  │
  ▼
is age >= 7  ──No──▶  is age < 7?  ──No──▶  OUTPUT "Sorry! You are too old."
AND <= 10?                │                        │
  │                      Yes                       │
 Yes                      │                        │
  ▼                       ▼                        │
OUTPUT              OUTPUT                         │
"You are the        "Sorry! You are                │
correct age."       too young."                    │
  │                       │                        │
  ▼                       ▼                        │
Stop  ◀────────────── exit() ◀─────────────────────┘
```

5. a. If the player is too young or too old, the program should give appropriate feedback and then use the function `exit()` to stop running.

   b. Save the program that you have developed as **TimesTableGameV3.py**.

6. Copy and complete the table on the next page and develop the test plan to check that your new sub-program works correctly. Make use of normal, extreme and invalid test data in your test plan. An example test has been included to get you started.

Unit 9.6 An array of skills

Test number	Data entered	Expected outcome	Pass/fail
1 Correct feedback when the age is between 7 and 10	`username = "Superstar"` `age = 10`	Welcome to the game. You are the correct age.	
2			
3			
4			

7 Get your partner to use your test plan to check that your code works as it should.

> **KEYWORD**
>
> **conditional statement:** completes a check to see whether set criteria is either True or False

Tracing through the lines

Learn

When creating algorithms or writing programs, you should always test them thoroughly. You are already used to doing this using a test plan.

As you explored in previous units, you can use **trace tables** alongside test plans to follow each line of an algorithm or program through step by step.
- A test plan provides you with the data to be input and the expected outcome.
- Trace tables allow you to see the value of each variable as each line of code is **executed** and can be used to identify any potential errors.

The program below uses two variables, 'x' and 'y'. If 'x' is greater than or equal to 'y' then it should add the contents of the two variables; otherwise, it should multiply them.

```
1 x = 20
2 y = 15
3 if x >= y:
4     print(x*y)
5 else:
6     print(x+y)
7 print("Program complete")
```

Remember: a trace table has headings for the line number and all the variables, as well as a column for the output. You may also find it helpful to include a column heading for the condition checks in an **IF statement**, to record the Boolean result.

Here is a trace table for the program on the previous page.

Line	x	y	x >= y	Output
1	20			
2		15		
3			True	
4				300
7				Program complete

This example has helped to identify a logic error. The program has multiplied the two values when 'x' is greater than 'y', when it should have added them.

Trace tables are extremely helpful when checking algorithms and programs that use iteration as they can include a column to track the value of the loop variable.

Look at the pseudocode algorithm below.

```
1   value = 3
2   FOR number = 1 to 5
3       x = value * number
4       y = x * 2
5       IF y > 20 THEN
6           OUTPUT y
7       ENDIF
8   ENDFOR
```

Work through the trace table below to see how the values of the variables change for each line of the algorithm.

Line	Variable value	Variable number	Variable x	Variable y	Condition y > 20	Output
1	3					
2		1				
3			3			
4				6		
5					False	
2		2				
3			6			
4				12		
5					False	
2		3				
3			9			
4				18		
5					False	

Unit 9.6 An array of skills

Line	Variable	Variable	Variable	Variable	Condition	Output
2		4				
3			12			
4				24		
5					True	
6						24
2		5				
3			15			
4				30		
5					True	
6						30

A simplified version of the trace table could show just the values at the end of each iteration.

Line	Variable	Variable	Variable	Variable	Condition	Output
	value	number	x	y	y > 20	
6	3	1	3	6	False	
6		2	6	12	False	
6		3	9	18	False	
6		4	12	24	True	24
6		5	15	30	True	30

Note that the 'Variable' and 'Output' columns do not always have to contain a value. It is usual to enter a value only if it has changed.

> **KEYWORDS**
> **trace table:** technique for predicting step by step what will happen as each line of an algorithm or program is run, and to identify errors
> **execute:** carry out the instructions described in a computer program
> **IF statement:** in Python, this evaluates a condition which determines the path of the program depending on whether the condition is true or false

Practise

1. Copy and complete the trace table for the program below:

```
1  x = 20
2  y = 15
3  z = 10
4  if x >= y:
5      if z > 9:
6          print(x*y)
7      else:
8          print(x-y)
9  else:
10     print(x+y)
11 print((x+y+z)/3)
```

Line	x	y	z	x >= y	z > 9	Output

2. Open the file **TraceTablesActivity1.py** provided by your teacher and run the program. Do the outputs in your trace table match those from the program? Have you managed to trace a Python program successfully to ensure that it is free from errors?

3. Copy and complete the trace table for the program below.

```
1  a = 5
2  b = 10
3  for i in range(a,b):
4      print(i+2)
```

Line	a	b	i	Output

4 Open the file **TraceTablesActivity2.py** provided by your teacher and run the program. Do the outputs in your trace table match those from the program?

5 Create trace tables for the following programs to demonstrate that you can follow pseudocode algorithms that use loops.

a
```
1 num1 = 3
2 num2 = 2
3 total = 0
4 FOR x = 1 to 3
5     num1 = num1 * x
6     num2 = num2 * 2
7     total = num1 + num2
8 ENDFOR
9 OUTPUT total
```

b
```
1 x = 1
2 y = 1
3 z = 0
4 FOR x = 1 to 2
5     FOR y = 1 to 3
6         z = (x * y) * 3
7         OUTPUT z
8     ENDFOR
9 ENDFOR
```

It's all in the lists

> **Learn**

When you want to store a single **item** of data in a program, you use a **variable**. A variable is a named memory location that can store a value: for example, `name = "Petra"`. The contents of a variable can be changed at any point in a program.

If you wanted to store five names using variables, you would have to use five different variables to store the names: for example,

```
name1 = "Petra"
name2 = "Adnan"
name3 = "Amir"
name4 = "Mira"
name5 = "Rayah"
```

This is fine if you have only a few different names to store, but imagine you wanted to store 100 different names. It would not be very practical to have 100 different variables, each storing one name. Instead, you can use a **one-dimensional array**: for example,

```
name1 = ["Petra", "Adnan", "Amir", "Mira", "Rayah"]
```

> Remember: an array is a data structure that allows you to store multiple pieces of data under a single identifier.

You can think of an array as a series of boxes, each of which contains one item of data. These items of data can be **indexed**. This means that they can be accessed individually using their index number, and the first item always has the index 0: for example,

name				
0	1	2	3	4
Petra	Adnan	Amir	Mira	Rayah

If you wanted to print the name Amir from the array above, you would use the code `print(name[2])`. The number in square brackets after the name of the array is the index number or position where the element can be found.

A drawback of arrays is that they allow only data of the same data type to be stored.

`name = ["Petra", "Adnan", "Amir", "Mira", "Rayah"]`	Allowed; all use the string data type
`topScores = ["Petra", 55, "Adnan", 46, "Amir", 44]`	Not allowed; this a combination of string and integer data types

Python uses data structures called **lists** and **tuples** to create arrays. These work in a similar way to arrays, but they allow a mixture of different data types to be stored in them. The difference between a list and a tuple is that the elements inside a list can be changed, but the contents of a tuple cannot be changed.

Unit 9.6 An array of skills

In Python, a list is created using square brackets: [ ]. Each item in the list is separated from the next element by a comma.

Look at the program below. Can you work out what will be printed when the program is run?

```
words = ["closed", "shops", "The", "today", "were"]
print(words[2], words[1], words[4], words[0], words[3])
```

The program retrieves and prints elements from the list to create a sentence.

```
The shops were closed today
```

The data contained in a list can also be used to perform calculations. Look at the program below. Can you work out what will be output when the program is run?

```
scores = [15, 24, 18, 32, 12]
firstLast = scores[0] + scores[4]
print("The total of the first and last scores is",firstLast)
```

This program adds together 15 (index 0) and 12 (index 4) to give the answer 27.

```
The total of the first and last scores is 27
```

In this list, there are no quotation marks. This is because the values are stored as integers and not strings.

> **KEYWORDS**
> **data item:** piece of information that represents part of the data that makes up a person, place or thing, e.g. some of the data items that represent a person are their first name and second name
> **variable:** named memory location that can store a value
> **one-dimensional array:** series of items grouped together under one identifier
> **index:** numerical reference for a location of a piece of data stored in an array
> **list:** data structure in Python that can store multiple items of data of mixed data types under a single identifier; data items can be changed
> **tuple:** data structure for storing multiple items of data in a single variable; values cannot be changed

Practise

1 Copy and complete this paragraph about the purpose of a one-dimensional array by filling in the blanks. Select from the words below.

> When you want to store multiple items of data about the same thing, instead of using lots of ... you should use an .... In Python, this can be done using lists or .... Lists allow you to ... the data they contain; tuples ... you from changing the data. To retrieve the value 5 from the list `points = [4,7,5,3,8]`, you would write the code ....
>
> | tuples | variables | array | `points[3]` |
> |---|---|---|---|
> | change | `points[2]` | prevent | |

2 Open a new program file in Python, and create a program that does the following.
   a Creates a list called 'countries', which stores the following countries: Belgium, Andorra, Malta, Mali, Sri Lanka.
   b Displays the countries in alphabetical order by accessing them from the array in Python using the `print` command: for example,

   ```
   Andorra
   Belgium
   Mali
   Malta
   Sri Lanka
   ```

   c Save the program as **CountriesList.py** and test it to ensure that it produces the output shown above.

3 Follow the pseudocode below and copy and complete the table to determine the output from each calculation.

   `score = [25, 34, 15, 17, 20]`
   `OUTPUT score[2] + score[3]`
   `OUTPUT score[4] - score[2]`
   `OUTPUT score[2] * score[4]`
   `OUTPUT score[1] / score[3]`
   `OUTPUT (score[0] + score[2]) / score[4]`

Calculation	Output
`score[2] + score[3]`	
`score[4] - score[2]`	
`score[2] * score[4]`	
`score[1] / score[3]`	
`(score[0] + score[2]) / score[4]`	

4 Open your file **TimesTableGameV3.py** (from the 'String manipulation' section). You are now going to add a sub-program called `character()` to allow the user to choose their character name.

   a Choose the names for five characters and store them in a list with a suitable name.
   b Use the `print` command to display each character name in turn.
   c Once all five names have been displayed, ask the player to enter their choice of character, and store this in a variable.
   d Confirm the character they have chosen by printing the character's name as part of a sentence.
   e Return the character name to the main program.

   > The number that the player enters as their choice will be one higher than the index number you need to use to print the character's name.

   Here is an example of what the sub-program may look like when it is run.

   ```
   Please choose your character name:
   1. Vivo
   2. Netta
   3. Quix
   4. Wenzo
   5. Poppa
   Enter the number of your choice: 2
   You have chosen Netta
   ```

5 Add code to the end of the main program, to call the sub-program `character()` and assign the value that is returned to a variable called 'charName'.

6 Save the updated program as **TimesTableGameV4.py**. Test your code to make sure that it is working correctly. Improve your code further so that if the user enters a number that is not between 1 and 5, the program will automatically assign them the first character name.

7 Save the updated program as **TimesTableGameV5.py**. Test your program to make sure that it is working correctly.

8 Make sure that your program meets all the requirements listed in task 4.

> **DID YOU KNOW?**
>
> The maximum number of values you can store in a list varies depending on the computer you are using. This is because it is dependent on the amount of RAM in your computer. This means that if you have a large list in Python, it may work correctly on one computer but not on another.
> Don't worry too much, though; you would probably need over 500 million items in your list even to get close to this being a problem!

Using iteration with lists

Learn

Lists are incredibly useful for storing multiple pieces of data without the need for lots of variables. However, retrieving each item from a list individually can require a lot of lines of code:

```
highScores = [150,120,110,90,70]
print("The top five high scores are:")
print("1",highScores[0])
print("2",highScores[1])
print("3",highScores[2])
print("4",highScores[3])
print("5",highScores[4])
```

If this list contained 100 scores, using this approach would require a separate line of code to print each piece of data. Instead, it is possible to use iteration to simplify and shorten the code:

```
highScores = [150,120,110,90,70]
print("The top five high scores are:")
for x in range(0,5):
    print(x+1,highScores[x])
```

Both of these examples give exactly the same output:

```
The top five high scores are:
1 150
2 120
3 110
4 90
5 70
```

The example using iteration would always use just four lines of code, even if the program displayed the top 100 scores.

Look at the second program in more detail.

`highScores = [150,120,110,90,70]`	This creates a list called 'highScores' that contains five values
`print("The top five high scores are:")`	This displays the text between the quotation marks using the `print` function
`for x in range(0,5):`	This is a loop that repeats five times; 'x' is the loop variable
`print(x+1, highScores[x])`	**x+1** displays the number of the high score; 'x' has a value of 0 to begin with, so we need to add 1 to display the correct number **highScores[x]** retrieves the value from the list with the index 'x'

Iteration can be used to handle the data in lists for a range of different purposes. The program below uses iteration to add together all the scores in the list.

```
scores = [7,6,9,10,4,5,6]
total = 0
for x in range(0,7):
    total = total + scores[x]
print("The total of the scores is:",total)
```

When the program is run, it gives the following output.

```
The total of the scores is: 47
```

The trace table below shows how this is achieved.

Line	Variable x	Variable total	output
2		0	
4	0	7	
4	1	13	
4	2	22	
4	3	32	
4	4	36	
4	5	41	
4	6	47	
5			47

Of course, the number of items in a list may vary, which can cause problems when using a **for loop** that repeats a set number of times. To overcome this problem, you can use the `len()` function to set the number of times the loop needs to run.

> **KEYWORD**
>
> **for loop:** the Python or MicroPython loop for a count-controlled loop

In the program below, the `len()` function is used in line 3 to find the number of items in the list, and the value is stored in the variable 'length'. In line 4, 'length' replaces a fixed value for the upper boundary of the loop. If the number of items in the list increases or decreases, then the program adjusts automatically to run the loop the correct number of times: for example,

```
scores = [7,6,9,10]
total = 0
length = len(scores)
for x in range(0,length):
    total = total + scores[x]
print("The number of items in the list is:",length)
print("The total of the scores is:",total)
```

When the program is run, it gives the following output.

```
The number of items in the list is: 4
The total of the scores is: 32
```

Practise

1. Copy and complete the trace table to check the algorithm below for any bugs and predict the outcomes. The first three lines have been completed for you.

```
1   scores = [7, 9, 14, 10, 3, 6, 9, 1]
2   total = 0
3   bonus = 0
4   FOR x = 0 to 7
5       total = total + scores [x]
6       IF scores [x] > 8 THEN
7           bonus = bonus + 2
8       ELSE
9           bonus = bonus + 1
10      ENDIF
11  ENDFOR
12  finalScore = total + bonus
13  OUTPUT finalScore
```

Line	Variable	Variable	Variable	Variable	Output
	x	total	bonus	finalScore	
2		0			
3			0		
9	0	7	1		

2. Look at the pseudocode below.

```
1   words = [Good morning, Goodbye, you, today?, how, are, Good afternoon]
2   day = INPUT
3   IF day == "AM" THEN
4       OUTPUT words[0], words[4], words[2], words[5], words[3], words[1]
5   ELSEIF day == "PM" THEN
6       OUTPUT words[6], words[4], words[5], words[2], words[3], words[1]
7   ELSE
8       OUTPUT "You haven't entered AM or PM.", words[1]
9   ENDIF
```

Unit 9.6 An array of skills

a Copy and complete this table to predict the output if the following values are entered.

Day	Output
AM	
AP	
PM	

b There is an error in the code on line 4, resulting in the output being displayed incorrectly. Rewrite this line of code so that the program works correctly.

3 Open your file **TimesTableGameV5.py** (from the previous section).
   a Improve the code in the sub-program `character()` using iterative development processes so that it uses a count-controlled loop to retrieve and display all the names from the array, rather than a series of print commands.
   b Save the updated program as **TimesTableGameV6.py**.
   c Test your program to make sure that it still works correctly.

4 Add a new sub-program called `timesTable()` that asks the player which times table they would like to practise. Return the value to the main program.

5 Add code to the end of the main program to call the sub-program `timesTable()` and assign the value that is returned to a variable called 'table'.

6 Save the updated program as **TimesTableGameV7.py**. Test your code to make sure that it is working correctly.

Computational thinking – algorithms

During this unit, you have been exploring lists in Python. As part of this, you have created programs that retrieve information from lists. When dealing with lists of values or numbers, there are different ways in which you can search through them to see whether they contain a specific value.

Two common methods of searching lists are the **linear search** and **binary search**. A linear search simply starts at the first value in the list and checks each element in turn. It continues doing this until it finds the value that is being looked for, or until it reaches the end of the list, in which case it can output that the value is not in the list. In a linear search, the list does not have to be in any particular order.

The other method is called a *binary search*. A key difference between a linear search and a binary search is that the list must be in numerical or alphabetical order to perform a binary search.

KEYWORDS

linear search: sequential method of searching a list from start to end, checking each element in turn

binary search: divide-and-conquer algorithm that splits an array in half each iteration, checking the middle value to determine whether it is higher or lower or it has found the required value

Here is an example of a binary search to see whether the number 9 is in the list below.

Index	0	1	2	3	4	5	6	7	8	9
Value	2	6	9	12	**16**	18	20	23	45	99

First, you need to find the middle value in the list. If there are an even number of elements in the list then there isn't a true middle value, so it is usual to take the value to the left of the mid-point. In this example, this would be index 4 with a value of 16.

Next you need to see whether the middle value is the one being searched for. If it is, then the algorithm finishes. However, if it is not, then the bottom half of the list plus the middle value is discarded if the middle value is lower than the one being looked for, or the top half of the list plus the middle value is discarded if the middle value is larger than the one being looked for.

In this example, 16 is larger than 9, so 16 and all the values to the right (that are higher than the target number) are discarded. The remaining numbers form a new list:

Index	0	1	2	3
Value	2	**6**	9	12

The process is then repeated. This time, the middle value is 6. This is not the value being searched for and is smaller than the target value, so 6 and the numbers below it are discarded. This leaves two values that create a new list:

Index	0	1
Value	**9**	12

This time the middle value is 9. This is the number being searched for, so the search is complete.

A worst-case scenario for a linear search is that the value you are looking for is the last item in the list. In a binary search, you are discarding half of the values each time and therefore the search is usually much quicker.

1 Perform a binary search on the following values to find the number 42.

6	9	15	18	20	24	27	33	37	40	42	49

2 Perform a binary search on the following list to find the string 'Blue'.

Black	Blue	Green	Orange	Pink	Purple	Red	White	Yellow

3 Explain the steps a binary search follows to look for a number in a sorted list.

Identifying errors and debugging

Learn

Being able to identify errors and correct them is a fundamental skill in programming. To recap, there are two main ways in which you can identify errors and debug them.

- The first is through trial and error. This requires you to write some code, run your program and see whether it works. If it doesn't work, then you need to make changes to your code and try to run it again until it does what you want it to do.
- Another method of identifying errors is through using a test plan. You should develop a test plan before you write your program. It should clearly identify what tests you are going to carry out when you have developed the program and what the program should do. When you have finished developing the program, you should carry out these tests to find any potential issues.

You have already written and used test plans, and these have usually focused on making sure that the program works and produces the outputs that you are expecting. A thorough test plan includes three different types of data. Can you remember what these are?

- **Normal**
- **Extreme**
- **Invalid**

When you try to run and test your program, there are three main types of errors that you may come across. These are:

- **syntax errors**
- **logic errors**
- **runtime errors.**

Here's a reminder of these errors.

Syntax errors

A syntax error is something that breaks the grammatical rules of the programming language. This can include misspelling a keyword or variable, missing brackets or speech marks, incorrect indentation or using assignment incorrectly. Syntax errors stop a program from running.

Common syntax errors include the following.

Error	Example	Explanation
Misspelling a keyword	``1 name = inpt("Enter your name")`` ``2 print("Hello",name)``	On line 1, **input** is spelled incorrectly
Missing brackets	``1 name = input("Enter your name"`` ``2 print("Hello",name)``	On line 1, there is a bracket missing from the end of the line

Error	Example	Explanation
| Missing quotation marks | ```
1 name = input("Enter your name")
2 print(Hello,name)
``` | On line 2, `Hello` should be in quotation marks as it is a string |
| Incorrect indentation of code | ```
1 age = input("Enter your age: ")
2 if int(age) > 13:
3 print("You can play the game")
4 else:
5     print("You are not old enough to play")
``` | On line 3, the `print` statement needs to be indented |

Logic errors

A logic error is an error in the algorithm that produces an incorrect or unexpected output. The program will still run, but the desired output is not produced. Logic errors are harder to spot because it is not always obvious that there is an issue with the program.

Common logic errors include the following.

Error	Example	Explanation
| Using Boolean operators incorrectly | ```
1 age = int(input("Enter your age: "))
2 if age > 12 or age < 20:
3     print("You are a teenager")
4 else:
5     print("You are not a teenager")
``` | On line 2, `or` has been used instead of `and`; this will give the output 'You are a teenager' for any age that is entered |
| Incorrect use of BIDMAS in calculations | ```
1 num1 = 10
2 num2 = 20
3 num3 = 30
4 average = num1 + num2 + num3 / 3
5 print(average)
``` | On line 4, the average is calculated incorrectly as `num3` will be divided by 3 before being added to the other variables; `num1 + num2 + num3` needs to be inside brackets so that this part of the calculation is completed first |
| Using logical operators incorrectly | ```
1 age = int(input("Enter your age: "))
2 if age < 12 and age > 20:
3     print("You are a teenager")
4 else:
5     print("You are not a teenager")
``` | On line 2, the incorrect operators have been used; it should be `age > 12` and `age < 20` |

Runtime errors

A runtime error occurs when Python understands the code but runs into a problem when it tries to execute it. In English, a runtime error would be something like the sentence 'Jump on the ceiling'. It makes sense but it is something that cannot be completed. The name *runtime error* comes from how it is encountered once the program is running.
```

Unit 9.6 An array of skills

Common runtime errors include the following.

Error	Example	Explanation
| Trying to use a variable that doesn't exist or has been misspelled | ```
1 myAge = 14
2 print(myage)
``` | The program would give a NameError, as `myAge` and `myage` are not the same |
| Dividing by zero | ```
1 num1 = 6
2 num2 = 0
3 num3 = num1 / num2
4 print(num3)
``` | A ZeroDivisionError would be produced, as dividing by zero makes no sense in maths |
| Trying to access items in a list that do not exist | ```
1 age = [13,14,16]
2 print(age[3])
``` | The program would give an index error as there is no item at 'index 3' in this list |

> **KEYWORDS**
> **normal test data:** data of the correct type that should be accepted by a program
> **extreme test data:** acceptable input but at the ends of the possible input range
> **invalid test data:** data that should be rejected by a program
> **syntax error:** error in program code that stops the program from running
> **logic error:** error that allows a program to run but not output what is expected
> **runtime error:** error that occurs while a program is running; the instructions cannot be completed

Practise

1. Identify the syntax errors in the program below. For each error, say which line it is on, describe the error and write a corrected version of the program code.

   ```
   1 name = input("Enter your name: )
   2 age = int(inpt("Enter your age: ")
   3 for x in range(0,age):
   4     print(x+1,"Your name is",naem)
   ```

2. The algorithm below should ask the user to enter three numbers and then calculate the average of the three numbers. If the average is more than 50, it should output 'Well done'; otherwise, it should output 'Try again'. Identify the logic errors in the code that prevent the algorithm from working correctly. For each error, say which line the error is on and how to correct it.

   ```
   1   total = 0
   2   FOR x = 0 to 5
   3       number = INPUT
   4       total = total * number
   5   ENDFOR
   ```

227
   ```

```
6    average = total / 3
7    IF average < 50 THEN
8        OUTPUT "Well done"
9    ELSE
10       OUTPUT "Try agin"
9    ENDIF
```

3. Open the file **RuntimeErrorsProgram.py** provided by your teacher. This program should add together all the numbers in the array and multiply them by the number entered by the user. Correct the runtime errors in the program.

4. Develop a test plan for the 'age' sub-program of your game. Open the latest version of your game (this should be **TimesTableGameV7.py**). Make sure that you include all types of test data in your test plan.

Test number	Data entered	Expected outcome	Actual outcome
1			
2			
3			
4			

Go further

Previously, you have looked at how you can retrieve data from lists in Python using one-dimensional arrays. There are a number of ways in which the contents of an array can be altered, including adding data, changing data and removing data.

Here are some examples of ways in which the contents of a list can be altered.

List method	Example	What it does

`append()`	`fruit = ["apple","banana","grapefruit"]`
	`fruit.append("orange")`
	`print(fruit)`
	
	`['apple', 'banana', 'grapefruit', 'orange']`
		`append()` adds an item at the end of a list

`insert()`	`fruit = ["apple","banana","grapefruit"]`
	`fruit.insert(2,"orange")`
	`print(fruit)`
	
	`['apple', 'banana', 'orange', 'grapefruit']`
		`insert()` adds an item to a list at a specific index position; this alters the index numbers of all the items that follow it

Changing the contents using 'index'	`fruit = ["apple","banana","grapefruit"]`
	`fruit[1] = "orange"`
	`print(fruit)`
	
	`['apple', 'orange', 'grapefruit']`
		The value of an item in a list can be changed by assigning a new value to the index position; in this example, 'banana' is overwritten by 'orange' at index 1

Unit 9.6 An array of skills

List method	Example	What it does
remove()	fruit = ["apple","banana","grapefruit"] fruit.remove("apple") print(fruit) ['banana', 'grapefruit']	remove() removes the first occurrence of an item with a specific value
pop()	fruit = ["apple","banana","grapefruit"] fruit.pop(0) print(fruit) ['banana', 'grapefruit']	pop() can be used to remove an item using its index

1. Open the file **Altering Lists.py** provided by your teacher. This program stores in a list the names of the five countries with the highest population and displays them in order.

   ```
   Top 5 most populated countries in the world.
   1 China
   2 India
   3 United States of America
   4 Indonesia
   5 Nigeria
   ```

2. The program needs editing to display the ten countries with the highest population. Update the code that uses a one-dimensional array and use `.append()` to add Brazil, Bangladesh, Russia, Mexico and Japan to the list. The finished program should look like this.

   ```
   Top 10 most populated countries in the world.
   1 China
   2 India
   3 United States of America
   4 Indonesia
   5 Nigeria
   6 Brazil
   7 Bangladesh
   8 Russia
   9 Mexico
   10 Japan
   ```

3. There has been an error in the order of countries. Insert Pakistan between Indonesia and Nigeria. The finished program should look like this.

   ```
   Top 10 most populated countries in the world:
   1 China
   2 India
   3 United States of America
   4 Indonesia
   5 Pakistan
   6 Nigeria
   7 Brazil
   8 Bangladesh
   9 Russia
   10 Mexico
   11 Japan
   ```

4. Now there are eleven countries in the list, the final country, Japan, needs to be removed from the list. Update your code to reflect this.

Challenge yourself

Now that you know how to alter the contents of a list, you are going to develop your game further so that the player can add a character of their choice to the list or alter the other characters that are available.

Your sub-program will still need to display the original list of characters, but will then need to give the player some options to choose from.

You will need to edit the sub-program `character()` so that the program allows the player to:

- add a character to the list
- change a character that is stored in the list for a character of their choice
- remove a character from the list
- choose a character from the existing list.

The updated list should be displayed to the user before allowing them to make their final choice.

Use the pseudocode below as a guide for the options that your sub-program will need to include.

```
OUTPUT "What would you like to do?"
OUTPUT "1. Add a character?"
OUTPUT "2. Change a character"
OUTPUT "3. Delete a character"
OUTPUT "4. Choose a character from the existing list"
INPUT option
IF option == 1 THEN …
```

1. Add the required code to the latest version of your times-table game program from previous sections (this should be **TimesTableGameV7.py**). Ensure that your developments complete each of the operations outlined.
2. Save your edited program as **TimesTableGameV7cy.py** and test it to make sure that it works correctly.

Final project

Look back at the start of this unit to remind yourself of the Scenario. You have already created several parts of the game, but you now need to develop the code to ask the questions and keep a score.

> Criteria for this part of the game are as follows.
> - The game must ask the player five multiplication questions that are phrased as sentences. For example, instead of 2 × 5, it would ask questions such as 'In the cave, you see 2 trunks each containing 5 coins. How many coins do you have?'
> - Each question will include the name of a room, the name of a container and the name of something that is inside the container. These items will need to be stored in three lists.
> - The player will get two attempts to answer each question. If they get it right first time, they will receive 2 points. If they get it right second time, they will receive 1 point. Otherwise, they will receive 0 points. After the five questions have been asked, they will be told how well they have done, including how many correct answers they got and how many were right at the first attempt.

Complete the following tasks.

Part 1

1. Open your file **TimesTableGameV7.py** or **TimesTableGameV7cy.py** if you completed the 'Challenge yourself' tasks.
   a. Import the 'random' library at the top of the program, as you have previously learned, by adding the code `import random` on line 1.
   b. Define a new sub-program called `question()` and pass 'table' into it as a parameter by adding `table` into the parentheses: `question(table)`.
   c. Create three lists, called 'rooms', 'containers' and 'items'. Each list should contain at least five different items.
2. The code `random.choice()` will retrieve an item randomly from a list:

   ```
   import random
   fruit = ["apple","banana","grapefruit"]
   food = random.choice(fruit)
   print(food)
   ```
   ```
   apple
   ```

   a. Use `random.choice()` to select an item from each list and store these in separate variables.
   b. Generate a random number between 2 and 12 and store it in a variable called 'number'.
3. Use the pseudocode on the next page to help you to write the program code to display the question and get the player's answer. The letters 'V', 'W', 'X', 'Y' and 'Z' have been used to indicate where you should insert certain variables into the output.

```
V = table
W = random number (2,12)
X = random choice(rooms)
Y = random choice(containers)
Z = random choice(items)

OUTPUT "In the X you see V Y containing W Z."
OUTPUT "How many Z do you have?"
answer = INPUT
```

4 Use the flowchart on the right to help you to write the program code to check whether the answer is correct and award the appropriate number of points. If the answer is not correct the first time, then the program will need to give the user a second chance to answer the question. The number of points scored should be returned to the main program.

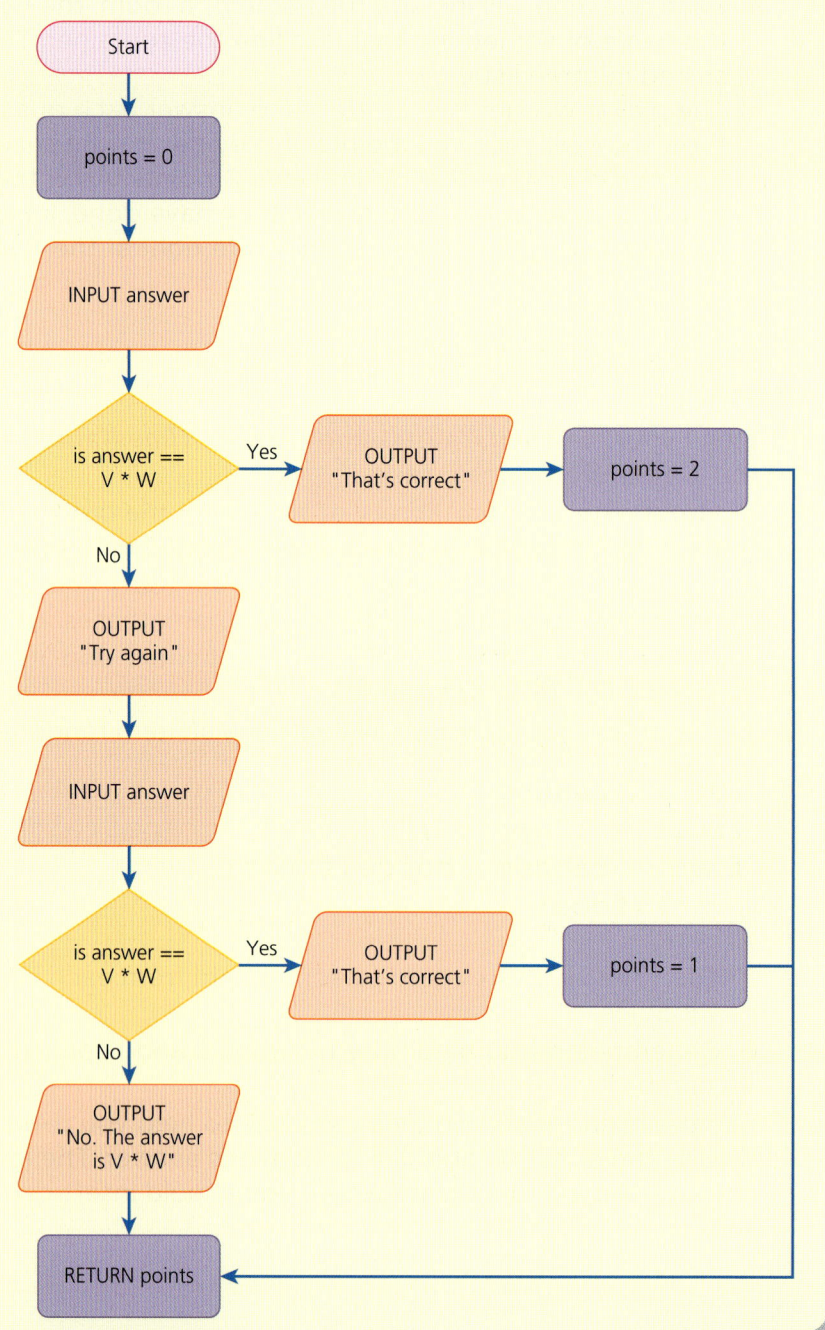

Start → points = 0 → INPUT answer → is answer == V * W?
- Yes → OUTPUT "That's correct" → points = 2
- No → OUTPUT "Try again" → INPUT answer → is answer == V * W?
  - Yes → OUTPUT "That's correct" → points = 1
  - No → OUTPUT "No. The answer is V * W"

→ RETURN points

5 a Create two variables in the main program called 'score' and 'first'. They should both have a value of 0.
  b Use the pseudocode below to help you to call the function **question()**, store the value that is returned and update the values of 'score' and 'first'. You will need to use a for loop to make this section of code run five times so that five questions are asked.

```
FOR i = 1 to 5
    points = SUBROUTINE question(table)
    score = score + points
    IF points == 2:
        first = first + 1
    ENDIF
ENDFOR
```

  c Save your program as **TimesTableGameV8.py**.
  d Test your program with appropriate data to check that it is working, before progressing to the next stage.

Part 2

1 The final stage of the game should tell the player how well they have done and give them some feedback.

> - First, address the player by name and tell them how many points they scored and how many questions they answered correctly at the first attempt.
> - Then give them some feedback based on the score that they achieved.
> - Include the number of the times table that they were practising. This is shown as V in the examples below.
>   a 8 or more points: 'Well done! You know your V times table.'
>   b 5 or more points: 'A good effort. You know some of your V times table.'
>   c Less than 5 points: 'You need to practise your V times table.'
>
> Here is an example of how this might look when the program is run:
>
> ```
> Poppa you scored 9 points and got 4 question(s) correct at the first attempt.
> Well done! You know your 5 times table.
> ```

  a Create a flowchart algorithm for the 'feedback' sub-program. It will need to use 'charName', 'score', 'first' and 'table' as parameters passed in from the main program.
  b Create a new sub-program called **feedback()** that takes in the four parameters 'charName', 'score', 'first', 'table'.
  c Use the flowchart algorithm you have just made to help you to write the code for the **feedback()** sub-program.
  d Save your finished program as **TimesTableGameV9.py**.

2. Copy the table below and create a test plan for the 'feedback' sub-program. Include normal, extreme and invalid test data.

Test number	Data entered	Expected outcome	Pass/fail
1			
2			
3			
4			

3. Copy and complete the table below, listing the variables used throughout your whole program, their data types and a justification for the data type you have chosen.

Variable name	Data type	Justification

4. Copy and complete the trace table for the following part of the algorithm if the points returned from the sub-routine are 2, 1, 0, 1, 2.

```
1   FOR i = 1 to 5
2       points = SUBROUTINE question(table)
3       score = score + points
4       IF points == 2:
5           first = first + 1
6       ENDIF
7   ENDFOR
```

Line	Variable i	Variable points	Variable score	Variable first

Unit 9.6 An array of skills

Evaluation

1. Swap programs with your partner and play each other's games. Comment on the following.
   a. Does their game cover all the requirements?
   b. Is their game easy to use?
   c. Are the messages easy to understand?
   d. Does the game calculate the score correctly depending on how many attempts it takes to get the correct answer?
2. Now open your own program and look at the code. Reflect on what you could improve in your game. Things you might want to think about include:
   - Is it easy to get full marks? How could you make the game easier/harder?
   - How could you develop the game further? Could you add additional levels? What would they look like? How could you use lists in your programming to do this?
3. Based on these evaluations, make a list of recommendations to improve your game.
4. Attempt to make the improvements to your game.

What can you do?

Read and review what you can do.
- ✔ I can identify and explain the purpose of a one-dimensional array.
- ✔ I can develop a Python program with count-controlled loops.
- ✔ I can access data from an array using Python.
- ✔ I can develop Python programs using string manipulation, including length, uppercase and lowercase.
- ✔ I can use iterative development on Python prototypes to create solutions to problems.
- ✔ I can develop and apply test plans using test data that is normal, extreme and invalid.
- ✔ I can identify and describe a range of errors, including syntax, logic and runtime errors.
- ✔ I can use a trace table to debug a Python program.
- ✔ I can follow, understand, edit and correct algorithms that are presented as pseudocode.
- ✔ I can use a sub-routine in flowcharts or pseudocode.
- ✔ I can explain and use iteration statements with count-controlled loops in either pseudocode or flowcharts.
- ✔ I can describe how a binary search is carried out, and perform a binary search on a given list.
- ✔ I can predict the outcome of algorithms that use iteration.

Glossary

5Vs: the terms used to describe the concept of Big Data: volume, velocity, variety, value, veracity

accelerometer: detects a change in direction of a device

accessibility: how successfully a new product or piece of software can be used by anyone

accumulator (ACC): holds the results of processing carried out by the arithmetic logic unit

active internet connection: where a device has a working connection to the internet

administrator: account with top-level access, with the ability to change settings or add and remove users from a network

algorithm: step-by-step instructions to solve a particular problem

analogue: continually varying signal, e.g. a sound signal

analogue-to-digital converter (ADC): converts analogue signals, e.g. the human voice, to digital signals

applications software: software designed to do a particular task, e.g. a word processor, spreadsheet, web browser, mobile-phone app

arithmetic logic unit (ALU): carries out the calculations needed during the execution of a program

array: data structure in a program that can store more than one item of data of the same data type under a single identifier; data items can be changed

artificial intelligence (AI): ability of a computer system to learn and develop its own programming from the experiences it encounters

assembler: translates assembly-language instructions into machine code and creates one line of machine code for each assembly-language instruction

assembly language: set of codes or symbols that represent each instruction, rather than a group of 1s and 0s

attribute: heading for organising data in a relational database

authenticate: confirm a user's details to ensure that they should be allowed access to a system

backup: copying files to another location in case the original is lost or damaged

Big Data: datasets that are too large or complex for traditional data-processing applications, e.g. databases or spreadsheets, to process

Big Data analytics: the analysis of sets of data known as *Big Data*

binary data: data that is represented as a 1 or a 0

binary digit: 0 or 1; the smallest unit of binary data represented on a digital device

binary search: divide-and-conquer algorithm that splits an array in half each iteration, checking the middle value to determine whether it is higher or lower or it has found the required value

biometric security: security method that identifies people using a physical attribute (e.g. a fingerprint) or a behaviour (e.g. a hand gesture)

bit: short for 'binary digit': 0 or 1

bit depth: the number of bits used to store a single sound sample

block: string of data (0s and 1s)

block-based program: individual code blocks connected together to create a program

Boolean expression: expression that contains conditional operators; symbols, e.g. >, < and =, used to carry out comparisons between two values

brute-force attack: type of unauthorised access to a computer system that uses a large dictionary to try multiple password combinations until it is successful

bus topology: network in which all devices are connected together via a main cable running down the centre of the network

byte: eight bits of data, e.g. 01010011

camelCase: all lowercase, and from the second word the first letter is capitalised

cast: change the data type of a variable

Central Processing Unit (CPU): the part of the computer that carries out program instructions, sometimes known simply as the *processor*

character: single letter, digit or symbol

chatbot: software application that uses text to ask questions to help a user

cloud computing: using servers on the internet for services

colliding: when data 'bumps into' other data, which often causes errors or lost data

command line: way of using an operating system that is navigated by typing commands

Glossary

compiler: translates an entire computer program into machine code and creates a file containing machine code for the entire program

complex query: where more than one criterion can be used to search a database, or a query can be used to combine data from more than one table, or calculations can be performed using the data in a query

concatenation: joining two strings together

conditional operator: symbol, e.g. >, < and =, used to carry out comparisons between two values

conditional statement: completes a check to see whether set criteria is either True or False

control unit (CU): issues commands to the other hardware components to help ensure programs are carried out correctly

convert: change from one unit to another, e.g. storage units (e.g. bits/bytes/kilobytes)

count-controlled loop: set of instructions repeated a set number of times

cookies: small pieces of data, collected from websites and stored as text by web browsers

COUNT function: checks all the cells in a specified range in a spreadsheet and outputs how many contain a numeric value

counter variable: variable that stores the number of times an iteration has iterated

criteria: set of rules that must be met

crocodile clips: cable for creating a temporary electrical connection between devices

current instruction register (CIR): stores the address of the instruction the Central Processing Unit is currently executing

cyber-attack: attempt to gain unauthorised access to a network, to damage or destroy a computer system

data: raw facts and figures

data dictionary: table that represents the structure of a database table at the design stage of developing a database; often contains details, e.g. data type, field length and details about validation checks applied to data items

data-entry error: error that occurs when data is being entered into a database

data item: piece of information that represents part of the data that makes up a person, place or thing, e.g. some of the data items that represent a person are their first name and second name

data packet: small unit of data that is packaged to be sent across a network

data redundancy: when data is unnecessarily repeated in a database

data type: classification applied to a data item specifying which type of data that item represents, e.g. in a spreadsheet some of the data types available include currency, text and number

database: application that organises data for storing, processing and accessing electronically

dataset: collection of related information that a computer can manipulate

decode: work out what an instruction means/what it is telling the Central Processing Unit to do

defragmentation: reorganising files stored on a hard drive to ensure that all parts of the same file are located one after the other on the drive

device driver: software program that operates a hardware device connected to a computer

digitise: convert into digital format, i.e. into 1s and 0s

domain name: part of a URL that specifies the location on the internet, e.g. google.com

dry run: process of working through an algorithm manually to trace the values of variables

efficient: the efficiency of a program can be measured by how quickly it runs

emerging technologies: new technologies that can be incorporated into a design to improve how the product operates

encryption: converting information into a scrambled form, so that it cannot be understood if it is intercepted

entity: person, place or object represented in a table in a relational database

entity relationship diagram (ERD): diagram that illustrates the relationships between two entities in a relational database

ergonomics: how a product or piece of software is designed or arranged so that it can be used efficiently

evaluation: checking the suitability of a solution to a problem

evolving: changing and improving

execute: carry out the instructions described in a computer program

extreme test data: acceptable input but at the ends of the possible input range

facial recognition: system that matches a real-time image of a human face with a database of saved facial representations to allow a user access to a digital device

feedback: comments made to help improve a product

fetch: collect an instruction from another location

file server: server that stores users' files and enables them to be shared on a network

fingerprint recognition: system that matches a real-time image of a human fingerprint with a database of saved fingerprint representations to allow a user access to a digital device

firewall: restricts the network traffic entering and exiting a network, to ensure that it is safe

fit for purpose: something that is well designed for its purpose

flat-file database: database that stores all data items using one table

float: decimal number

flowchart: visual representation of an algorithm

for loop: the Python or MicroPython loop for a count-controlled loop

foreign key: when the primary key from one table appears in another table to establish a link between two entities

fragmentation: situation that occurs when pieces of files are scattered across the surface of a hard disc when the operating system is storing the file

function: sub-program that can exist as part of a bigger program

general-purpose input output (GPIO): pins at the bottom of the micro:bit that allow additional inputs and outputs to be added through crocodile clips

Global Positioning System (GPS): satellite-based system that keeps track of users' physical locations and helps with navigation

graphical user interface (GUI): way of using software that is navigated by pointing and clicking on graphics on a screen

hacker: somebody who tries to gain unauthorised access to a computer system or network

hard disc drive: removable disc in computers for storing large amounts of data, typically measured in gigabytes or terabytes

hardware: physical parts of a computer that you *can* touch and see, e.g. the processor, storage devices, input devices, output devices

hertz (Hz): unit of measurement of how many sound samples are taken in 1 second

high bandwidth: connection that can send and receive a large amount of data per second

high-level language (HLL): programming language that uses commands and terms that are linked to the words or symbols a human would use when carrying out the same task

Hypertext Transfer Protocol (HTTP): set of rules for communicating with web servers

Hypertext Transfer Protocol Secure (HTTPS): set of rules for communicating with web servers, with added encryption to improve security

IF statement: in Python, this evaluates a condition which determines the path of the program depending on whether the condition is true or false

incremented: when the value of a variable is increased by 1

index: numerical reference for a location of a piece of data stored in an array

industrial revolution: rapid change in how society works following the introduction of new developments, e.g. machines, computers, robots, AI, machine learning

Industry 4.0: refers to how industry is combining electronics with new technologies, e.g. machine learning, artificial intelligence, robotics and green energy

input mask: control added to a field in a database table to control the format of data being added

instruction set: all the instructions in machine code that a Central Processing Unit can execute

integer: whole number

integrated development environment (IDE): software that includes all the tools needed to develop a program in a particular language

interference: when electronic signals disrupt data transmissions

Internet Service Provider (ISP): company that provides users access to the internet, and is often responsible for the network equipment that connects LANs to WANs

interpreter: translates each line of high-level language code into machine code

invalid test data: data that should be rejected by a program

IP address: unique number assigned to a computer on a network

iterate/iterative/iteration: repeat/repeated/repetition

linear search: sequential method of searching a list from start to end, checking each element in turn

list: data structure in Python that can store multiple items of data of mixed data types under a single identifier; data items can be changed

Local Area Network (LAN): type of network where devices communicate over a small geographical area, e.g. a single building

logic circuit: combination of logic gates for solving a problem in a digital device

logic error: error that allows a program to run but not output what is expected

Glossary

login system: method of accessing different systems using a username and/or password

loop variable: variable that counts the number of times code has been repeated in a count-controlled loop

low-level language (LLL): programming language that uses commands that are similar to the type of instructions the processor understands

MAC address: number programmed into a network interface card that identifies each device on a network

machine code: combination of 1s and 0s that represent each instruction in the instruction set of a digital device

machine learning: ability of a computer system to learn over time

main memory: another name for RAM, which is used to store the programs and data the Central Processing Unit is currently using

many-to-many relationship: a primary key can exist many times as a primary key on one table in a relational database and many times as a foreign key to link a second table in the relational database

MAX function: returns the highest value in a specified range of cells in a spreadsheet

memory address register (MAR): holds the address of the memory location being accessed, either to read data from or write data to

memory data register (MDR): any data or instructions that pass into or out of main memory must pass through the MDR

meteorology: study of climate and the weather

microprocessor: device that has one circuit but the input, process and output functions of a computer

MicroPython: programming language used on the micro:bit

MIN function: returns the lowest value in a specified range of cells in a spreadsheet

multiple-criteria query: query that uses more than one criterion to select data items from a database

multi-table query: query that uses data from more than one data table

naming convention: the way a variable or array is named in programming

nesting: one programming construct, e.g. selection, occurring inside another construct, e.g. a count-controlled loop

network: collection of computing devices connected to each other, either by wires or wirelessly

network interface card (NIC): every device that connects to a network includes a NIC, which has a pre-programmed MAC address so that it can be identified on the network

network operating system (NOS): computer operating system that supports networks, often including additional administrator software and monitoring tools

network switch: switch that connects devices together to form a wired network

network topology: diagram that shows how devices in a network are connected to one another, and shows the network hardware

network traffic: amount of data travelling through a network, split into small parts for transmission

normal test data: data of the correct type that should be accepted by a program

one-dimensional array: series of items grouped together under one identifier

one-to-many relationship: a primary key can exist once as a primary key on one table in a relational database and many times as a foreign key to link a second table in the relational database

one-to-one relationship: a primary key can exist once as a primary key on one table in a relational database and once as a foreign key to link a second table in the relational database

online storage services: using file storage servers on the internet to store files

operating system: software that manages all the computer hardware and software; it also acts as an interface between computer hardware components and the user, and provides a platform where applications can run

parameter: value that is passed into a function to be used as part of a sub-program

parameter query: query where the end user provides the search criteria

parity bit: bit added to a byte to make the total number of 1 bits either even or odd

parity byte: byte added to a block of data to check whether the data is valid or invalid

parity-checking: type of error check that ensures data has been transmitted correctly

password: code made up of numbers or numbers and letters and other characters (depending on the device), which allows a user access to a digital device

Personal Area Network (PAN): type of network where devices communicate over a small area of no more than 10 metres, usually connecting devices a person wears to a smartphone or computer

personal identification number (PIN): sometimes called a *PIN number* or *PIN code*; a numerical passcode that allows a user access to a digital device

physical computing device: device that can be programmed using block or text-based programming languages

plaintext: text that has not been encrypted and can be read if it is intercepted

platform: hardware and operating system that runs an application

plug-and-play device: device that is detected automatically and set up correctly for use by the operating system; no human intervention is needed

primary key: field in a database table that provides a unique identifier for a record/entity

process: carrying out an operation on data, e.g. querying a database or doing a calculation using data in a spreadsheet

processor: electronic circuitry that executes the instructions described in a computer program; often called the *central processor* or *central processing unit*

program: instructions that tell a computer system how to complete a task

program counter (PC): stores the address of the next instruction waiting to be executed (carried out) by the Central Processing Unit

protocol: agreed set of rules that computers follow to communicate with each other over a network

prototype: initial product created for testing and reviewing, before a final product is released

pseudocode: textual representation of an algorithm

query: tool that allows users to search for data that meets specific rules or criteria

Query by Example (QBE): interface that allows users to select fields and criteria for use in a query in a database application

radio frequency identification (RFID) tags: technology that uses radio signals to send data to another device

Random Access Memory (RAM): memory used to store programs and data currently being used by the processor

random value: randomly generated number in a program that can be set within a range

real: also known as a *float*; a decimal number

register: location in main memory that temporarily stores data about memory locations, instructions and data used during the execution of an instruction

relational database: database that stores data using two or more linked tables

relationship: feature in database applications for linking tables together

remotely: connecting to a network from another location via an internet connection

report: feature in MS Access for displaying data in a user-friendly format

ring topology: network in which all devices are connected together to form a ring

router: hardware device that connects networks together

rule-based chatbot: chatbot with a set of questions built in that it asks and the user answers

runtime error: error that occurs while a program is running; the instructions cannot be completed

sample rate: number of sound samples taken each second

sampling: taking samples of a sound wave at fixed intervals

scalability: capacity to make something larger, e.g. a network enlarged with more devices

search criterion: data item used for comparison when carrying out a search

security software: any type of software that secures and protects a digital device

selection: choice to be added to a program using `if… elif… else` and the next instruction executed in the program is decided by the outcome of a condition

sequence: order that program code needs to be in to work correctly

server: usually a powerful computer that offers a range of services to a network, e.g. file storage, user management, printer sharing, email access or web servers

simple query: where only a single search criterion is used to select data items from a database

snake_case: all lowercase, and spaces are replaced with underscores (_)

social-media application: web-based software that allows users to share ideas, information and thoughts in an online community

software: program or set of instructions that tell a computer what to do to complete a task; aspects of a device you *cannot* touch

spreadsheet: application that uses rows and columns to organise data and carry out calculations using that data

spreadsheet model: spreadsheet containing data that represents a real-life scenario

star topology: network in which each device is connected separately to a central switch

Glossary

storage units: number of bits used to store a data item in a digital device

string: sequence of characters that can be text, numbers or symbols; quotation marks around the characters define it as a string

string manipulation: process of changing the format of a variable/string to allow it to be analysed

Structured Query Language (SQL): specialised language for accessing data in relational databases

sub-program: small program that can be called from the main program to run at any time

sub-routine: standalone section of code that can be called from the main program

sustainably: when a network is built in a way that it is easy to maintain in the future

syntax: specific rules used in a programming language

syntax error: error in program code that stops the program from running

systems software: software that helps a user run a computer

table: set of facts or figures that are set out in a column and row structure

terminator: ending to a network cable that absorbs the signal to stop it bouncing back

test plan: document that details the tests to be carried out when a program is complete and whether or not they are successful

text-based programming: written lines of code using a specific programming language, e.g. Python

traceback message: displayed when a runtime error is encountered to help identify where the error occurred and what went wrong

trace table: technique for predicting step by step what will happen as each line of an algorithm or program is run, and to identify errors

traditional manufacturing: the making of products before computerisation; it often relied on human production lines, where people completed individual tasks, which were passed along the production line until the final product was complete

transistor: tiny switch activated by electrical signals – when the transistor is ON it represents 1; when the transistor is OFF it represents 0

translator: converts program instructions into machine-code format so the processor can carry out the instructions

Transmission Control Protocol/Internet Protocol (TCP/IP): protocol for transferring data between devices

truth table: breakdown of a logic circuit, listing all possible operations the logic circuit can carry out

tuple: data structure for storing multiple items of data in a single variable; values cannot be changed

two-dimensional parity check: check for finding where an error exists within a parity check

two-factor authentication: method of signing into a system that requires two types of authentication (e.g. a password and a one-time SMS message code)

user experience: how intuitive the product is based on the user's previous experience with digital products or applications

user management: adding or removing users to control access to a network

user requirements: tasks a user expects of an application

utilities software: software that helps maintain the smooth functioning of a digital device by helping the operating system manage tasks and resources

validation: automatic checks applied to individual fields in a database table to help reduce the chance of error when adding data to the table

value: how useful data is to an organisation

variable: named memory location that can store a value

variety: the range of data formats and data types collected

vehicle telematics: information monitored and transmitted from vehicles, e.g. their location and speed, using GPS, engine diagnostics and driving style

velocity: how quickly data is generated, processed and turned into useful information

veracity: accuracy and quality of data

version control: saving each development iteration as a new filename to track changes

virtual learning environment (VLE): online classroom where teachers and students can share learning materials

virus scanning: checking files on a computer system for malicious content

voice-pattern recognition: software that can understand and carry out spoken instructions

volume: the massive amounts of data collected and analysed on an ongoing basis

Wide Area Network (WAN): type of network where devices communicate over a large geographical area, such as across a city or country

wildcard query: query where special characters are used to stand in for unknown characters (this is useful when trying to find lots of data items that are similar but not exactly the same)

wireless access point: allows devices to connect to a network using Wi-Fi

Index

A

accelerometers 93, 97, 126
active internet connections 56
AI *see* artificial intelligence (AI)
algorithms 4, 5, 13
   code tracers 19–23
   fragmentation 133
   see also flowcharts; pseudocode
analogue sound 135
   digitisation of 130, 131, 135–7
analogue-to-digital convertor (ADC) 135–7
AND logic gate 11, 147, 149
antivirus software 57, 133
applications software 129, 132
the APRAnet 57
arrays 6, 35–8, 49–50, 51, 52, 53, 198
   altering contents of 228–30
   indexed items 98, 100, 216
   on the micro:bit 97–102
      musical notes 111, 113, 115, 117
      storing images 116–25
   see also lists; one-dimensional arrays
artificial intelligence (AI) 12, 153
   and machine learning 150
   and network security 76–7
assembly language 140–1, 142, 145
authentication 75–6

B

Big Data 4, 5–6, 160–97
   and the 5Vs 163
   analytics 164, 165
   applications of 163–5
   complex queries 176–81
   data items 161, 163
   data searches 161
   evaluating models of real-life systems 185–8
   social media 160, 163
   see also databases; relational databases; spreadsheets
binary data 71, 135, 138–9, 140
binary search 223–4
biometric security 75–6, 133, 134, 135, 150
block-based programs 91
Boolean expressions/operators 130, 131, 147–9, 156, 158, 200
   data types 9, 13, 200
   IF statement 211, 213
   string manipulation 207
bus topology 61

C

casting 13
Central Processing Unit (CPU) 140, 141, 142, 143, 144, 145, 156
chatbot program 5, 10, 38–53
   code tracers 19–23
   development iterations 16–18, 38–44, 52–3
   error processing 23–8, 45–8
chatbots 8, 11–12, 152
cloud computing 68, 76–7
code tracers 19–23
command lines 80–4
compilers 130, 131, 141, 142
computerisation 5, 129, 151–3, 157
concatenation 13
conditional operators 24, 27, 46, 48, 90, 147–8
conditional statements 11, 24, 44, 49, 90
   combining logic gates 147–8
   and the micro:bit 94, 124
   in Python 210, 211
cookies 152, 153
count-controlled loops (for loops) 5, 9, 28–30, 37, 44
   in game development 88, 124, 127
      creating a musical sequence 112–14, 115
   and the micro:bit 103–11
   in pseudocode 29–30, 33–5, 51–2
   Python 199, 202–6
counter variables 106
crocodile clips 91
cyber-attacks 67

D

data accessibility 67–8, 70
databases 4, 163, 186, 187, 188–9
   see also relational databases
data storage 130, 131, 138–9, 157
   datasets 74
   logic gates 129
data types 5, 9, 11, 12–15
   in arrays 216
   evaluating database models 186
   MicroPython 88
   Python 9, 11, 200, 207
   test plans 9, 47, 48, 53, 225
decomposition 201–2
defragmentation programs 69, 131, 133–4
device drivers 130, 131, 133
disc defragmentation 69, 131, 133–4
domain names 66
dry-run testing 22, 27, 53

E

emerging technologies 154, 155
encryption software 69, 76
entity relationship diagrams (ERDs) 170
ergonomics 154
error processing 23–8
   changing contents of an array 228–9
   identifying errors and debugging 225–30
   logic errors 9, 24, 27, 45, 46, 48, 227–8
   networks 5, 71–3
      parity-checking systems 72–3, 78–80, 85
   runtime errors 9, 24, 45, 46–7, 48, 225, 228
   syntax errors 9, 24, 45–6, 48, 91, 199
ethernet cabling 60
extreme test data 9, 47, 48, 53, 225
   for the micro:bit 95
   Python 199, 206, 210–11

F

facial recognition 76, 133, 135, 150, 151
fetch-decode-execute cycle 5, 130, 131, 143–4, 145, 146, 157
file servers 60, 67, 68, 69
file storage and retrieval 133
fingerprint recognition 76, 133, 134
firewalls 57, 60, 63, 67, 69, 70, 75, 133
flat-file databases 165, 166, 168, 169
floats (real data types) 12, 13, 14
flowcharts 9, 9–10, 11, 15, 16, 19
   game development 88, 90, 127, 232
   iteration 31–3, 38–9, 204, 205
   Python 199, 200
   spreadsheet models 185
for loops *see* count-controlled loops (for loops)

G

game development 5, 6, 88–128
   creating a musical output 111–15

Index

creating your own image 120–3
microprocessors 88
physical computing devices 88, 89
Python 200, 207, 210–11, 231–5
Tetris 89
'What am I?' game 90, 111, 125–7
see also micro:bit
general-purpose input output (GPIO) 91
graphical user interface (GUI) 80

H

hackers 71, 75
high bandwidth connections 56
HLL (high-level languages) 140, 141, 142, 145
HTTP (Hypertext Transfer Protocol) 66
HTTPS (Hypertext Transfer Protocol Secure) 66, 76

I

icons 129
IDLE (Integrated Development and Learning Environment) 11, 200
industrial practices, computerisation of 130, 151–3
Industry 4.0 4, 5, 152–3
integers 9, 12, 13, 14, 21, 97, 99, 217
integrated development environments (IDEs) 46, 48
Internet Service Providers (ISPS) 58
interpreters 130, 131, 141, 142
invalid test data 9, 47, 48, 53, 225
the micro-bit 95, 96, 123
Python 199, 206, 210–11
IP addresses 64–5
iteration 6, 9, 16–18, 28–38, 52–3, 198, 199
error processing 23–8
game development 88, 120–7
login systems 202
program development 38–44
Python 9, 17–18, 52–3, 198, 199, 200–6
using with lists 220–4
statements 9
version control 120
see also count-controlled loops (for loops)

L

LANs (Local Area Networks) 58, 59, 61
linear search 223
lists 35–7, 216–19, 231
altering contents of 228–30
searching 223–4
storing 131
using iteration with 220–3
see also arrays
LLL (low-level languages) 140, 142, 145
logic circuits 5, 130, 131, 147, 148–9, 156, 158
logic errors 9, 24, 27, 45, 46, 48, 227–8
Python 199, 212
logic gates 129, 132, 147–8

M

machine code 141, 142, 145
machine learning 129, 130, 131, 150–1, 153, 157
chatbots 12
in network security 4, 5, 76–7
potential uses of 151
malware 71, 133
manufacturing
computerising tasks in 130, 131
machine learning and computerisation in 129
many-to-many relationships
in relational databases 170
micro:bit
accelerometer 93, 97, 126
arrays 97–102
and count-controlled loops 103–11
game development 5, 88, 90, 91–7, 111
creating images 116–25
creating a musical output 111–15
inputs and outputs 91
programming 88, 90, 91–7, 100–1
random library 99, 100–1, 102
MicroPython 91
accessing 90
arrays 97, 98
creating the program 110, 115
game development 5, 88, 90
displaying an image 116–23
pseudocode plan 93
MS Access 160, 162, 173–4, 190
MS Excel 160, 162, 182
multiple-criteria queries 176, 180–1
multi-table queries 176, 179–80
music 111–15

N

naming conventions 14, 97
nesting 124, 125
network interface cards (NICs) 59
network operating systems (NOS) 68–9, 70
networks 4, 5, 55–87
accessibility 67–8, 70
administrators 68, 69, 75
command lines 80–4
connections 56, 57–60
data packets 55, 64, 65, 71, 74
disconnection due to interference 56
error detection 55, 71–3
fit for purpose 55
hardware 59–60, 61, 63
packet switching 65
parity bits 55
protocols 55, 64–6, 76
scalability factors 55, 67–70
storage 67, 70
sustainable 55
topologies and architecture 55, 56, 58–9, 61–3, 85–7
traffic 60
user management 69
Nintendo Switch 88, 89
normal test data 9, 47, 48, 53, 225
the micro-bit 95, 96, 123
Python 199, 206, 210–11
NOT logic gate 11, 147, 149

O

one-dimensional arrays 4, 5, 9, 199
chatbot program 45
game development 88
Python 216, 217, 218, 228
one-to-many relationships
in relational databases 170, 172, 174
one-to-one relationships
in relational databases 170
operating systems 130, 131, 132, 133, 134
command lines 80
MOS (network operating systems) 68–9
network operating systems (NOS) 68–9
OR logic gate 11, 147, 149

P

packet switching 65
PANs (Personal Area Networks) 57
parameter queries 176, 177–8
parity-checking systems 72–3, 78–80, 85
passwords 75, 133, 134
PINs (personal identification numbers) 133, 134
PlayStation 89
plug-and-play devices 133, 134
Pong 89
power surges 71
programming languages 140–2, 145
prototypes 4, 5, 18, 130

243

improving technology 154, 155, 158
micro:bit program codes 126
Python 23, 199
pseudocode 9, 11, 14, 15, 16–17, 19
  count-controlled (for) loop in 29–30, 33–5, 106, 107–8, 110, 111, 204–5
  creating an image 121–2, 123
  error processing 25
  iterative development 16–17, 40, 43–4, 125
  for a micro:bit program 92, 96, 117, 125, 127
  Python 199, 200, 231–2, 233
  trace tables 19–23, 212–13
Python 5, 9, 198–235
  count-controlled loops 199, 202–6
  data types 9, 11, 200, 207
  decomposition and sub-programs 201–2
  identifying errors and debugging 225–30
  IDLE 11, 200
  IF statement 211, 213
  iterative development 9, 17–18, 52–3, 198, 199, 200–6
  lists 35–7, 216–19
    using iteration with 220–3
  prototypes 23, 199
  running 145
  string manipulation 9, 199, 207–11
  test plan 11, 199, 206, 210–11
  trace tables 9, 23, 211–15, 221, 222–3
  tuples 216, 217
  variables 211, 216, 233
  see also chatbot program

Q

Query by Example (QBE) 190–1, 192
questioning 8, 10

R

radio frequency identification (RFID) tags 152, 153
random access memory (RAM) 133, 134
relational databases 5–6, 161, 162, 165–75
  creating 170–5, 192–4
  data dictionaries 171, 172
  foreign keys 167, 168, 169, 170, 174
  input masks 171, 172
  primary keys 167, 168, 169, 170, 171, 174
  validation 171, 172
ring topology 62, 63

robotics 150
routers 59, 61, 63, 69
runtime errors 9, 24, 45, 46–7, 48, 199, 225

S

security 5, 55, 67, 70, 74–84
  breaches 71
  machine learning 4, 5, 76–7
  software 75–6, 130, 131, 133, 134, 135, 150
selection 6, 9, 28, 30, 198
  chatbot program 38, 41
  game development 88, 90, 124
  nested 124, 125
sequence 6, 9, 28, 38, 198
  in game development 88, 90
servers 58, 60
smartphones 96
Snake 89
social media 160, 163
software 4, 129, 132–5
  applications software 129, 132
  encryption software 69, 76
  network utilities 69, 70
  security software 75–6, 130, 131, 133, 134, 135, 150
  spreadsheets 181–4
  systems software 68–9, 70, 129, 132, 157
  utilities software 130, 131, 132, 134, 136, 157
  see also operating systems
spreadsheets 4, 161, 163, 189–90
  data analysis 161
  models 6, 161, 162, 181–4, 191
    creating 194–5
    evaluating 187–8, 197
star topology 62–3, 63
strings 12, 13, 14, 21
  in arrays 36, 97
  converting variables to 109
  len(i) function 209
  manipulation 4, 5, 49
    in Python 9, 199, 207–11, 219
Structured Query Language (SQLs) 190, 192
syntax errors 9, 24, 45–6, 48, 91, 199
systems software 68–9, 70, 129, 132, 134, 135, 157
  see also operating systems

T

TCP/IP Protocol 64–5
terminators 61

test plans 15, 16, 19
  chatbot program 45–8, 53
  data types 9, 47, 48, 53, 225
  micro:bit 88, 90, 95, 96, 102, 118–19, 123
  Python 11, 199, 206, 210–11
Tetris 89
times tables 6
traceback messages 47, 48
trace tables 6, 9, 16, 18, 19–23, 45, 52–3
  debugging a Python program 199
  error processing 24, 25–8
  for the micro:bit 88, 103–7, 110, 124–5
    creating a musical output 113, 115
    displaying an image 117
  Python 9, 23, 211–15, 221, 222–3
traditional manufacturing
  computerising tasks in 130, 131, 151–2
translators 5, 130, 131, 141, 142, 157
truth tables 156
tuples 216, 217

U

user access controls 75
user requirements 186
utilities software 130, 131, 132, 133, 134, 136, 157

V

variable data collection 12–15
variables 18, 19, 211, 216, 233
  counter variables 106
vehicle telematics 164
version control 120
virus scanning backup 69
VLE (virtual learning environment) 161–2, 192, 194, 195, 197
voice-pattern recognition 133, 134

W

WANs (Wide Area Networks) 58, 59, 61
while true code 99
wildcat queries 176, 178–9, 181
wireless access point 59

X

Xbox 89

Acknowledgements

The Publishers would like to thank the following for permission to reproduce copyright material.

Photo credits

p. 8 *t* © Coosh448/stock.adobe.com, *b* © Thapana_Studio/stock.adobe.com; **p. 11** © Zapp2photo/stock.adobe.com; **p. 55** © Metamorworks/stock.adobe.com; **p. 56** © Parilov/stock.adobe.com; **p. 57** *t* © Aitorserra/stock.adobe.com, *b* © Yurakrasil/stock.adobe.com; **p. 58** *t* © Metamorworks/stock.adobe.com, *m* © Paisan1leo/stock.adobe.com; **p. 59** *in descending order* © Vadim/stock.adobe.com, © Sergey Ilin/stock.adobe.com, © An-T/stock.adobe.com, © Quality Stock Arts/stock.adobe.com; **p. 60** *in descending order* © Cybrain/stock.adobe.com, © MicroOne/stock.adobe.com, © RankSol/stock.adobe.com; **p. 64** © PCH.Vector/stock.adobe.com; **p. 66** © WENN Rights Ltd/Alamy Stock Photo; **p. 68** *t* © WrightStudio/stock.adobe.com, *b* © Chaosamran_Studio/stock.adobe.com; **p. 71** © Vitalii/stock.adobe.com; **p. 74** © Issaronow/stock.adobe.com; **p. 75** © Kt Stock/stock.adobe.com; **p. 88** © Rosinka79/stock.adobe.com; **p. 89** *t* © Bohdan/stock.adobe.com, *m* © Oleksandr/stock.adobe.com, *b* © Gorodenkoff/stock.adobe.com; **p. 91** © Gargantiopa/Shutterstock.com; **p. 96** © Jeler/stock.adobe.com; **p. 129** © Macrovector/stock.adobe.com; **p. 130** © Adam121/stock.adobe.com; **p. 133** © Prostock-studio/stock.adobe.com; **p. 135** © DGTL Graphics sro/stock.adobe.com; **p. 142** © ZinetroN/stock.adobe.com; **p. 147** © Frozen Design/stock.adobe.com; **p. 150** © Sammby/Shutterstock.com; **p. 151** © Ico Maker/Shutterstock.com; **p. 154** *t* © Bongkochrut/stock.adobe.com, *ml* © Gorodenkoff/stock.adobe.com, *m* © Gorodenkoff/stock.adobe.com, *mr* © Gorodenkoff/stock.adobe.com; **p. 155** *t* © Sakinakhanim/Shutterstock.com, *b* © Stakes/Shutterstock.com; **p. 156** *in descending order* © Flatvector/Shutterstock.com, © Agatha-vector/Shutterstock.com, © Andrii/stock.adobe.com; **p. 160** © Scanrail/stock.adobe.com; **p. 161** © Natee Meepian/stock.adobe.com; **p. 162** © Merla/stock.adobe.com; **p. 176** © Dimon_ua/stock.adobe.com; **p. 181** © Wachiwit/stock.adobe.com; **p. 185** © Worawut/stock.adobe.com; **p. 202** © Jane Kelly/stock.adobe.com.

Text credits

The following brands mentioned in this book are trademarks or registered trademarks:

- Android
- Google Drive
- Javascript
- Mozilla
- Microsoft Access
- Microsoft Powerpoint
- MS-DOS
- Pong
- Dropbox
- Google Maps
- Linux
- micro:bit
- Microsoft Excel
- Microsoft Windows
- Nintendo Switch
- Python
- Google.com
- iOS
- macOS
- MicroPython
- Microsoft OneDrive
- Microsoft Word
- Netflix
- Python's Integrated Development and Learning Environment

CAMBRIDGE LOWER SECONDARY COMPUTING 9

- Playstation
- Snake
- UPS
- Xbox
- MakeCode
- Spotify
- Wi-Fi
- Scratch
- Tetris
- Windows Explorer

BBC micro:bit images and screenshots © Micro:bit Educational Foundation microbit.org

Google, Google Drive and Google Maps are trademarks of Google LLC and this book is not endorsed by or affiliated with Google in any way.

MicroPython copyright © 2013-2022 Damien P. George, https://github.com/micropython/micropython/blob/master/LICENSE

Microsoft product screenshot(s) used with permission from Microsoft.

Python copyright © 2001-2022 Python Software Foundation; All Rights Reserved.

Every effort has been made to trace all copyright holders, but if any have been inadvertently overlooked, the Publishers will be pleased to make the necessary arrangements at the first opportunity.

Although every effort has been made to ensure that website addresses are correct at time of going to press, Hodder Education cannot be held responsible for the content of any website mentioned in this book. It is sometimes possible to find a relocated web page by typing in the address of the home page for a website in the URL window of your browser.